Teaching Reading
to Struggling Learners

Teaching Reading
to Struggling Learners

by

Esther Minskoff, Ph.D.

·P·A·U·L·H·
BR∞KES
PUBLISHING C⁰ ®

Baltimore • London • Sydney

Paul H. Brookes Publishing Co.
Post Office Box 10624
Baltimore, Maryland 21285-0624

www.brookespublishing.com

Typeset by Integrated Publishing Solutions, Grand Rapids, Michigan.
Manufactured in the United States of America by
Versa Press, Inc., East Peoria, Illinois.

The vignettes in this book are composite accounts that do not represent the lives or experiences of specific individuals, and no implications should be inferred.

Library of Congress Cataloging-in-Publication Data

Minskoff, Esther H. (Esther Hirsch)
   Teaching reading to struggling learners / by Esther Minskoff.
      p.   cm.
   Includes bibliographical references and index.
   ISBN 1-55766-669-5
   1. Reading—Remedial teaching.   I. Title.

LB1050.5.M59 2005
428.4'2—dc22   2005001072

British Library Cataloguing in Publication data are available from the British Library.

Contents

About the Author

Esther Minskoff, Ph.D., is Professor Emerita of Special Education at James Madison University in Harrisonburg, Virginia. She taught graduate and undergraduate courses in special education at James Madison University and served as Project Director for two federally funded grants—Steppingstones of Technology Innovations and a Model Demonstration Postsecondary Education Project. She has published extensively in journals and co-authored *Academic Success Strategies for Adolescents with Learning Disabilities and ADHD* (written with David Allsopp, Paul H. Brookes Publishing Co., 2003) and *Phonic Remedial Reading Lessons* (written with Samuel A. Kirk & Winifred D. Kirk, Academic Therapy Publications, 1985). Dr. Minskoff served as President of the Division for Learning Disabilities of the Council for Exceptional Children and was a member of the Professional Advisory Board of the Learning Disabilities Association of America.

Foreword

> My experience at the Wayne County Training School also biased me toward a belief in the power of intervention. (Kirk, 1984, p. 35)

Given changes in state and federal laws since the 1990s, all teachers must be prepared for the complex, challenging task of teaching children to learn to read. Although many children appear to learn to read with relative ease, others do not. Some children have trouble acquiring basic word identification skills, some read accurately but too slowly, some have trouble understanding the content of what they read, and some have trouble with all aspects of reading performance. This book is written for the teachers of these children—children who have challenges in any aspect of reading development from the beginning to the advanced stages of development.

This book is an amalgam of both past and present knowledge regarding reading difficulties. Dr. Esther Minskoff and I were both students of the late Dr. Samuel A. Kirk, who is often referred to as the "father of the field of learning disabilities." Clearly, our understanding of reading difficulties was influenced and shaped by this great educator. Dr. Kirk taught us the power of assessment that leads to an accurate diagnosis and targeted intervention. Dr. Minskoff recalled, "As a student in Kirk's course on learning disabilities in 1962, I repeatedly heard him say, 'Diagnosis and remediation are inseparable'" (1998, p. 15). Dr. Kirk firmly believed that the purpose of assessment was for treatment purposes, not just classification

Throughout his writings, lectures, and speeches, Dr. Kirk would frequently reiterate his basic beliefs and tenets regarding effective reading instruction. As early as the 1940s, Kirk observed that a good thorough reading program should 1) consider the child's level of maturation, 2) use instructional materials at the appropriate difficulty level, 3) provide direct and systematic instruction, 4) provide opportunities for enjoyable reading, 5) provide instruction in word attack skills, 6) motivate students with interesting materials, and 7) introduce the practical reading activities of daily life (Kirk, 1949; Lerner, 1998). Not only has Dr. Minskoff embedded these basic beliefs throughout the chapters of this book, she has integrated these fundamental principles of special reading instruction with current research findings and best practices to create a comprehensive guidebook that addresses all major aspects of systematic reading instruction for students of all ages.

Teaching Reading to Struggling Learners will help teachers build a solid foundation of understanding the nature of reading difficulties and ways to create and implement effective instructional programs. Chapter 1 sets the stage for the three-pronged instructional model for providing reading instruction to students who struggle: the foundation of skills needed for efficient reading (pre-reading skills, word identification, fluency, and comprehension); the various stages of reading development; and the strategic, explicit methods that guide the reading instruction. Each subsequent chapter builds on this model and provides specific examples of explicit, teaching methods.

A central premise throughout the book is that one method of instruction will not work with all children; this premise is based on Kirk's belief that reading teachers need to be eclectic in their selection of methodology. He advised,

> Instead of being an evangelist for one method or approach for all children, we can delineate the specific approach for a specific child and his specific problem. Phonics may be valuable for one child and of little use to another. The Fernald method may be useful to one child and not to another. Each of the procedures . . . may be of value, each in its own place for a particular group of children. (1993, p. 124)

To maximize learning, reading teachers need to be careful and thoughtful in their selection of methodologies. Thus, an accomplished reading teacher possesses a toolbox of effective methods, strategies, and techniques that will be carefully matched to a student's unique needs and developmental level.

Chapter 2 describes the approach used in the book to reading instruction, strategic, explicit teaching (S.E.T.). The early pioneers in the field of reading disabilities—including Drs. Samuel Orton, Marion Monroe, and Grace Fernald—promoted the use of reading methodologies for struggling readers that were individualized, multisensory, systematic, sequential, repetitive, and intensive. Students who struggle to learn to read require more repetition, more practice, and more review to acquire basic skills, and the instruction needs to be more systematic and more carefully designed—aimed at improving the overall level of skill, as well as the efficiency of the learner. In describing the results of remedial intervention, Monroe found that "children who have difficulty in learning to read do not usually overcome the difficulty under ordinary school instruction but are able to make normal and accelerated progress under special methods adapted to their difficulties" (1932, p. 143). The S.E.T. approach described in this book embodies the essential characteristics and elements of the special methods of structured reading instruction.

Chapter 3 covers the pre-reading skills, such as phonological awareness and letter–sound relationships that provide the foundation for reading development. The activities described ensure that early intervention efforts will make a difference.

Chapters 4 and 5 explain clearly how to teach structured phonics and then structural analysis skills so that children can pronounce words without assistance. These chapters are particularly valuable for teachers working with children who are struggling to acquire the alphabetic code.

Chapter 6 describes the visual analysis skills that are needed for successful reading and clarifies how accurate word reading requires more than just phonic skills. The reader must also note the distinctive features and readily recognize the common spelling patterns that exist. As Fernald (1943) noted many decades ago, children with difficulty forming visual images can be helped to learn words through multisensory instruction—that is, by incorporating visual, auditory, kinesthetic, and tactile clues. These types of procedures are clearly explained with examples of ways to facilitate the recall of letters and words.

Chapter 7 is devoted to teaching fluency skills, aptly referred to as the bridge between word identification and comprehension. One noted criticism from the past has been that instruction in fluency has been neglected or insufficient for many developing readers. Once students have learned how to pronounce words with accuracy and ease, they must make the transition to smooth, rapid reading with expression. Various strategies to improve rate and fluency are described.

Chapter 8 centers on providing instruction in all types of reading comprehension. As with other chapters, the emphasis is placed on differentiated instruction and finding the specific methods that will be most efficacious for specific students. Practical strategies are described that will help students become active participants in the reading process.

Both Chapters 8 and 9 remind educators of the complexity of reading comprehension as well as the intricate, reciprocal connections between reading comprehension and the reader's cognitive and linguistic abilities and experience. A strong foundation in oral language and metalinguistic abilities provides the support for strategic reading.

Chapter 10 describes many strategies for helping students to engage actively in problem solving and the reading process, thus improving their comprehension. The significance of the intricate link between higher-order thinking processes and reading comprehension is explained, as well as how teachers can make thinking visible through modeling and explicit strategy instruction.

Chapter 11 describes how to vary instruction for the three types of text structures: narrative, expository, and electronic. Reading comprehension for electronic text has rarely been addressed in books on reading. As students encounter an increasing amount of reading in electronic formats and on the Internet, reading teachers must instruct their students about how to meet the changing demands of the reading process.

Chapter 12 describes a comprehensive model of assessment for planning and monitoring reading instruction that incorporates both standardized assessments and informal techniques. An important component of all effective reading programs is that the teacher must carefully monitor and document student progress. As described in Chapter 12, teachers need to "use daily monitoring, and after each lesson ask [themselves], 'Did the student learn what I wanted to teach and if not, why? What can I do to help the student learn?'" This book emphasizes the importance of teacher modeling and guided instruction that is dynamic, interactive, and informed. Gradually, the teacher transfers the responsibility and control from teacher-directed reading tasks to student-directed tasks. Finally, the book's appendices provide teachers with a glossary, informal assessments, a record for tracking reading skills, a graph for estimating readability, and an array of interesting games and reading programs to enhance the effectiveness of intervention.

Teaching Reading to Struggling Learners is an invaluable resource for teachers who provide prevention, intervention, or remediation for struggling readers. It is organized to promote success and mastery of all aspects of reading. The first step toward the development of an appropriate treatment plan is to understand a child's level of reading development. As described, this understanding can be gained through careful observation of a child's present reading abilities. After the student's needs have been identified, a comprehensive program for reading improvement is developed, implemented, and monitored. Through the employment of targeted research-based reading interventions, children become better readers. The central message of this book is that students who struggle with reading can be helped when knowledgeable, competent, relentless teachers provide intensive, systematic, structured, comprehensive, and strategic instruction. These teachers will be able to wield the power of intervention that Dr. Kirk so passionately advocated.

Nancy Mather, Ph.D.
Professor
Department of Special Education,
Rehabilitation, and School Psychology
University of Arizona, Tucson

REFERENCES

Fernald, G.M. (1943). *Remedial techniques in basic school subjects.* New York: McGraw-Hill.

Kirk, S.A. (1949). Characteristics of slow learners and needed adjustments in reading. *Supplementary Educational Monograph, 69,* 172–176.

Kirk, S.A. (1984). Introspection and prophecy. In B. Blatt & R.J. Morris (Eds.), *Perspectives in special education: Personal orientations* (pp. 25–55). Glenview, IL: Scott, Foresman, & Co.

Kirk, S.A. (1993). Our current headaches in learning disabilities. In G.A. Harris & W.D. Kirk (Eds.), *The foundations of special education: Selected papers and speeches of Samuel A. Kirk* (pp. 115–124). Arlington, VA: Council for Exceptional Children.

Lerner, J.W. (1998). The Milwaukee years and their unending influence. *Learning Disabilities Research & Practice, 13,* 8–10.

Minskoff, E.H. (1998). Sam Kirk: The man who made special education special. *Learning Disabilities Research & Practice, 13,* 15–21.

Monroe, M. (1932). *Children who cannot read.* Chicago: The University of Chicago Press.

Introduction

The purpose of this book is to describe how to teach reading to struggling learners at the elementary, middle, and secondary levels. The assumption underlying this book is that all students can become successful readers if they are taught in ways that fit their instructional needs. *Struggling learners prove that they are hard to teach because they fail to learn through conventional methods used in general education.* These methods do not fit their unique needs. It is the responsibility of teachers to meet the challenges presented by these students and find the methods that work the best. Reading instruction should not be based on the concept of "one size fits all"; rather, it should be customized to the individual.

The focus of this book is not on teaching reading to all students but only to those who are struggling. These students struggle for a number of reasons. They may

- Have learning disabilities (e.g., dyslexia)

- Have attention-deficit/hyperactivity disorder (ADHD)

- Not speak English as their first language and are labeled as English language learners (ELLs) or students with limited English proficiency (LEP) who may or may not be enrolled in ESL (English as a Second Language) programs

- Speak nonstandard English dialects based on regional or cultural differences (e.g., African American Vernacular English)

- Be culturally diverse and are being reared in homes that do not support literacy development

- Be economically disadvantaged and are not exposed to the experiences that are supportive of school learning

The numbers of these various types of struggling students have increased dramatically in recent years. Students diagnosed with learning disabilities have grown nationally from about 800,000 in 1976–1977 to about 2,800,000 in 1998–1999. In 1976–1977, students with learning disabilities constituted 1.5% of the overall student population, whereas in 1998–1999, the number of these students was 5.99% (LD Online, n.d.). In a National Center for Health Statistics (2002) report, 3% of children from 6 to 11 years old were diagnosed with ADHD, 4% were diagnosed with only learning disabilities, and 4% were diagnosed with both conditions. The number of ELLs enrolled in the nation's schools in 2000–2001 was about 4,500,000 or 9.6% of the total school population. This represented a 32% increase over the number of ELLs in

1997–1998 (Padolsky, 2002). In 1999, 16% of all children from ages 5 to 17 lived in households where the annual income was below the poverty level (National Center for Education Statistics, 2003). These statistics clearly demonstrate the daunting challenge presented to American education by the large numbers of struggling students in the nation's schools.

The significantly lower levels of reading achievement of students who are African American or Hispanic, who are ELLs, or who have disabilities as compared with students who are middle class, Caucasian, and typically developing support the need to provide more appropriate education to meet the critical needs of struggling students (Nation's Report Card: Reading Highlights, 2003). Congress enacted the No Child Left Behind (NCLB) Act of 2001 (PL 107-110) in an attempt to meet the needs of all children in America's schools, especially the ones who struggle. One aspect of NCLB involves the Reading First initiative, which is designed to assist schools in making all children successful readers by the end of the third grade. The recommendations of the Reading First initiative (The Partnership for Reading, 2001) have been incorporated into the instructional model for teaching reading that is presented in this book.

This book is a how-to manual written for prospective teachers enrolled in reading methods courses and practicing teachers who are faced with the challenge of teaching reading to struggling students. This book differs from textbooks frequently used in courses on teaching reading because it does not emphasize theory, history, viewpoints, case studies, pictures of children and teachers, lists of books, and so forth. This book is a technical manual rather than an informational resource like many textbooks on reading. It is important to recognize that both technical manuals and informational resources are needed for teachers to learn how to be competent guides who can lead their students along the difficult path of becoming successful readers.

This book is designed for prospective teachers and practicing teachers who have limited background knowledge in the field of reading. Consequently, it is written in an easy-to-understand style with as little jargon as possible. An extensive glossary is presented in Appendix A to help the reader understand the vocabulary that is necessary for comprehension of the basic concepts in the field of reading.

All the methods and strategies described in this book are anchored to evidence-based research and/or have been identified as best practices in reading. In order not to overwhelm the reader with comprehensive reviews of research, only major studies relevant to a topic are cited. As is often found in reading textbooks, this book does not contain lengthy reviews of similar teaching methods and strategies. Instead, one or two methods or strategies that have been found effective for teaching specific skills are highlighted.

Acknowledgments

I want to thank the countless James Madison University (JMU) undergraduate and graduate students from whom I have learned so much over my years of teaching. I especially want to recognize the following JMU special education students who used the first manuscript of this book as the textbook for their course on specialized reading methods: Sarah Bosler, Leigh Buckley, Julie Foley, Lauren Gardner, Amanda Henrikson, Ginny Johnston, Katie Kingsley, Kevin Lancor, Eunice Lee, Jennifer Masi, A.J. Romero, Cary Schulte, Amber Shingler, Ashley Silsbe, Lynn Stephens, Laura Tarrant, Sarah Tulchin, Jennifer Turner, Kim Weirich, Jennifer Westley, Sara Whitney, and Jennifer Wutka. They used the ideas from the book as the basis for creating and delivering excellent reading instruction to the children in their field experience. Their feedback was most helpful.

Thanks also to my graduate assistant, Jessica Brooks, who provided support with a smile no matter how many times I changed my mind. To my JMU colleague, Dr. Margaret Kyger, who co-taught the special education reading course with me, I extend my deep appreciation for turning abstract concepts into teachable classroom activities.

To my grandchildren, Sam, Ally, and Katy,
who brighten my life
with both their joy of learning
and their joy of living

A Three-Legged Instructional Model for Teaching Reading to Struggling Learners

CONCEPTS EXPLORED

- Instructional model for specialized reading instruction
- Four skill areas of reading instruction
- Six stages of learning to read
- Strategic, explicit teaching methodology

INSTRUCTIONAL MODEL FOR SPECIALIZED READING INSTRUCTION

There are two unique aspects of the instructional reading approach advocated in this book. One involves the use of an underlying instructional model as the basis for designing and delivering reading instruction to struggling learners. The second involves the integration of reading instruction with instruction in language and cognitive processes (or thinking).

The instructional model for teaching struggling students rests on three legs: 1) the skill areas of reading instruction that must be taught; 2) the stages of reading that students must pass through on their way to attaining adult literacy; and 3) strategic, explicit teaching methods that must be used to develop these skill areas. A graphic showing this instructional model is in Figure 1.

Students must master different reading skills at each of the six stages of learning to read, and the skills mastered at one stage are prerequisites for learning the skills at the next stage. This model helps teachers design and provide instruction to develop these skills at each of the six stages using strategic, explicit teaching methods. The model enables teachers to identify *when* to teach *what* reading skills to struggling students and *how* to do so.

As noted, a second unique aspect of this book is the assumption that reading is a complex skill that does not develop in isolation. Rather, mastery of reading is intertwined with the development of skills in language and cognitive processing or cognition (i.e., thinking). *Teaching Reading to Struggling Learners* presents an integrated plan for teaching reading, language, and cognition together. To learn to read, students must first master certain language and cognitive skills. As children become good readers, their reading abilities lead to growth of their language and cognitive abilities. Therefore, not only is reading important for its own sake, but it is also important for enhancing students' language and cognitive abilities.

Students who are *not* struggling may learn readily by whatever teaching methods are used in general education, even holistic methods that do not systematically teach specific reading skills (e.g., whole language methods). Struggling learners do not learn to read on their own. They need carefully orchestrated guidance by competent teachers, which is possible with use of the strategic, explicit teaching methods described in this book.

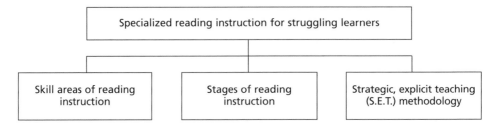

Figure 1.   Instructional model for teaching reading to struggling learners.

Teaching Reading to Struggling Learners is not designed to teach only beginning reading, but rather to help struggling students attain competency in reading at all levels, culminating at the adult literacy level. Some think that reading is mastered by third grade and that no special instruction is needed after this level, but this viewpoint ignores the higher level comprehension skills that are necessary for attaining adult competence in reading (Stevens & Bean, 2001). The challenges of instructing struggling students to understand their high school textbooks are as overwhelming as teaching students to master primary level word identification skills.

FOUR SKILL AREAS OF READING INSTRUCTION

In response to a Congressional mandate to improve the teaching of reading in America, the National Reading Panel issued a report recommending that reading instruction be focused on five skill areas: phonemic awareness, phonics, fluency, vocabulary, and text comprehension (National Institute of Child Health and Human Development, 2000). Based on this report, the document *Put Reading First: The Research Building Blocks for Teaching Children to Read* was produced to assist teachers in designing instruction for these five skill areas (The Partnership for Reading, 2001).

These five areas are critically important and constitute a starting point for reading instruction, but they do not include all areas necessary for a comprehensive reading program that will make struggling learners proficient readers. The instructional model presented in this book expands the skill areas to be taught to meet the different instructional needs of struggling students.

One of the reasons for the narrowness of the skill areas included in *Put Reading First*, often called the Reading First initiative, is the focus on teaching reading from kindergarten to third grade. This book focuses on teaching reading from kindergarten through the secondary level because only then can students attain mastery of the reading process. The goal of reading instruction must be the attainment of adult competency in reading (i.e., the ability to read all types of material in one's environment). Reading cannot be narrowly defined as the ability to identify words or sound out words; rather, reading must be defined as a process for getting meaning from the printed page. With this definition, it becomes apparent that students must be taught many different skills so that they can understand all types of print materials that they have to read.

Another reason for the narrowness of the skills included in the Reading First Initiative is the swing that takes place in the field of reading instruction. Periodically, the emphasis in the field of reading moves from a code-breaking, or phonics, approach to a meaning-based, or literacy, approach. In the 1970s and 1980s, the meaning-based approach, typified by whole language with no systematic teaching of specific reading skills, was popular. In the 1990s, emphasis in the field of reading shifted to a code-breaking approach. This shift is reflected in the stress placed on phonics in the National Reading Panel report. Both code breaking and phonics are necessary, but not sufficient, for teaching reading to struggling students.

One of the legs of the instructional model for struggling learners includes the four skill areas of reading instruction: pre-reading, word identification, fluency, and comprehension. Phonemic awareness is included as one of a number of important skills needed before learning to read. Vocabulary is subsumed under the broader category of comprehension. Each of the four major skill areas of reading and the specific skills included in each are shown in Table 1.

Pre-Reading

Before students can learn to read, they need to develop prerequisite skills involving language, visual processes, cognitive processes, experience, and motivation.

Language

Reading is best viewed as one level of a four-level verbal communication system that all children master.

- Receptive oral language (understanding oral language)
- Expressive oral language (talking)
- Receptive written language (reading)
- Expressive written language (written expression)

At the first level of communication, children understand language that they hear, which usually starts before age 1 in typically developing children. They then learn to use language to express their ideas, usually beginning be-

Table 1.   Four major skill areas and specific skills of reading instruction for struggling students

Pre-reading	Language
	Visual processes
	Cognitive processes
	Experience
	Motivation
Word identification	Phonics
	Visual analysis
	Structural analysis
	Combined methods
Fluency	Automatic word identification
	Reading smoothly and with inflection
	Speed
Comprehension	Language-based factors
	Cognitive processess
	Text structures

tween ages 1 and 2. After children have a strong foundation of receptive and expressive oral language (usually by age 5 or 6), they are ready to apply these skills to written language. At the third level of the communication system, children learn to understand language in written form (reading), which generally starts at age 6 in typically developing children. They learn to associate the words that they hear or speak with the words that are represented by print symbols. Finally, they reach the fourth level of the communication system in which they express their ideas through writing, which starts at about age 6 or 7.

It becomes apparent, through the use of the four-level communication system, that reading is a form of verbal communication built on a foundation of oral language and that effective reading instruction must link to this foundation. This communication system makes clear the need to tie reading and writing instruction together. For example, after students can read words with a particular sound, they need to learn to spell words with the sound. This communication system shows a basic principle of child development—that is, that learning at the receptive level precedes learning at the expressive level. Teaching receptive and then expressive mastery is one of the basic principles incorporated into the strategic, explicit teaching methodology in the instructional model.

The methods of reading instruction in general education are based on the assumption that children have mastered prerequisite receptive and expressive oral language skills. Children lacking the prerequisite language skills (e.g., students with language learning disabilities, students who are English language learners [ELLs]) do not learn to read by general education methods and may become hard to teach. Instruction for such children must include consideration of the development of both language and reading skills.

It is necessary to consider the five areas that compose oral language—phonology, morphology, semantics, syntax, and pragmatics—in order to build reading instruction on a strong foundation of oral language. These areas of oral language, their definitions, and relationships to reading are presented in Table 2.

Phonology deals with the sounds, or phonemes, of language. Children first master discrimination of different sounds followed by the production of words with different sounds. By school age, they can produce all of the sounds in English. The skill of discriminating and analyzing sounds in spoken words is called *phonological awareness*.[1] There is strong research support showing that phonological awareness skills are exceedingly important for learning to read (Torgesen, 1999). However, phonological awareness is necessary for learning to read primarily through phonics. Children must first attend to sounds they

---

[1]*Phonological awareness* is a broad term encompassing different ways of analyzing sounds. *Phonemic awareness* is a narrow term focusing on some ways of analyzing sounds. (See p. 29 for further information.)

Table 2. Areas of oral language, their definitions, and relationships to reading

Phonology	Discrimination and expression of sounds in spoken words
	Related to the pre-reading skill of phonological awareness and word identification skill of phonics
Morphology	Discrimination and expression of the smallest meaningful units of oral language
	Related to the word identification skill of structural analysis of word parts
Semantics	Meaningful understanding and production of spoken words
	Related to the comprehension skill of understanding written words or vocabulary
Syntax	Understanding and use of grammar or sentence structures in oral language
	Related to the comprehension skill of understanding written sentences
Pragmatics	Appropriate use of oral language with different speakers and in different settings
	Related to the fluency skill of reading with expression
	Related to skills involving literal, inferential, and evaluative comprehension of reading material

hear in words before they can attend to sounds they read in words. Therefore, it is necessary to teach phonological awareness skills so that students can break the code of the relationship between sounds that they hear (phonemes) and sounds represented by written letters they see (graphemes).

It is especially important to teach phonological awareness skills to students with learning disabilities who may not have mastered such skills like typically developing children (Torgesen, 1999). It may also be necessary to teach phonological awareness to ELLs because they have learned the sounds of their native language, which are often different from the sounds in English. For example, in Spanish, *j* is pronounced /h/, as in the word jalapeño (*Phonetics: The Sounds of Spanish and English*, n.d.).[2] In addition, students who speak different dialects may need phonological awareness instruction because their dialect may have sounds different from Standard American English, the dialect that is used in the schools. For example, children who speak African American Vernacular English (AAVE) may use the /f/ sound instead of the /th/ sound and say the word *teef* for the word *teeth* (*Salient Features of African American Vernacular English*, n.d.).

A second area of language that is a prerequisite for learning to read is morphology, which has to do with morphemes, or the smallest unit of meaning in language. Morphology is a prerequisite for learning to read using structural analysis methods in which students are taught to read multisyllabic words by analyzing the parts of words. Phonics help students read one-syllable words, but structural analysis is needed to learn to read multisyllabic words. For

---

[2]When letters are separated by hyphens within slash marks, the letter sounds, not the letter names, are represented. For example, when the word *cat* is written as /k-a-t/, the sounds of the letters are to be used. When the word is presented with spaces (*c a t*), then the letter names are to be used.

example, to learn to read the word *unlock*, students must understand the meaning of the two morphemes in the word (the base word *lock* and the prefix *un*) when they are spoken so they can apply this understanding when they read them. Three groups of children may have difficulty with morphology and may not be able to make the leap to reading larger, complex words: children with language learning disabilities, ELLs, and speakers of dialects other than Standard American English. For example, ELLs whose first language is Spanish may use *mas* (more) to show comparison rather than adding *er* onto a word (e.g., *more* fast versus fast*er*).

A third area of language that is tied to reading involves semantics, or understanding the meaning of spoken words. This area encompasses vocabulary. Children must first understand the meanings of words they hear so that they can subsequently associate these meanings to words when they read them. The semantic aspect of language may present difficulties for ELLs because they may not have the meanings of words in their oral vocabularies to correspond to the words that they are reading. They may be able to read a word aloud, but they may not understand its meaning. It must be emphasized that correctly reading a word aloud is not the same as knowing the meaning of a word.

The fourth area of language has to do with syntax or grammar, or how words are combined to form sentences. Children must understand sentences they hear before they can understand sentences that they read. Knowing the unique grammar of English is also imperative. For example, in English, the article preceding singular and plural nouns may be the same (*the* boy versus *the* boys), whereas in Spanish, the article changes for singular and plural nouns (*el* niño versus *los* niños). Consequently, children who are ELLs may have difficulty understanding the meanings of sentences because they do not understand the grammar of the sentences. Students who speak dialects other than Standard American English may also have difficulty understanding sentences that they read. Students who speak AAVE and substitute the word *is* for the word *be* may read the sentence *It is raining* and translate it into *It be raining*. Translating Standard American English material into the student's dialect makes the reading process harder for these children.

Pragmatics has to do with the uses of language for interpersonal communication, or how we vary our language when we speak to different people in different settings for different purposes. For example, middle school students speak respectfully to authority figures in school settings but speak familiarly to their peers on the baseball field. Understanding how language is used orally is transferred to understanding how language is used for reading purposes, especially higher level comprehension skills. For example, understanding how people speak to each other when reading the dialog of a play requires pragmatic language skills. In addition, the fluency skill of reading with meaning involves analyzing how material is read based on pragmatic factors.

Visual Processes

Learning to read requires visual as well as auditory processes (or phonological awareness). Visual processes are necessary for learning to read words that cannot be decoded by phonics or cannot be sounded out. For example, the word *was* cannot be sounded out, so it has to be visually recalled. It would be written as *wuz* if it were spelled phonetically. For nonphonetic words, of which there are many in the English language, it is necessary for students to have visual processing skills in discriminating letters and recalling letter sequences that make up words. Other visual processing skills are required for reading skills such as tracking print from left to right, going from one line to another, and going from one text box to another on a web page.

Any teacher who has worked with a student who needs help reading the word *the* on every line of a six-line, first-grade story is working with a student who has deficient visual memory skills. These impede the student from mastering the basic sight words that are the glue of reading material. Visual processing skills are also important for the fluency skills of automaticity and speed. These skills have also become important for reading electronic materials, especially web pages with complicated visual configurations.

Cognitive Processes

Reading is not a process of just decoding words; it is a process of gaining meaning from the printed page and using this meaning for the purpose of thinking. Decoding words is the means to the end, and the end is understanding, or comprehension, of the printed page. Comprehension requires many different cognitive processes ranging from simple understanding to higher order abstract thinking. At the pre-reading stage, students begin to develop different cognitive processes based on oral language and experiences. When they hear stories read by their parents or teachers, they begin to understand that stories have beginnings, middles, and ends. When they learn to read stories, they apply this knowledge learned from hearing stories. Children at the pre-reading stage have experiences that help them learn more advanced cognitive processes (e.g., understanding cause and effect based on building block towers and seeing how many can be stacked before they fall). Later, they apply this understanding of cause and effect to ideas that they read. Students with some types of learning disabilities may have difficulties mastering higher order cognitive processes and may need instruction to develop both cognitive processes and reading skills.

Experience

Having experiences (or prior knowledge) with the ideas that are in the reading material facilitates comprehension of the material. If a child has never seen or heard of an elephant, then a story about an elephant will be difficult to understand. If you were reading a story about yak butter, then you would likely find it more difficult to understand than a person who comes from Nepal where experiences with yak butter would be common. Children may have limited experiences because they come from different cultures or economically deprived backgrounds in which educational experiences have not been provided. These students need special instruction to supplement their lack of experiences so that they can be better equipped to understand reading material dependent on such experiences.

Motivation

Children must want to learn to read if reading instruction is to be successful. Some children are not motivated to learn to read for cultural reasons (e.g., their parents do not read, education is not valued in the home). Other children were motivated at one time, but when they experienced failure they turned away from reading because of the damage done to their fragile self-concepts. Ways to increase motivation for reading must constantly be interwoven into reading instruction for struggling students. Use of games and fun activities is especially important for motivating students to perform tasks that are not easy for them.

Word Identification

Word identification skills are those that are needed to figure out how to read specific words or how to decode words. There are three ways children learn to read one-syllable words, such as *cat:* one involves phonics or sounding out the letters of the word; another involves recalling visual aspects of the word and associating them with the word; and a third involves a combined phonics/visual approach in which part of the word is sounded out and is combined with visual recall of the word. With phonics, children sound out the three sounds in the word /k-a-t/; with visual methods, they remember that they saw the three letters in the word *c a t* in a book and they associate the letters with the oral word *cat;* and with a combined method, they may sound out the first sound /k/ that sparks an association to the word *cat* that they remember seeing.

Instruction on reading one-syllable words will not take students very far. They must be systematically taught multisyllabic words. There are also three ways to teach reading of multisyllabic words, such as *rabbit*. First, children use structural analysis in which they separate the word into two syllables, *rab bit*, sound each syllable out, combine them, and then say the word. Second, children visually recall that they saw some or all of letters in the word (e.g., they may recall the double *b's* in the middle) and associate it with the oral word. Third, children combine the two methods and sound out the first syllable and then visually recall the word that goes with those letters.

Therefore, students use four methods to decode both single and multi-syllabic words: phonics, visual analysis, structural analysis, and combined methods. The more methods students can use to decode words, the more likely they will become successful readers.

Phonics

Phonics involves learning to associate written symbols (e.g., graphemes) with the corresponding sounds of the language (e.g., phonemes), which is called grapheme–phoneme association. Most phonics instruction starts by teaching students to associate consonant sounds (e.g., /s/) with the corresponding written symbol (*s*). After consonant sounds are learned, then vowel sounds are taught (e.g., the short /a/ sound). Once the vowels are learned, children are ready to learn to decode words by sounding them out (e.g., /s-a-t/). Students must have mastered phonological awareness preskills in order to read phonetically.

The major reason that phonics is effective is because it enables children to *independently* read words containing sounds that they have been taught. They do not need a teacher to tell them words. However, the problem with phonics is that some words in the English language cannot be decoded because they do not follow phonetic rules (e.g., the word *work* should rhyme with the word *cork*, but it rhymes with the word *jerk*). Because of this, word identification cannot be based solely on phonics methods but must also involve visual analysis methods.

Visual Analysis

Visual analysis occurs when the teacher reads a word aloud as the word is visually presented. The students associate the orally presented word with the written word. The teacher points out what is special about how the word looks, or the students may independently notice this (e.g., the two *o*'s in the word *look* appear to be eyes). The students recall the sequences of letters in the word, the shape of the word, or an association with a picture. For example, students may recall the three letters *c a t* that they saw as the word was spoken by the teacher and a picture of a cat was shown. Or, the students may recall the *r* and the two *b*'s in the word *rabbit* and associate it with the spoken word and picture of a rabbit. Visual analysis methods are necessary for learning words that cannot be decoded phonetically (e.g., *was*). The disadvantage of visual analysis methods is that students have to be repeatedly told the word before they can read it. They usually cannot independently identify a word without the teacher's assistance.

Structural Analysis

It is not possible to sound out all the letters in a long word such as *civilization*. Therefore, students must be taught to analyze multisyllabic words into shorter, more manageable parts. For the word *rabbit*, they need to separate the two syllables and decode each. A prerequisite phonological awareness skill for reading using structural analysis is the ability to break orally presented words into syllables. Structural analysis builds on phonetic skills for reading one-syllable words. Once students separate words into syllables, they must apply decoding skills to read the syllables, which is often done phonetically.

Combined Word Identification Methods

Students who become competent readers use a number of decoding skills and combine these with context clues in which they use the meaning of the reading material to help decode a word. For example, when a student reads a sentence such as, "The rabbit can hop," the student may use the meaning of the word *hop*, which he can read, to help decode the word *rabbit*, which he cannot read. It is necessary to instruct struggling students to use these different methods to create effective word decoders and to develop a strategy in which they try different methods to see what works. We need to give these children all possible tools for unlocking words.

Fluency

After students can identify words and read sentences, they must attain automatic word identification and smooth reading of text with proper inflection. In addition, students must learn to adjust their speed of reading based on the purpose of the reading. Fluency is necessary so that students have quick access to word identification so that they can turn their attention from decoding to understanding the words that they read.

Automaticity results when students can identify words accurately and quickly. During the initial stages of learning to read, students often laboriously analyze words before identifying them. Struggling learners often linger at this initial stage of word identification; therefore, explicit instruction has to be directed at helping them to automatically identify words.

Fluency also involves reading of sentences and passages that is smooth and has proper inflection, or reading with meaning. Students must learn to process meaning while reading and use inflection to demonstrate this understanding, which is usually done through oral reading. However, students must also learn to do this when reading silently. For example, when reading a sentence such as, "He hit the ball out of the ballpark!" students must process the meaning of the exclamation point and read the sentence accordingly. Mastery of prerequisite pragmatic language skills involving how to use language is necessary for use of inflection when reading.

As students gain higher levels of reading achievement, it is important that they learn to increase their speed of reading text. This becomes especially important as students move through the grades and have more textbook reading and research to do for their content area classes. Students must also learn to adjust their speed of reading depending on the purpose of their reading. They need to learn to read slowly when reading for studying purposes but read quickly to skim for specific information. Skimming is an especially important reading skill for reading electronic text, such as web sites.

Comprehension

The ultimate goal of learning to read is to understand the meaning of the reading material and to use this understanding for the purpose of thinking. Comprehension skills are harder to develop than the other types of skills because of the different linguistic and cognitive skills that must be integrated with the identification of words and the long time period that is necessary for reaching complete mastery. There are three variables involved in teaching comprehension skills: language, cognitive processes, and text structures.

Language-Based Factors

Students must be systematically taught words (vocabulary) and syntax to develop comprehension. When teaching word understanding, they must be taught to associate words that they read with the meanings of these words in their oral vocabularies. This comprehension skill is built on pre-reading semantic skills that students develop in oral language. Through the primary grades, student vocabulary growth is based on words that they hear in their environment, but as they are exposed to more content area learning, their vocabulary grows through reading books. Initially, students associate word meaning with words they read, but when they have no associated meaning for a word, they must acquire it from the reading material by using context clues. Struggling learners must be taught how to systematically analyze reading material to identify and define new words.

A second area of language-based comprehension involves analysis of sentences to gain understanding. This is tied to the pre-reading syntax skills that students develop in oral language. Sentences are short and relatively easy to understand in the early stages of reading. They become increasingly longer and grammatically more complex as students read higher level materials, especially content area textbooks. Struggling students need strategic, explicit instruction on how to analyze the parts of such sentences so that they can grasp the underlying meaning.

Cognitive Processes

Students must be taught to apply different types of cognitive processes for the purpose of understanding the material in order to develop comprehension. Simple understanding of words and sentences, especially main ideas and details, is primarily required in the early stages of reading. Students can usually understand this material by tying it to the cognitive processes that they developed at the pre-reading level. At the early levels, literal comprehension skills (e.g., main idea, details, sequence) are mainly developed. However, students must develop inferential and evaluative comprehension skills as they are exposed to more advanced reading material and higher level expectations for thinking in content area subjects. These types of comprehension skills require thinking processes such as comparing, contrasting, categorizing, problem solving, inferring, predicting, and criticizing. Some struggling learners do not develop these thinking skills unless they are systematically taught using content area textbooks and carefully constructed teacher questions.

Text Structures

Students must be able to analyze the structure of the text they are reading and use strategies that best fit it to develop an understanding of advanced reading materials. There are three types of text: narrative (e.g., stories), expository (e.g., information from textbooks), and electronic (e.g., reading search engine web sites). Most reading at the primary grade level involves narrative text. Expository text is introduced as content area textbooks are used. Electronic text is not usually systematically taught but needs to be included in instructional programs for struggling learners. Systematic, explicit teaching of strategies to meet comprehension demands of these three types of text structures must be provided to struggling learners.

SIX STAGES OF LEARNING TO READ

The purpose of this book is to describe how to teach reading to struggling learners from the pre-reading level to adulthood. It is not enough to get these students through the early reading stage because they continue to have linguistic, cognitive, or experiential challenges for meeting the demands for reading at higher levels. These students must be equipped to meet the reading demands of secondary and postsecondary education and the challenges of working and living in a print-rich world. Therefore, the second leg of the instructional model includes the stages of learning to read from pre-reading to adult mastery.

The stages of reading in the instructional model are based on the stages put forth by Jeanne Chall (1983)—the great reading pioneer. She proposed six stages that typically developing children pass through.

1. Pre-reading (from birth to age 6)

2. Initial reading (from grades 1 to 2)

3. Fluency (from grades 2 to 3)

4. Reading to learn new information (from grades 4 to 8)

5. Reading from multiple viewpoints (from grades 8 to 12)

6. Construction and reconstruction of knowledge (at the college level)

The stages in the instructional model described in this book are the same as Chall's, but the fifth and sixth stages have been condensed, and the adult literacy stage has been added. There is also greater emphasis on electronic reading because so much of our knowledge today is web based. The six stages of learning to read along with the major skill areas developed at each stage are shown in Table 3.

These stages should be used as guides for understanding how reading should be taught. It is important to teach all the skills at a particular stage using strategic, explicit teaching methods for students who are at risk for reading failure. The stages should be used as a guide for *preventing* reading failure in children who are at risk by ensuring that all skills at each stage are explicitly taught.

For students who have already failed in reading (e.g., those diagnosed with learning disabilities), there must be instruction to develop skills that they missed at earlier stages. These stages serve as a guide for providing them with

Table 3.   Six stages of learning to read

1. Pre-reading stage	Develops before age 6 in typically developing children
	Development of skills in the areas of language (including phonological awareness), visual processes, cognitive processes, and experiences
2. Early reading stage	Develops at grades 1–2 in typically developing children
	Development of word identification skills using phonics, visual analysis, and structural analysis
	Development of word comprehension skills of words in students' oral vocabulary
	Development of literal comprehension of narrative text
3. Fluency stage	Develops at grades 2–3 in typically developing children
	Development of automatic word identification and comprehension skills mastered at previous stage
	Application of word identification and comprehension skills mastered at previous stage to more advanced reading materials
4. Reading to learn stage	Develops at grades 4–8, using content area reading, in typically developing students
	Development of word comprehension skills of words not in students' oral vocabulary
	Development of literal, inferential, and evaluative comprehension skills of expository text
	Development of metacognitive strategies for monitoring reading
5. Advanced reading stage	Develops at grades 8–12 and postsecondary education, using content area reading, in typically developing students
	Development of word comprehension skills of words not in students' oral vocabulary
	Development of literal, inferential, and evaluative comprehension of all types of text in wide range of content areas
	Development of metacognitive strategies for study skills and test taking
6. Adult literacy stage	Lifelong learning
	Continuous development of comprehension skills adapted to the changing literacy demands of a technological society

Note: Based on Chall's six stages (1983).

remedial instruction. In addition, it is necessary to analyze two stages—the stage that corresponds to their reading level and the stage that corresponds to their grade placement. For example, if a sixth grader was reading at the second-grade level, then it would be necessary to teach the skills at the early reading stage. In addition, the reading expectations for a sixth grader at the reading to learn stage would need to be analyzed to determine how they could be modified. This student would not have the word identification and fluency skills necessary to read content area texts or be ready to learn the comprehension skills that are the focus of this stage. The devastating cumulative effect of reading failure becomes apparent by analyzing student performance and expectations using these six stages of reading.

At the pre-reading stage, the skills necessary for learning to read in the subsequent stages are established. The major skills at this stage involve the development of language, visual processing, and cognitive processing and exposure to educationally supportive experiences. At the early reading stage, word identification skills involving phonics, visual analysis, structural analysis, and combined methods are developed. The major comprehension skills developed at this stage are reading comprehension for words in the students' oral vocabulary. Students need to learn to decode words and then associate the words with the corresponding meanings they previously learned. Literal comprehension of narrative text is also developed.

At the fluency stage, the skills developed at the early reading stage are emphasized so that students learn to read automatically. In addition, the word identification and comprehension skills developed in the earlier stage are further developed with more advanced words, sentences, and different types of texts.

The reading to learn stage constitutes a significant shift in the reading process because at the two preceding stages students learned how to read, but at this stage, they know how to read and must apply this ability to learn new information. This stage introduces content area reading in which students learn to read their textbooks. They learn to read new words that are not in their oral vocabularies and they learn inferential and evaluative comprehension skills as applied to expository material. They begin to develop metacognitive reading skills in which they monitor their reading to make sure that they understand what they read.

At the advanced reading stage, which encompasses the secondary and postsecondary levels, students continue to grow in vocabulary and literal, inferential, and evaluative comprehension skills with all types of texts. They develop higher order cognitive skills as they learn to read the materials for their classes. They also learn metacognitive strategies for use with study skills and test-taking skills.

Once the adult literacy stage is reached, individuals can use reading for lifelong learning. They can adapt the comprehension skills they have developed in the five previous stages to changing literacy demands of the complex, technological society in which we live. This is the ultimate goal for teaching struggling learners because only then do they have the reading knowledge to be successful in all areas of their lives.

STRATEGIC, EXPLICIT TEACHING METHODOLOGY

Children who are not struggling usually learn by the various methods used in general education. Struggling students do not learn by most general education methods because the onus is on the student to learn independently and not on the teacher to teach. They do not learn by discovery-type methods. They learn by carefully planned step-by-step methods focused on development of specific reading skills at each stage of learning to read.

The strategic, explicit teaching methodology used with this instructional model is tied to scientifically based research with struggling students. This instructional approach has two aspects: systematic steps using explicit instruction and principles of effective teaching. The strategic, explicit teaching methodology used with this model is similar to the direct instruction approach (Carnine, Silbert, Kame'enui, & Tarver, 2004), but it is more comprehensive and flexible in its use. The strategic, explicit teaching methodology uses the following five steps in the sequence of teaching specific reading skills.

1. *Advanced organizers*, which show the student the objective of the instruction and link the target skills being taught with previously taught skills

2. *Teacher modeling*, so it is clear what skill is to be learned

3. *Guided practice*, in which the student uses the skill with the help of the teacher

4. *Independent practice*, in which the student uses the skill without the help of the teacher

5. *Generalization*, in which the student applies the skill to different settings and materials

The principles of effective teaching are based on research on instructional practices that have been found effective with students with learning disabilities (Carnine, 1999; Swanson, 1999; Vaughn, Gersten, & Chard, 2000). Some of the major principles of effective teaching include small group or one-to-one teaching, strategy instruction, and controlling task difficulty.

Model lessons are provided at the end of Chapters 3–7 that demonstrate how to apply strategic, explicit teaching to different skill areas. These model lessons incorporate the steps of strategic, explicit teaching and the principles of effective instruction so that you can see how reading skills are most effectively taught to struggling students.

2

S.E.T.

Strategic, Explicit Teaching

> **CONCEPTS EXPLORED**
>
> - Evidence-based reading instruction
> - Explicit instruction
> - Strategy instruction
> - Steps and accompanying procedures for S.E.T.
> - Principles of designing effective reading instruction

EVIDENCE-BASED READING INSTRUCTION

Struggling learners can only become competent readers if they are given instruction that is carefully designed to meet their individual needs. This chapter describes how you can provide such reading instruction. The instructional approach advocated in this book is scientifically based (i.e., based on evidence from studies on methods that have been demonstrated as effective for teaching struggling students to read). Reviews of research studies on teaching reading to students with learning problems have shown that direct instruction and strategy instruction are two necessary ingredients for effective teaching (Carnine et al., 2004; Gersten, Fuchs, & Williams, 2001; Swanson, 1999; Vaughn, Gersten, & Chard, 2000). Both direct instruction and strategy instruction serve as the third leg of the specialized reading approach described in Chapter 1. Although direct instruction is stressed more for word identification and fluency skills, and strategy instruction is emphasized more for comprehension skills, both are essential for teaching all reading skills.

This chapter describes strategic, explicit teaching (S.E.T.) so that you can incorporate it into teaching your struggling learners. In addition to S.E.T., the principles of good teaching based on research-demonstrated effectiveness and best practices that are needed for teaching struggling students to read are also described in this chapter.

EXPLICIT INSTRUCTION

Although direct instruction is one of the ingredients of S.E.T., this term is not used in this book. Instead, the term *explicit instruction* is used. The term *direct instruction* is often associated with a specific reading program (i.e., DISTAR, also called Reading Mastery; Engelmann & Bruner, 1988). However, direct instruction can be used with a number of instructional methods and does not necessarily mean the use of one particular reading program. To avoid confusion that may result from the automatic association of the instructional approach advocated in this book with DISTAR or another program, the term *explicit instruction* is used in lieu of *direct instruction*.

To understand explicit instruction, it is best to contrast it with constructivist or discovery methods of learning, which are frequently used in general education. With these methods, students independently discover what they are to learn and teachers play a limited role in helping with the learning process. With explicit instruction, what is to be learned is made clear to the students and teachers play a dominant role in helping students with the learning process.

A discovery method that has been popular for teaching reading in general education is the whole language approach. The underlying assumption of this approach is that students *naturally* learn to read and learn by just being exposed to reading material (Goodman, 1986). There are no textbooks with this approach; rather, students read trade books (story books). There is no teaching of word identification or comprehension skills because it is assumed that students will learn to identify words based on understanding the overall meaning of the reading material (Carnine et al., 2004). In contrast, explicit reading instruction is delivered through lessons that are designed to build in a variety of specific word identification and comprehension skills. There is no assumption that students can learn to read on their own. Rather, it is assumed that they will only learn if effective methods are used to teach specific word identification and comprehension skills. Research has shown that constructivist or discovery methods, such as the whole language reading approach, have not been effective with struggling students (Carnine et al., 2004; Swanson, 1999). Struggling students do not learn on their own; that is why they are hard to teach. They learn best if carefully guided by competent teachers.

Explicit instruction is *comprehensive, performance-based*, and *systematic*. It is *comprehensive* because it includes a scope and sequence of all reading skills that must be taught to the students by the teacher. These skills extend from the pre-reading to the adult literacy stage. Identifying students' level of mastery for each skill determines what skills the students need to learn. This can best be done with comprehensive assessment using standardized tests, informal assessment, curriculum-based assessment, and teacher constructed tests, which are described in Chapter 12.

Once a student's level of reading mastery of a particular reading skill is determined, you know where to start teaching. You know the student's level of mastery in terms of where she is in the sequence of steps in learning a target reading skill. In this way, the difficulty level of instructional tasks is controlled, and the student is not expected to perform at levels that are too high for her.

Explicit instruction is *performance-based* because it incorporates the pretest-teach-posttest process. I first proposed this process in a 1973 article on creating and evaluating remediation, or specialized teaching, for students with learning disabilities (Minskoff, 1973). With this process, testing is used before teaching to discover what skills a student has not mastered. Testing is necessary after teaching to ascertain the degree to which the skills have been mastered. There is a presentation of a stimulus to which a student makes a response with both testing and teaching. However, with teaching, strategies are used between the stimulus and response to build in the desired response. The essential ingredient of remediation involves these strategies.

For example, pretesting has shown that a particular student does not know any short vowel sounds. Therefore, the teacher wants to instruct her to produce the short *a* vowel sound. The first step involves learning the sound in isolation with the help of strategies such as key word associations (e.g., the word *apple* starts with the /a/ sound). Once testing shows that she can do this, the student is moved to the second step in which she decodes isolated words with the /a/ sound. After demonstrating that she can do this, the student goes to the third step and reads words with the /a/ sound in sentences. When posttesting indicates that she has mastered these three steps, the student is ready to move to the next step and learn the short *o* sound.

Explicit instruction is *systematic* because sequential steps are followed to take the student from limited or no mastery to complete mastery of a skill. These steps are effective in aiding the learning of struggling students and include the following procedures (Carnine et al., 2004; Swanson, 1999; Vaughn et al., 2000):

- Clear instructional goals: teachers must have goals for what they want to teach their students based on skills they have not mastered

- Modeling of the target skill to be learned: teachers must provide a clear demonstration of how to perform a reading skill

- Providing prompts and cues for the correct demonstration of the skill: teachers must use as many prompts and cues as necessary to assist the students in acquiring the skill

- Use of think-alouds: teachers need to verbally describe how a skill is performed so that the students become aware of what they need to do

- Corrective feedback: teachers need to show the students how to perform a skill when they have done so incorrectly

- Positive reinforcement: teachers need to firmly implant correct responses by providing reinforcers that the students value

- High levels of student engagement: teachers need to make sure that students are active participants in the teaching–learning interaction

Explicit instruction emphasizes the teacher as the guide who clearly shows students what skills they need to learn and how they can achieve them.

STRATEGY INSTRUCTION

The term *strategy* is used in education in two ways, which can lead to confusion. It is used to refer to techniques that *students* use to improve their mastery of learning a particular skill, and it is used to refer to techniques that *teachers* use to help students learn. In this book, the term *strategy* is only used to refer to what students use. The term *technique* is used to describe what teachers use to help students learn.

This book incorporates two different definitions of strategy instruction when pertaining to students. First, strategy instruction is targeted at teaching students efficient ways to acquire, store, and express information and skills (Mercer & Mercer, 2001). This definition of strategy instruction is similar to the view expressed previously (i.e., strategies are the ingredients used for teaching in the pretest-teach-posttest process). Teachers model how to use these strategies so that students will incorporate them into their behavior. For example, a teacher might use the strategy of having students put their fingers over their lips as a signal for quiet when learning the /sh/ sound.

A different definition of strategy instruction is more general and involves how a person thinks and acts when planning, executing, and evaluating performance of a task and its outcomes (Lenz, Ellis, & Scanlon, 1996). This definition of strategy instruction is related to development of metacognition, or students' ability to control and manage their cognitive activities in a reflective, purposeful fashion (Gersten, Fuchs, & Williams, 2001). For example, a teacher might teach the metacognitive strategy of monitoring for meaning when reading by having the students ask themselves, "Does this make sense?" after reading each paragraph in a passage.

With S.E.T., students are taught specific strategies to facilitate their mastery of different reading skills. In addition, they are taught metacognitive skills so that they can manage their mental activities when reading.

STEPS AND ACCOMPANYING PROCEDURES FOR S.E.T.

The basic principles of explicit instruction and strategy instruction have been used as the basis for S.E.T. Table 4 shows the five steps in S.E.T. and accompanying procedures: advanced organizer, modeling, guided practice, independent practice, and generalization.

Advanced Organizer

The purpose of the advanced organizer step is to set the stage for what will be taught and to establish an anticipatory set in the students (i.e., a knowledge of what will come). A frequently used acronym for the three procedures used is LIP (Minskoff & Allsopp, 2003).

- **L:** linking of the target skill to be learned to previously learned skills or prior knowledge relevant to the task

- **I:** identifying the objective of the instruction so that the students know what they are to learn

- **P:** providing an explanation of why the skill to be learned is important

You need to review previously learned skills so that you are sure that the students are ready for this next step. For example, when introducing reading of the short *o* sound, review the short *a* sound to make sure that the students have retained a high level of mastery. Thus, the next step in the sequence of learning short vowel sounds is based on mastery of the previous step. In addition to reviewing previously learned skills, it is also important to link what will

Table 4.   Steps and procedures of strategic, explicit teaching (S.E.T.)

Steps	Procedures
Advanced organizer	**L:** Link the target skill to be learned by reviewing previously learned skills or prior knowledge relevant to the task.
	I: Identify the objective of the instruction.
	P: Provide an explanation about why the skill to be learned is important.
Modeling	Demonstrate how to perform the skill using strategies.
	Provide prompts and cues to focus students' attention on important aspects of performing the skill using think-alouds.
	Use multisensory teaching to provide students multiple avenues for mastering the skill.
Guided practice	Provide a high level of support and gradually fade as students demonstrate mastery of the skill.
	Provide corrective feedback for students' incorrect responses.
	Provide positive reinforcement for students' correct responses.
	Monitor and chart student performance to determine pace of instruction and movement to independent practice step.
Independent practice	Provide multiple opportunities for practice of the skill.
	Monitor and chart student progress to determine when to move to the next step, generalization.
	Return to previous steps if students have difficulty.
Generalization	Provide opportunities for students to use the new skill with different materials and in different settings.
	Periodically review skills and return to guided or independent practice steps, if necessary.

be learned with prior knowledge. For example, when teaching comprehension of a story about whales, it is important to discuss what the students already know about whales so that they can use this as a foundation for understanding what they read in the story.

The second and third parts of LIP inform the students what they are going to learn and why. So often, students are clueless about what they are learning. They have no direction and, consequently, little motivation to learn to read. The second part of LIP has the teacher tell the students what they are going to learn so they can "see" where the instruction will take them. The third part of LIP has the teacher give the students information on why learning the skill is important. This helps the students become active participants in the teaching–learning interaction. The purpose of LIP is for students to have a high level of involvement in and motivation for learning the target skill.

Modeling

Struggling students are not independent learners. They do not easily master reading skills because they have difficulties with memory, attention, metacognition, and are passive learners (Lerner, 2003). Students who are struggling cannot just be *told* what to do; they need to be *shown*. You must model a strategy for learning a skill by providing a clear demonstration of the skill as you use think-alouds to describe what you are doing. Use think-alouds and bombard the students with prompts and cues to focus their attention on the important aspects of performing the skill. Also, use multisensory approaches to provide students with different avenues to master the skill. Whenever possible, techniques involving visual, auditory, kinesthetic, and tactile (VAKT) senses should be used.

Guided Practice

The movement from the modeling to the guided practice step represents the shift from teacher control of the teaching–learning process to student control. The purpose of this shift is to gradually give total control to the students. Struggling students require many opportunities to practice the target skill starting with a high level of support and gradually fading the support as they demonstrate mastery of the skill. It is vitally important that practice of new skills be carefully scaffolded, or supported, because of student difficulties with retention. Providing high levels of support in the early stages leads to success and increased student motivation to continue trying to master the skill.

At this step, control the task difficulty by starting with examples that you have modeled. As the students progress, gradually introduce new examples. Also, control task difficulty by gradually eliminating prompts and cues. For example, in the early stages of learning the short /o/ sound, have the students say the associated word and sound before they read words with the short *o* sounds. "We're reading short *o* words. The short *o* is at the beginning of the word *octopus*. Octopus. /o/. Now we're going to use this sound to read these words with the short *o* sound." After the students can correctly decode words with the short *o*, drop the use of think-alouds involving associated words.

Give positive reinforcement for students' correct responses. Identify what students find reinforcing and use these (e.g., if a student likes stickers, then use them; if another student likes a token system leading to classroom store purchases, then use tokens). Be sure to vary what you say when using verbal reinforcers, and do not say the same reinforcer repeatedly (e.g., do not say the word *good* after each correct response, but say *awesome, cool,* or *nice* instead). When students respond incorrectly, provide immediate corrective feedback to help them identify why they made the error and assist them in producing the correct response.

Provide visual representations of the students' progress as they move from less to more difficult tasks. Seeing their progress charted increases their motivation to continue learning. Monitor student performance as the basis for determining the pacing of instruction and when to move to the independent practice step.

Independent Practice

As students gain mastery of a target skill, it is important that they practice it without any assistance from the teacher. This step is especially important for students with learning disabilities who demonstrate learned helplessness and come to rely on their teachers and others to perform difficult tasks for them instead of trying on their own. At this step it is important to carefully monitor the students progress and provide corrective feedback when students have difficulty and decide if it is necessary to return to the guided practice step. As students demonstrate independent mastery of the target skill, they can be moved to the generalization step.

Generalization

At this step, students apply the newly learned skill to different settings and with different materials. This step is critical for students to transfer skills they have learned in special settings to authentic settings so that they can meet the classroom demands for reading. Without planned opportunities for students to generalize the reading skills they have learned, they will not meet with success in the real world. For example, at the generalization step, students who have been taught to phonetically decode materials in their special reading program would be required to apply these skills to decoding the reading materials in their general education classroom. This step is also important for students to transfer skills so that they can perform better on statewide assessments. This step is critical for students with learning disabilities because they frequently have problems with generalization of skills (Lerner, 2003). You need to continue monitoring student progress at this step. It may be necessary to return to additional instruction at the guided or independent practice steps for students who have difficulty generalizing newly learned skills to new materials and different settings.

Chapters 3–7 contain model lessons showing how S.E.T. is used to develop the specific reading skills described in each chapter.

PRINCIPLES OF DESIGNING EFFECTIVE READING INSTRUCTION

If a strategic, explicit approach, such as S.E.T., is to be successful, then it is necessary to incorporate principles that have been shown to be effective for enhancing learning.

1. Reading instruction for struggling learners should be prioritized over all other areas of instruction. Reading should be the cornerstone of the curriculum for struggling students. The more severe the students' reading problems, the more instructional time needs to be devoted to reading. Research has demonstrated that the more time devoted to learning a task, the more likely the task will be mastered (Carroll, 1963). Ironically, struggling readers, who need to spend as much time as possible on reading, spend less time on reading than skilled readers (Stanovich, 2000). Maximizing academic learning time (ALT), the time students spend actively engaged and meaningfully involved in literacy activities at a level at which they can be both challenged and successful, has been identified as a best practice for helping struggling readers (Allington, 2001). Some reading instruction programs lack the intensity necessary to remediate students' deficits in reading. Students who are 2 or 3 years delayed in reading will not "catch up" in 1 year, even if they make up a year's progress in 1 school year. They need to have more intense academic instructional time devoted to reading over a long period of time so that they can catch up.

When we want students to improve in other skill areas, we make sure that we provide a lot of time for practice. For example, students with an interest in basketball spend a lot of time practicing shooting baskets. Students with an interest in playing the piano spend a lot of time practicing playing. We need to use the same approach with reading. However, devoting more time to reading instruction becomes a problem as students get into fourth grade and beyond, when instructional time is usually channeled away from language arts to content area instruction. If, at these higher grades, additional time is devoted to reading rather than content area instruction, this causes the students to fall behind in science or social studies. The schools are faced with a daunting choice for children who need extra time for reading instruction—where the additional time will come from.

2. Reading should be provided on an individual or small-group basis. Research has demonstrated that reading instruction delivered individually or on a small-group basis results in greater gains than classroom instruction (Vaughn et al., 2000). Students with reading problems cannot have their unique needs met when they are in a large classroom where teachers often teach to the average student, which is at a higher level for struggling students. Delivering instruction to individuals or small groups is difficult and expensive for public schools. Reading instruction that might have been effective had it been delivered individually or in small groups is not effective when delivered in large groups.

3. Continuous evaluation should be done. Student progress needs to be examined at daily, weekly, grading period, and semester points. If students are not making adequate progress, then the instructional program must be changed. Continuing to use an instruction approach when it is *not* working is educational malpractice. Changing an instructional approach is difficult, especially at mid-year, for most public schools. Flexibility is not a characteristic of most schools, especially large ones.

4. A variety of instructional methods and materials must be used. Reading materials need to be varied so that the students apply reading skills to the different types of materials that they will meet. It is especially important to include technology, both in terms of computer-assisted instruction and reading different forms of electronic print. To motivate students to want to read, it is important to use materials that are of interest to them. For example, if students are interested in NASCAR or wrestling, then materials with such content should be emphasized. Also, games are important for practicing reading skills in a fun way.

5. Reading should be embedded in social interactions with teachers, peers, and others. Learning to read is facilitated when there is an interactive relationship between the teacher and the students. The see-saw relationship between teacher control of the learning process to student control can only be accomplished by active interaction between the teacher and the learners. Reading with peers, as in peer tutoring arrangements, has been demonstrated as an effective means for improving reading in struggling students (Vaughn et al., 2000). Students should read with many other people such as parents, para-professionals, volunteers, and younger children.

6. Success must be programmed into all lessons. The best motivator for learning to read is success. It is human nature for people to want to do what they do well and to avoid doing what they do not do well. Likewise, students with reading problems avoid reading. They must experience success so that they are motivated to read.

7. A knowledgeable, competent, relentless teacher is key to success for teaching reading. A teacher must be knowledgeable about the many reading skills and stages of reading that students pass through to finally attain adult reading competency. They must be competent in techniques for teaching these skills. They need to know many methods, not just one or a few. No one reading method works for every student with a reading problem. Teachers must be proficient in using many methods so that they can find the ones that meet each student's unique needs. Finally, teachers have to be relentless in their quest to teach all students to read. They cannot give up on any student. They have to believe that each and every student can become a successful reader.

3

Building a Solid Foundation

Teaching Pre–Reading Skills

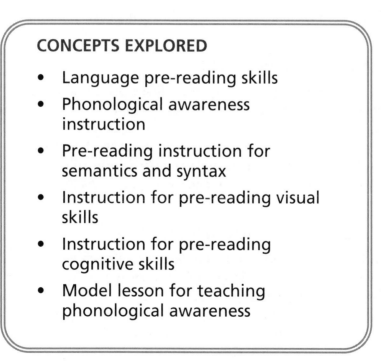

CONCEPTS EXPLORED

- Language pre-reading skills
- Phonological awareness instruction
- Pre-reading instruction for semantics and syntax
- Instruction for pre-reading visual skills
- Instruction for pre-reading cognitive skills
- Model lesson for teaching phonological awareness

Pre-reading skills in oral language, visual processing, and cognitive processing provide the building blocks for specific reading skills learned at later stages. For most children, these skills start developing at birth and culminate at age 6 when they are strong enough to support the building of reading. However, these pre-reading skills primarily develop from ages 3 to 6, also known as the reading readiness period. Some in the field of reading believe that these pre-reading skills develop naturally and do not have to be explicitly taught and call this the emergent literacy period (Leu & Kinzer, 2003). These skills do not emerge naturally for children who are at risk for reading difficulties (e.g., ELLs, those who are economically disadvantaged, those who are culturally diverse, those with learning disabilities) and must be explicitly taught. Therefore, preschool education at this level is necessary for learners who are at risk. The nature of such preschool education should be both developmentally based, in which play and socialization are emphasized, and academically based, in which pre-reading skills are systematically taught. Such preschool programs are often provided through Head Start and early childhood special education. A remedial program emphasizing pre-reading skills—which can be provided through special education, ESL, Title I, and general education programs—is necessary for children who are older than age 6 and have not developed these skills.

LANGUAGE PRE-READING SKILLS

In order to learn to read, students must first master oral language skills in phonology, morphology, semantics, syntax, and pragmatics. Pre-reading skills involving phonology are referred to as *phonological awareness* and are developed by general education and special education teachers. Language pre-reading skills involving semantics, syntax, and pragmatics are usually taught by speech-language therapists, ESL teachers, and some special educators.

PHONOLOGICAL AWARENESS INSTRUCTION

The need to teach phonological awareness before teaching phonics has long been recognized. Two specific phonological analysis skills that were taught with the *Remedial Reading Drills* (Hegge, Kirk, & Kirk, 1936) are auditory discrimination and sound blending. These drills have been revised by Sam Kirk, Winifred Kirk, and the author of this book. Now titled the *Phonics Remedial Reading Lessons* (Kirk, Kirk, & Minskoff, 1985), they continue to emphasize these two prerequisite phonological awareness skills. The importance of teaching phonological awareness skills is strongly supported by past (Liberman & Shankweiler, 1985) and current (Torgesen, 1999) research. From a logical point of view, it is also apparent that phonological skills are necessary for learning to read because children cannot attend to sounds in written words without first being able to attend to sounds in spoken words.

Dyslexia is caused by deficits in phonological awareness, according to The International Dyslexia Association's definition of *dyslexia:* "a specific learning disability . . . characterized by difficulties with accurate and/or fluent word recognition and by poor spelling and decoding abilities. These difficulties typically result from a deficit in the phonological component of language" (Lyon, Shaywitz, & Shaywitz, 2003). Some researchers believe that there are two subtypes of dyslexia. One subtype is phonologic dyslexia, which is caused by deficits in phonological awareness. The second subtype, orthographic dyslexia, is caused by visual deficits. Unfortunately, orthographic dyslexia has been ignored compared with the attention given to phonological dyslexia (Roberts & Mather, 1997).

There has been a great deal of emphasis on phonological awareness in terms of both assessment and instruction. Statewide assessments often include assessment of phonological awareness skills. For example, at the first-grade level, the Virginia Standards of Learning include assessment of the phonological skills of sound counting, adding and deleting phonemes, creating rhymes, and blending sounds (*Standards of Learning Currently in Effect,* n.d.). Some of the major standardized tests that have been developed to assess various aspects of phonological instruction are listed in Appendix B. There have also been programs and books devoted to phonological instruction, including the LiPS Program (Lindamood & Lindamood, 1998) and Fundations (Wilson, 2002).

Phonological awareness is necessary for learning to read by a phonics method. However, there is a current overemphasis on training only phonological awareness. This can be dangerous because it leads to a simplistic view of reading instruction. Some believe that phonological awareness training is the magic bullet. It is not. Training in phonological awareness will not automatically result in improved reading. Skills in a number of different areas, including phonological awareness, are needed to become a competent reader.

There has been some confusion about two frequently used terms: *phonological awareness* and *phonemic awareness.* Phonological awareness is best used as a broad term that includes analysis of **phonemes** (individual sounds), **syllables, rhymes, words,** and **onsets** and **rimes,** whereas phonemic awareness includes only the ability to hear, identify, and manipulate individual sounds, or **phonemes,** in spoken words (The Partnership for Reading, 2001). In this book, the term *phonological awareness* is used to represent the broad category of skills in analyzing words, sounds, and syllables.

Mastery of phonological awareness skills represents a significant transition in the development of children. They move from responding to words based on their meanings (semantics) to also responding to words based on their sounds (phonology). Initially, children respond to a word such as *cat* by associating it with its meaning of an animal that meows. In the preschool years, they start to respond to a word such as *cat* in a different way; they associate it

Table 5. Phonological awareness skills

Phonological awareness for sounds
Auditory discrimination
Sound segmentation
Sound blending
Rhyming
Sound counting
Sound deletion and addition
Onsets and rimes
Phonological awareness for syllables and compound words
Compound words
Syllable blending
Syllable segmentation

with other words that sound like it (*bat, hat, mat*) and other words that start with the same sound (*cow, cub*).

Phonological awareness needs to be developed by teaching children the specific skills involved in this broad ability. Two major areas of phonological awareness must be taught: phonological awareness for sounds or phonemes (phonemic awareness) and phonological awareness for syllables. The specific subskills in each of these two major areas are shown in Table 5.

Phonological awareness instruction requires a high level of competency in the different skills on the part of the teacher. A test for phonological proficiency is included in Appendix C. Take this test with your professor, classmates, and/or colleagues. If you have difficulties with any of the skills, then make sure that you master them before you try to teach students these same skills. Students who need phonological awareness skills also need to have correct models presented by their teachers.

The specific subskills for phonological awareness of sounds include auditory discrimination, sound segmentation, sound blending, rhyming, sound counting, sound deletion and addition, and onsets and rimes. Although all seven subskills are important, sound segmentation and sound blending are most important for learning to read by a phonics method (Wanzek & Haager, 2003). If you have limited time available for phonological awareness training, give priority to these two subskills. A second type of phonological awareness involves syllables and compound words. Instead of focusing on specific sounds, this type of awareness focuses on word parts. Phonological analysis for syllables is necessary for learning to read by a structural analysis method. If students cannot separate spoken words into syllables, then they will not be able to separate written words into syllables.

Guidelines for Designing Phonological Awareness Instruction

Use the following general guidelines to design instruction for both types of phonological awareness.

1. Gradually sequence the instructional difficulty of tasks by controlling the number of sounds or syllables in the words presented. At the beginning of instruction, use words with two sounds (e.g., /g-o/). After these are mastered, move to words with three sounds (e.g., /m-a-t/) and finally four sounds (e.g., /s-p-o-t/). Do the same with phonological awareness training for syllables, starting with words with two syllables (e.g., *rab-bit*) and then three syllables (e.g., *com-pu-ter*). It is probably not necessary to go beyond three syllables for phonological awareness training because of the difficulty of such lengthy words.

2. Sequence the instructional difficulty of tasks by first placing the target sounds to be learned in the initial position in words, then the final position, and then the middle or medial position. For example, have students segment words based on the initial sound (e.g., "What is the first sound in the word *cat*?"), then the final sound (e.g., "What is the last sound in the word *cat*?"), and the middle sound (e.g., "What is the middle sound in the word *cat*?"). Sounds at the beginning of words are easiest to identify because they are heard first; sounds at the end are next easiest because they are heard last; and sounds embedded in between other sounds are most difficult because they must be "pulled out" from the other sounds.

3. Sequence the difficulty level of students' responses by first using receptive tasks and then expressive tasks. Receptive tasks are easier than expressive tasks because students can select the answer from the choices presented. Expressive tasks are open ended and require the students to produce the answer. Use receptive tasks in the early stages of teaching a skill, and as students demonstrate mastery, move to expressive tasks. For example, use a multiple-choice format for sound counting with a receptive response (e.g., "Does the word *go* have two or three sounds?"). Then, use an expressive task in which the students have to produce the response (e.g., "How many sounds does the word *go* have?").

4. In the initial stages of instruction, use words with continuous sounds that can be elongated. For example, when teaching students to segment initial sounds, start with the continuous sounds (*f, h, l, m, n, r, s,* and *sh*) as well as short vowel sounds. When presenting these sounds, emphasize them by drawing them out (e.g., "The first sound in the word *sun* is /sss-u-n/.").

5. When modeling words and their sounds, first say the whole word, then the separate sounds in the word, and then the whole word again. This will provide the contrast of the complete word and the word with separated sounds. For example, for modeling sound blending say, "The word *boy* can be said /b-oy/. Boy." Have students repeat the complete word and the target sounds after you so that they are isolating the target sound to be learned. For example, say, "Say *boy* . . . Say /b-oy/ . . . Say *boy*."

6. Use a multisensory, or VAKT, approach with as many different sensory inputs and varied motor responses as possible. To associate sounds with visual stimuli, use the Elkonin procedure (Elkonin, 1973) in which visual stimuli, such as blocks or chips, are associated with sounds. For example, when counting sounds, have students point to a chip for each sound as it is spoken. Structure tasks to include as much active student involvement as possible, requiring both fine and gross motor responses. For example, have students tap their thumbs and fingers for each sound that they hear, clap for each syllable that they hear in a word, or stand whenever they hear a specific sound spoken.

7. Make the instructional periods for phonological training short and frequent. Many children have difficulty sustaining attention to such tasks for long periods of time because of the abstractness of the nature of these tasks and the intense attention that they require. Remember, written letters are not usually presented at the phonological awareness stage. Only sounds are presented, which makes it harder for students to sustain attention for long periods of time.

8. Provide instruction on isolating words in sentences before beginning instruction on sounds and syllables. Awareness of words in sentences is the easiest level of analysis and provides an effective means for leading children to analyze different aspects of language they hear. For example, have the students put up a finger for each word that you say in a sentence. Also, have them identify words on the basis of their position in the sentences starting with the first and then the last words (e.g., "What is the first word in the sentence *Mary is smiling?*"). Also, have the students count words in sentences (e.g., "How many words are in the sentence *Jack is tall?*").

9. Use games and computer-assisted instruction. Phonological awareness training can be dry and of little inherent interest to many children; therefore, embed the content in fun activities to increase student involvement in instructional tasks as well as provide motivation.

Instruction on Phonological Awareness for Sounds

Instruction for the seven skills involved in phonological awareness for sounds are presented in this section. The description of each skill includes its definition, special techniques to facilitate its development, and several activities exemplifying how to teach the skill.

Auditory Discrimination

Definition

Auditory discrimination involves the ability to determine if spoken sounds are the same or different (e.g., *cat* versus *cat*, *cat* versus *sat*). This is the most basic skill involved in phonological awareness. If students do not hear the difference in sounds, then they cannot begin to manipulate them.

Techniques

- First, present word pairs that differ in the initial sound ("Are these words the same or different: *cat, mat?*"). After these are mastered, present pairs that differ in the final sound ("Are these words the same or different: *cat, cap?*"). After both initial and final sounds are discriminated, present tasks with pairs that differ in the middle or medial sounds ("Are these words the same or different: *cat, cut?*").

- Initially, provide visual cues by having students look at your lips as you say the words. Once they can discriminate words with visual cues, eliminate them, and have the students look away or shut their eyes as the words are presented.

Activities

- Play a game in which the students shut their eyes as you say word pairs that are the same or different. Have them stand when they hear you say words that are different and sit when the words are the same.

- Present word pairs on a tape recorder and have the students select a red chip for word pairs that are the same and a blue chip for word pairs that are different. At the end of the tape have them count the red and blue chips to see if there were more like or unlike pairs.

Sound Segmentation

Definition

Students isolate and analyze each sound in a word with sound segmentation. In most phonics instruction, students are taught to recall a particular sound for a grapheme by associating it with a key word. For example, to recall the /b/ sound, the word *ball* along with a picture of a ball is used as a key word. Students are expected to isolate the first sound in the word *ball* and use that sound when they see the letter *b* as a strategy for recalling the /b/ sound. They can only do this if they have the pre-reading skill of sound segmentation.

Techniques

- First, teach students to segment words by isolating the initial sounds in words ("What is the first sound in the word *cat?*"). After this is learned, teach them to isolate the final sound ("What is the last sound in the word *cat?*") and the middle or medial sound (e.g., "What is the middle sound in the word *cat?*").

- When modeling initial sounds, present continuous sounds that can be elongated (e.g., /f/, /h/, /l/, /m/, /n/, /r/, /s/, /sh/) as well as short vowel sounds. For example, say, "The first sound in the word *man* is /mmm/—mmman." Use the same procedure for the final sounds ("The last sound in the word *sun* is /nnn/—sunnnn.") and medial sounds ("The middle sound in the word *bat* is /aaa/—baat.").

- First, present tasks that require receptive responses from the students, and after these are mastered, presents tasks requiring expressive responses. For example, first present receptive tasks such as, "What is the first sound in the word *fish:* /f/ or /t/?" or "Which word starts with the /f/ sound: *fill* or *till*?" Then, present expressive tasks such as, "What is the first sound in the word *fish*?" or "What is another word that starts with the same sound as the word *fish*?"

Activities

- Have each student in the group represent a different sound, and have each stand when he hears his sound spoken at the beginning, end, or middle of a word. For example, have one student be the /n/ sound, another the /s/ sound, and a third the /l/ sound. As you say words that end with these sounds, have the students stand every time they hear a word spoken with their sound. Slowly read a list of words emphasizing the target sounds: *fannn, passs, hillll, busss, sunnn, balll.*

- Use worksheets with pictures in which each row includes four pictures, three of which have words that start (or end) with the same sound and one of which does not. Have the students identify the one that does not have the same target sound as the others. For example, for a row of pictures of a ball, boy, apple, and bug, the students would mark the picture of the apple because it does not have the same beginning sound. Have the children label the pictures before starting this task so that you are sure that they are using the correct word for each picture.

Sound Blending

Definition

Sound blending occurs when students hear a word spoken with separated sounds and then synthesize these sounds to say the word. This skill is important when students are learning to sound each of the letters in a word and then combine the separate sounds to say the complete word.

Techniques

- First, present short pauses between the sounds as if you were saying the whole word while drawing out each sound. Gradually increase the length of the pauses between the sounds.

- Elongate the sounds when presenting words initially, and gradually phase out this cue ("What is this word: /sss-aaaa-mmm/?").

Activities

- Say a word with the sounds separated, and have the students match the word to a corresponding picture. For example, show pictures of a bat and a hat and say, "What picture goes with this word: /h-a-t/?"

- Play a game in which the students tell if you are giving the correct or incorrect word for a series of sounds. For example, say, "Am I right or wrong? The word *cat* goes with /c-a-p/ . . . Am I right or wrong? The word *map* goes with /m-a-p/."

Rhyming

Definition

Rhyming involves both the ability to discriminate words that sound alike (a receptive task) and the ability to produce words that sound alike (an expressive task). Most phonics instruction presents words in sound groups or families (e.g., *cat, rat, sat*); therefore, students who can rhyme can readily apply this skill as an aid to reading such word groups.

Techniques

- Emphasize the rhyming element when presenting word families by saying the rhyming element in a louder voice and using a hand signal. Have the students repeat the words using these same two cues.

- First, use receptive tasks and then expressive tasks. Have students select words that belong in a rhyming category (e.g., "Which word doesn't sound like the others: *bat, hat, mud, rat?*"). Then, have them generate words in a rhyming category (e.g., "What words rhyme with *bat?*").

Activities

- Present rhyme words in a category, some of which are real words and some of which are not. Have the students raise their hands when they hear a rhyme word that is not a real word ("Raise your hand when you hear a word that is not a real word. *Bat. Sat. Lat. Rat. Gat.*").

- Read a story with rhymes (e.g., any Dr. Seuss book), and have the students stand every time they hear certain rhyme words.

Sound Counting

Definition

Counting each sound in a word helps students focus their attention on both the number and order of sounds in words.

Techniques

- Use blocks or chips as aids for helping students to count sounds. This creates an association between an auditory stimulus (sound) and a visual stimulus (block) that is extremely important for learning to read. As you say each sound, point to a block.

- Have students hold up a finger or clap after each sound in a word is spoken to provide a motor cue to aid in their recall.

Activities

- Present words with differing numbers of sounds, and have the students identify the word with more sounds (e.g., "Which word has more sounds: /g-o/ or /g-oa-t/?")

- Have the students match the written number to correspond to the number of sounds that they hear in a word. For example, show cards with the numbers 2, 3, and 4 on them and then say, "Which number shows the number of sounds in the word *by*?"

Sound Deletion and Addition

Definition

Sound deletion and addition involve the ability to delete or add sounds for given words and the ability to identify words spoken with missing sounds. Students are taught to compare words with and without specific sounds (e.g., having the students compare the words /s-t-o-p/ and /t-o-p/ and identify that the /s/ is missing from the word *top*).

With sound omission, also called auditory closure, students generate the complete word for a spoken word with missing sounds (e.g., hearing /teleone/ and identifying that the complete word is *telephone*). This is an important skill because students often omit sounds when they learn to read phonetically. If they have phonological awareness skills for sound omission, then they are able to read the word because it sounds similar to a complete word that they know.

Techniques

- Use blocks or chips to correspond to each sound in a word. When modeling, use blocks of matching colors to compare word pairs. For example, to contrast the sounds in the words /g-o/ and /g-oa-t/, present a block for the /g/ sound and a block for the /o/ sound, then show that there is no block for the /t/ sound in the word *go*.

- When presenting words with omitted sounds, pause at the place in the word where the sound is omitted. Also, use a hand motion when you come to the missing sound to provide a visual cue to attend to this part of the word.

Activities

- Say a word with missing sounds, and have the students select a picture that represents the word (e.g., show a picture of a television and telephone and say, "Which picture goes with the word *teleision*?").

- Play a game in which you say word pairs differing in one sound (e.g., *stop* versus *top*), and have the students identify where in the word the sounds differ by pointing to a picture of a train engine if it is at the beginning of the word and a caboose if it is at the end of the word.

Onsets and Rimes

Definition

Phonological awareness for onsets and rimes (the word *rime* should not be confused with the word *rhyme* although they are both pronounced the same) involves the combining of an onset (one or more consonant sounds) with a rime (two or more sounds containing a vowel). For example, when students change the word *cat* by dropping the /k/ sound and adding a /b/ sound to form the word *bat*, they are dropping the onset of /k/ and adding the onset of /b/ to the rime of /at/. Obviously, this area is related to rhyming and should be combined with instruction for rhyming.

Techniques

- To develop skills in identifying onset and rimes, use blocks or chips for the different word parts. For example, use a blue chip for the /b/ sound and a red chip for the /k/ sound and long black strip for /at/ to show that it is longer unit. When you model, say the word *bat*, pointing to the blue chip as you say /b/ and the black strip as you say /at/. Then, do the same with the red chip as you say /k/ and /at/.

- Have the students close their eyes and repeat words with the same rimes (e.g., *bat*, *cat*, *mat*). Say each rime in a loud voice, and have the students do the same.

Activities

- Play a game in which you give a word and the initial sound to be substituted, and have the students determine if the new word is a real word or not. For example, say, "Change the /b/ sound to the /g/ sound in the word *bat*. What word is that? . . . Is *gat* a real word?"

- Use riddles with meaning cues as aids to generate a word with a different onset. For example, say, "If I change the first sound in the word *bat* and add an /h/ sound, do I have something to wear on my head or something to wipe my feet on?"

Instruction on Phonological Awareness for Syllables and Compound Words

Students must be able to discriminate and identify the parts of words that they hear to make the jump from decoding one-syllable words to decoding multi-syllabic and compound words. Identifying compound words is the easiest level of this skill because each of the word parts is a complete word semantically. Next, students must learn to focus on syllables, first receptively by blending syllables that they hear spoken and then expressively by segmenting a word into syllables.

Compound Words

Definition

Compound words are made up of two small words, each of which can stand alone. Compound words that have small words with concrete meanings (e.g., *fireman*) are easier than compound words that have small words with abstract meanings (e.g., *everywhere*).

Techniques

- Initially, use word groups that share one little word (e.g., *bookcase, bookmark, bookshelf; policeman, fireman, mailman*) when training students to identify the two little words in a compound word. Also, initially use groups that have the shared word in the first position (e.g., *snow*man, *snow*storm), and then use groups that have the shared word in the final position (police*man*, mail*man*).

- Use a pause between each of the little words when modeling. For example, say, "There are two little words in the word *fireman*, *fire* (pause) *man*." Have the students repeat the word with the pause and then without the pause.

Activities

- Use pictures corresponding to compound words, and give one of the small words in the compound word and have the students supply the other (e.g., show a picture of a mailbox and say, "What is this? This is a mail____.").

- Give a compound word with the small words in the correct or incorrect order, and have the students determine if it is right. If it is not right, then have the students put them in the correct order. For example, say, "Are the two small words in the word *manfire* in the right order? Change the word to make it right. Are the two small words in the word *mailman* in the right order?"

Syllable Blending

Definition

Use the word *part* instead of the word *syllable* when teaching phonological awareness of syllables to young children because of the complexity and abstractness of the term *syllable*. If you are teaching phonological awareness to older students in a remedial program, then the term *syllable* can be used. Initially, teach students to blend words with two syllables and then three. It is not necessary to teach more than three-syllable words because of the difficulty of recalling lengthy auditory stimuli and the abstractness of many of these words.

Techniques

- Use pictures to help students recall the word that is being blended when modeling words in the early stages of instruction. For example, present a picture of a rabbit, say the complete word, the separated word (*rab-bit*), and the complete word again. Then, have the students imitate your modeling.

- Use clapping as an aid to recognizing syllables. The use of clapping incorporates the rhythm of the word, making it easier for students to analyze the syllables.

- Have older students in a remedial program say the words with exaggerated mouth movements and hold their palm under their chin. They are to count a syllable each time their jaw drops. Every syllable has a vowel sound in it. When you say vowel sounds, your mouth opens, and your jaw drops. Therefore, your jaw should drop every time you say a separate syllable.

Activities

- Say a word separated into syllables, and have the students point to a picture corresponding to the word. For example, present pictures of a hammer and a farmer and say, "What picture goes with this word: *ham-mer*?"

- Play a game in which you say a sentence with multisyllabic words spoken with separated syllables. Have the students perform the actions corresponding to the sentence. "Go to the win-dow and then touch your shoul-ders sev-en times."

Syllable Segmentation

Definition

Sound segmentation involves breaking a word into syllables, which is required for eventually breaking written words into syllables so each syllable can be decoded.

Techniques

- The ability to separate words into syllables is very difficult for some children, so be sure to use clapping, jaw dropping, and pictures as aids.

Activities

- Use tasks in which you give the first syllable in a word and the students produce the remaining syllables. For example, say, "The first part of the word *window* is *win*. What's the second part?"

- Use tasks in which each child has to give a syllable in word and then the whole word. For example, "Mary, you give the first syllable in the word *furniture*. Bobby you give the second syllable, and Timmy you give the third syllable. Then, everybody say the whole word together."

PRE-READING INSTRUCTION FOR SEMANTICS AND SYNTAX

Three groups need pre-reading instruction in the language areas of semantics and syntax: students with language learning disabilities, students who speak dialects other than Standard American English, and students who are ELLs. The nature of the instruction for these three groups differs, and the people who provide the instruction also differ. Students with language learning disabilities have reading difficulties associated with semantic and syntactic deficits which, in turn, are associated with cognitive or neurological factors (Kahmi & Catts, 1999). Students who speak nonstandard dialects or who are ELLs also have reading difficulties associated with semantic and syntactic deficits, but these are not necessarily associated with cognitive or neurological factors. Rather, their reading difficulties result, in part, because reading instruction does not match their unique linguistic and cultural characteristics (Labov, 2003).

Students with language learning disabilities in semantics and syntax have developmental delays in understanding and using words and sentences. They are best served by speech-language therapists who are trained to provide language instruction to meet their needs. The language instruction they provide should be coordinated with the reading instruction provided by special educators.

Students who speak nonstandard dialects need to be taught "school talk" but retain their "home talk" for home and social settings. They need to become bi-dialectal and learn Standard American English so that they can meet the reading and content area demands in school and future workplaces. Such language instruction needs to be provided by the students' classroom teachers. The reading instruction should be coordinated with the instruction on Standard American English. For example, when students learn to use *is* and *are* instead of *be*, they need to read sentences with these structures (e.g., *The boy is happy*) and contrast this with how they say the sentence with their dialect (e.g., *The boy be happy*). Do not present their dialect in a negative light, but rather present it as another way of talking that differs on the basis of where it is used.

Students who are ELLs need to be taught to first speak and then to read English. It is important to recognize the stages that students pass through as they learn a second language (Cummins, n.d.). Most students first learn Basic Interpersonal Communication Skills (BICS), also called playground English or survival English, in 2 years. BICS are learned through face-to-face interactions and help students meet the needs of communicating with their peers. However, for school purposes, students need to attain Cognitive Academic Language Proficiency (CALP), which takes 5–7 years for mastery. CALP is needed to understand textbooks that are written in formal English as well as the formal English that is used when teachers lecture. Because it takes so long to attain CALP, it is important that reading instruction be tied to English instruction. In this way, students can learn to apply newly acquired oral language skills to reading.

There are two general types of program models for ELLs based on the language used to provide instruction: bilingual education or ESL (Antunez & Zelasko, 2001). In bilingual education programs, content instruction is provided both through English and the student's native language, and the students are taught English at the same time. Some professionals recommend that if students do not speak any English but are proficient in their native language, then they should first be taught to read in their native language. After they have learned to read in their native language, they should be taught to read English. This approach can only be effective if there are teachers available who are proficient in the students' native language (Snow, Burns, & Griffin, 1998). In ESL programs, all content area instruction is in English, and students are also given instruction in speaking English. Whatever the type of program, reading instruction needs to be coordinated with the English instruction that is being provided.

For students receiving both English and reading instruction, certain techniques have been found useful for ELLs (Drucker, 2003), including previewing material before reading; choral reading; shared reading; paired reading; books on tape; multicultural literature; the language experience approach (LEA); and total physical response (TPR), which is built on the idea of teaching language through physical actions. These techniques are discussed in greater detail in subsequent chapters. However, it must be pointed out that learning to read English will not be the same for all ELLs. It will probably be especially difficult for students whose native language has a nonalphabetic writing system (e.g., Chinese) and languages that are not primarily written (e.g., some Native American languages) (Snow et al., 1998).

INSTRUCTION FOR PRE-READING VISUAL SKILLS

Instruction on visual pre-reading skills is necessary for students with orthographic dyslexia (i.e., reading disabilities associated with visual problems). Students with visually based reading problems experience confusion of similar-looking graphemes, letter reversals, difficulty mastering high-frequency sight words, slow reading rate, and problems with fluency, among other problems (Roberts & Mather, 1997). Reversals (e.g., confusing *b* and *d*) have long been considered the defining characteristic of dyslexia by the general public. In actuality, most people diagnosed with dyslexia do not have significant problems with reversals, but it is important to recognize that some with visually based reading problems do. Instruction on visual pre-reading skills is necessary so that students can learn to read by visual methods (see Chapter 6) and achieve fluency (see Chapter 7). Just as phonological awareness instruction is designed to teach students to focus on the auditory aspects of language and reading, visual pre-reading instruction is designed to teach students to focus on the visual aspects necessary for reading. Unlike phonological awareness, there are

Table 6. Pre-reading visual skills

Visual discrimination: Differentiation of letters and words based on shape, length, order, and detail

Directionality: Attention to left–right aspects of letters, words, and text

Visual memory: Recall of sequence of letters

Visual speed: Rapid naming of pictures and words

Visual closure: Identification of a picture or letter from an incomplete representation

few assessment instruments or published instructional programs for visual pre-reading skills.

The importance of visual pre-reading skills can better be understood by relating them to the dual deficit theory of dyslexia that asserts that dyslexia is caused by deficits in phonological awareness and/or rapid automatized naming (RAN) (Wolf & Bowers, 1999). RAN tasks in which students rapidly name pictures, colors, letters, or words involve a strong visual component. Because of the speed aspect, RAN has been related to the development of fluency skills.

The specific visual pre-reading skills that need to be trained include visual discrimination, directionality, visual memory, visual speed, and visual closure (see Table 6). One of the most important techniques for training all visual pre-reading skills is the use of a multisensory, or VAKT, approach in which visual, auditory, kinesthetic, and tactile cues are used. You can provide auditory cues by describing the visual stimuli so that the students focus on key visual aspects. Also, you can have them use movement (kinesthetic) or touch (tactile) to get additional cues. Whenever possible, emphasize important aspects of the visual stimuli by using color coding, underlining, or bolding.

Teach students to attend to words in text before beginning instruction on the separate visual pre-reading skills. When you read books to the students, point to each word as it is said. Indicate that the spaces between the written words show that each word is separate. Have the students point to each word as you read to them so that they learn to match a written word with a spoken word.

In the following sections, each of these five visual pre-reading skills is defined, and teaching techniques to facilitate development of the skill as well as activities exemplifying how to teach it are presented. Remember, the students do not need to know how to read the letters or words used in these tasks. However, if these tasks are being used remedially with older students who have some reading skills, then the letters and words can be identified.

Visual Discrimination

Definition

The ability to perceive visual stimuli as being the same or different is necessary for reading. Obviously, if students do not see any difference between the graphemes (or written letters) *m* and *n*, then they cannot learn to read these letters. Or, if students do not see the difference between the words *cape* and *cap*, then they cannot learn to read them. The purpose of visual discrimination instruction is to teach students to attend to letters and words based on differences in their shapes (e.g., the grapheme *c* versus *o*; the word *are* has no tall letters or letters that go below the line, whereas the word *boy* has a tall letter and a letter that goes below the line), lengths (e.g., the word *us* versus the word *use*; the word *elephant* is long, and the word *fox* is short), order (e.g., the letter order in the words *ate* versus *eat*), or details (e.g., the two *l*'s in the word *yellow* or the two *m*'s in the word *mom*).

Techniques

- Use color coding to draw the students' attention to the differences in the letters or words. For example, when teaching students to discriminate between the graphemes *m* and *n*, make the second hump in *m* in a different color. Also, use underlining, and make key visual aspects darker.

- When modeling, direct the students' attention to the critical differences between the visual stimuli. Describe what is unique about the stimuli, and have the students repeat what you said as they point to the visual stimuli. "There are two humps in this letter and there is one hump in this letter."

Activities

- Use worksheets in which there are three items, two of which are the same and one of which is not (e.g., *m*, *m*, *n*), and have the students mark the one that is different.

- Present written words with separate boxes for each letter, and have the students match the words that go with the different series of boxes (e.g., present a series of three boxes that are the same size for the word *are* and a series of three boxes with one tall box, one regular box, and one box with a tail for the word *boy*).

Directionality

Definition

Students need to learn to attend to the left–right direction in letters, words, and text. Reversals of letters (*b* versus *d*) and words (*was* versus *saw*) are frequently observed behaviors of students with visually based reading disabilities.

Techniques

- Tracing with different media is helpful to focus students' attention on directional aspects of reading. Have students trace frequently reversed letters using sandpaper, rice, cotton balls, and so forth.

- For discriminating directionality in words, line one word up under the other and contrast how each of the letters in one word corresponds to the letters in the other word (e.g., for the words *was* and *saw*, point out that the *w* is first in *was* and the *s* is first in *saw*).

Activities

- Use worksheets in which two or three letters (*b, d, b*) or words (*was, saw, saw*) are the same, and have the students mark the item that is different.

- Present a word that is frequently reversed (e.g., *was*), and have three students hold each of the three letters in the word. Have them line up so that they are holding the words in the same order as they appear in the word.

Visual Memory

Definition

Students recall nonphonetic sight words by recalling the sequence of letters and associating this sequence with the word. These words are learned through visual sequential memory (i.e., recall of letters in the order that they appear in a word).

Techniques

- Start with visual memory for sequences of pictures in which you present a picture of a horse, a car, and an apple. Then, shuffle the pictures, and have the students reproduce them in the same order as originally shown. Also, use sequences of colors and shapes. After the students can recall a sequence of four pictures, colors, or shapes, move to sequences of letters and then words (even if they cannot read the letters and words).

- Have the students label the pictures, colors, or shapes as they point to them to aid in recall of the sequence. If they know the names of the letters, then have them also label the letters as an aid to recalling the sequence.

- First, use completion tasks and then production tasks. For example, after you show a sequence of the three letters *s a t*, take the letters away, then present *s a _*, and have the students select the letter that is missing from several choices. Also, provide tasks in which the students select the first letter (*_ a t*) and the middle letter (*s _ t*). Finally, use production tasks in which the students place the letters in the same order as originally shown.

Activities

- Play a game in which you present a sequence of cards with numbers, letters, or words and then take them away. Have the students pull cards that were shown in the sequence from a bag and then put them in the order that they were shown.

- Have a scavenger hunt in which you show a series of pictures, shapes, colors, letters, or words. Hide items from the series around the room, and have the students find the items and put them in the order that they appeared.

Visual Speed

Definition

Students must learn to recognize letters and words quickly so that they can eventually read quickly and attain fluency. Present tasks in which students name pictures, colors, or shapes faster and faster. If older students know their letters, then use letters for the tasks.

Techniques

- Use timers to time the exposure of the visual stimuli to be named. Gradually increase the number of items to be recalled and the length of time for doing so.

- Use charts to demonstrate the number of items students recall on a task to demonstrate their improvement over time.

Activities

- Have each student use a tape recorder and name as many pictures as possible in a given time period (e.g., 1 minute using a 1-minute sand hourglass). Record the number the students get each time they do the task, and make a chart to show how they improve.

- Put the students on teams and see which team can produce more picture, color, shape, or letter names in a certain period of time.

Visual Closure

Definition

Visual closure involves the ability to see part of a letter and generate the complete letter or see part of a word and generate the complete word. This skill is required for learning to read quickly so that students do not have to look at each letter in a word before reading it or look at each word in a sentence before reading it.

Techniques

- When modeling, describe the different parts of the incomplete letter and contrast these to the parts in each of the complete letter choices. Have the students trace over the incomplete and complete letters. Also use cutouts so you can lay the incomplete letter over the complete one.

- Initially, use choices that are very different from the incomplete letter (e.g., for the *w*, use the choices of *b*, *f*, and *w*), and then give choices that are similar to the incomplete letter (e.g., for the *w*, use *x*, *v*, and *w*).

Activities

- Present worksheets in which the first item is an incomplete letter along with three choices, one of which is the complete letter. Have the students mark the choice that goes with the incomplete letter.

- Use pictures in which you have blackened out one part (e.g., black out one wheel on a car) and have the students tell which part has been blackened out. You can vary this task by having one student cover a part of a picture with a marker and the other students guess what part has been covered.

INSTRUCTION FOR PRE-READING COGNITIVE SKILLS

Pre-reading cognitive skills are necessary to provide both the prior knowledge that is needed to facilitate reading comprehension and the foundation of cognitive processes necessary for literal, inferential, and evaluative reading comprehension skills. It is much easier to understand reading material with which you are familiar. Children with extensive experiences at home and school can use these as the basis for understanding their school experiences, especially those involving reading. Children from educationally disadvantaged homes come to school lacking the experiences of middle-class children, either because they live in poverty or have different cultural backgrounds. Both books and computers are integral aspects of middle-class homes but not educationally disadvantaged homes. Preschool experiences for children from educationally disadvantaged homes need to provide enriched, varied experiences filled with books and computers so that these children become comfortable with the print and electronic worlds. In addition, students from educationally disadvantaged homes need to be exposed to educationally beneficial media such as the Public Broadcasting Service (PBS) television shows *Sesame Street* and *Between the Lions*. Parents should be encouraged to have their children watch such programs at home.

Cognitive processes can be developed by asking questions about stories that have been read aloud. It is imperative that students be read to as much as possible so that they become addicted to literature. They need to develop a love of books and be provided opportunities to hear these books read over and over. You probably have books that you loved as a child and always asked your parent to read.

When you ask questions about books that you have read aloud, have the students analyze the pictures to get visual cues to aid in their early understanding of the book content. Ask questions to build student understanding of the main ideas, details, sequence, cause and effect, associations, and evaluations. For example, these questions might be asked for the story *Officer Buckle and Gloria* by Peggy Rathmann (1995):

Main idea: "Who made the children listen to Officer Buckle's safety speeches?"

Detail: "Where did Officer Buckle take Gloria after every safety speech?"

Sequence: "What happened after Officer Buckle saw his safety speech on TV?"

Cause and effect: "Why did the children listen to Officer Buckle's safety speeches when he was with Gloria?"

Association: "Do you have any safety tips?"

Evaluation: "Did you like Gloria? Why?"

Asking questions dealing with main ideas, details, and sequence provides the foundation for literal comprehension skills that students will need to understand future material they read. Questions involving cause and effect and association provide the basis for inferential comprehension skills, and evaluations provide the basis for evaluative comprehension skills required at later stages of the reading process. Directions for how to ask these different types of questions are given in Chapter 10.

Model Lesson for Teaching Phonological Awareness
Find the Sound

OBJECTIVE

Students will identify and say the final sound in consonant-vowel-consonant (CVC) words with 100% accuracy (sound segmentation).

ADVANCED ORGANIZER

Play the I Spy game to review the previously learned skill of identifying and saying the initial sound in CVC words as well as to teach the new skill of identifying and saying the final sound in CVC words. Use picture cards in a wall chart as well as colored tiles to demonstrate the segmenting of the sounds. Give each student a flashlight to shine on the wall chart and the tiles during the I Spy game as you say the corresponding sounds of the words. If age appropriate, have the students wear detective hats. You can also wear a hat and use a magnifying glass to "search" for words and sounds. Have students hold up their fingers as you say each sound and move the tiles.

Link

Link to previous lessons on segmenting initial sounds.

"What do I have? . . . Right—my detective kit. We have been using our detective skills to help us figure out the sounds in words. Let's see if you can help me with the beginning sounds of these words. I spy something that begins with the /m/ sound . . . Right, *man* begins with the /m/ sound. I'm going to use my detective ears and listen to the sounds in *man*: /m-a-n/ *(draw out each sound and display a colored tile as you say each sound)*. The first sound in *man* is /mmm/ *(point to the first tile)*. /mmm/: *man*. Let's try another one. I spy something that begins with the /s/ sound . . . RIGHT! *Sun* begins with the /sss/ sound. *(As you continue with your review, use the colored tiles to provide visual cues. Have students move the tiles as they say the sounds.)* I spy something that keeps us cool. What is it? Shine your flashlight on that picture . . . Right, it's a fan. What sound does *fan* begin with? . . . /fff/: *fan*. I spy something that says meow. Shine your flashlight on that picture . . . You are sharp today! It's a cat. What sound does *cat* begin with? . . . /kkk/: *cat.*"

Identify

Identify the goal of the lesson.

"You are certainly good detectives! You can figure out all sorts of beginning sounds. Today we're going to work on *ending* sounds. We are going to use our detective skills to listen and figure out what sounds we hear at the *end* of words."

Provide Rationale

Explain the importance of the lesson.

"Good detectives need to listen closely to both beginning and ending sounds to figure out words."

MODELING

Use colored tiles to give students visual cues during segmenting, and have students hold up their fingers to represent sounds to give them motor cues.

"Let's look at this picture. It's a sun. Watch while I use my detective skills to find the *ending* sound in this word. *(As you say each sound, use a colored tile to represent each sound. Push the last tile out as you elongate the final sound.)* The ending sound in *sun* is /nnn/. *(Point to the last tile as you say the sound.)* How did I know when I came to the end sound? I touched the last tile, and I knew that was my ending sound. Watch me again. *(Repeat the activity two or three more times with* sun *before moving to the next word.)* Now, I want you to hold up your fingers each time I touch a tile." *(Initially, use words such as* jam, ham, *and* can *so you can elongate the final sounds.*

Model several more times using the tiles and having students hold up their fingers to correspond to each sound.)

GUIDED PRACTICE

Each student has a detective kit that has three colored tiles, five picture cards, and mini-flashlights for use in the following activities.

Tile Time

Have the students use the tiles to correspond to each sound that they say and then identify the last sound after they say it.

"It's time for you to be detectives. Get your tiles out of your detective kits and get ready. Look at this picture. What is it? . . . Right. It's a sun. Say the word and then lay out the tiles as you say each sound. What's the last sound you said? . . . Super! The last sound is /nnn/."

Same Sound Search

Show students a card and ask them to shine their lights on the card in their stack that has the same ending sound.

"Now I'm going to show you a picture and you're going to be a detective and find another picture that has the same ending sound as mine. Put your picture cards on the desk. Here is my picture. It's a picture of a can. The ending sound in *can* is /nnn/. Shine your light on your picture that has the same ending sound that you hear in *can*. Yes, the word *sun* has the same ending sound as *can*." Students have pictures of a sun, ham, bat, and cup.

INDEPENDENT PRACTICE

Have students practice the skill without assistance. Record the accuracy of the students' responses so you can evaluate their mastery of the objective.

File Folder Game

Use a file folder game with a game board drawn on the inside pages of the file folder. The board has a circular road of boxes, with a start and a stop point. Make the board attractive by decorating it with theme stickers, such as dinosaurs, Disney characters, or zoo animals. You can reuse the game board for other games by adding stickers with different themes to keep the students interested. Each student has a toy token to move (e.g., a small toy car or horse) when it is his turn. At his turn, the student selects a card with a picture, names the word for the picture, segments the sounds in the word, and then identifies the last sound in the word. If he is correct, the student rolls one die and moves the corresponding number of boxes on the road. If the student cannot identify numbers corresponding to the spots on the die, use cards with a picture on one side and a color on the other. Use different colors for each box on the road (e.g., start with a red box and then have a green one, a yellow one, and so forth). When the student responds correctly, have him move to the next box with the color corresponding to the color on the card. The students continue playing until one (or all) reaches the stop point.

Finding Sounds Worksheet

Provide students with a worksheet that has 10 pictures in column one and 10 pairs of pictures in column two. Students are to circle the picture in column two that has the same ending sound as the picture in column one (e.g., the picture in column one is a bat and the two pictures in column two are a rug and a hat).

Sound Detective Bingo

Give each student a Bingo card with pictures on it. Have the students listen to the ending sound you say and find a picture with that sound on their Bingo card. They are to cover matching pictures with plastic chips. When they have five pictures covered across or down, they have Bingo.

GENERALIZATION

Help students use this skill in different contexts. Read a story such as *Green Eggs and Ham* (Seuss, 1960). Have students raise their hands every time they hear a word with a particular ending sound.

4

Breaking the Code

Teaching Phonics Skills

CONCEPTS EXPLORED

- Role of phonics in the great debate
- Different approaches to phonics instruction
- Guidelines for effective phonics instruction
- Techniques for teaching different sounds in the phonics scope and sequence
- Model lesson for teaching phonics

ROLE OF PHONICS IN THE GREAT DEBATE

Phonics is the most important word identification skill for teaching struggling students. However, phonics is not the final goal of reading instruction. It is the means to the ultimate goal of reading instruction, which is understanding the meaning of words, sentences, and text.

Phonics is the only word identification technique that enables students to *independently* decode words. It helps them solve the mystery of the relationship between written letters and the sounds that they make. Phonics enables students to understand the alphabetic principle, which explains letter–sound associations (also called grapheme–phoneme relationships and sound–symbol correspondences). However, English is not a strictly phonetic language, so some words cannot be decoded phonetically. In some words—such as *cough*, *dough*, and *bough*—the sounds for the letters *ough* are very different. Phonics is the most important word identification technique, but it does not help with decoding nonphonetic or irregular words. Visual word identification methods and meaning cues are needed for these words.

Historically, there has been a great debate over the best way to teach all children how to learn to read (Chall, 1967). On one hand, there are those who advocate a code-breaking emphasis for beginning reading instruction. On the other hand, there are those who advocate a meaning-based emphasis. The code-breaking approach stresses the systematic teaching of sounds and words first (phonics) and later emphasizes understanding of words, sentences, and text. With this approach, students are first taught target sounds in isolation, then words with these target sounds, followed by reading of text containing these words. The goal of code-breaking systems is correct decoding of words, not understanding of words. With the meaning-based approach, sentences and stories are selected based on conveying a certain meaning, and students learn to read the words in them based on the overall meaning or by visual methods. Sounds and words are not taught first and are not preselected for separate instruction in a meaning-based approach. Whole language, basal readers, and the Language Experience Approach (LEA) are the major meaning-based approaches. The code-breaking approach has been called a bottom-up approach because students learn to put together the sounds in words, then put the words together, and finally achieve the meaning. The meaning-based approach is viewed as a top-down approach because the students get the overall meaning of the reading material first and then use it to analyze the words.

The debate between the code-breaking versus meaning-based approaches has raged for many years. In 1955, the book titled *Why Johnny Can't Read* (Flesch, 1955/1986) called for the use of phonics and elimination of meaning-based approaches for teaching reading to all students. In recent years, this debate has been called the *reading wars*. Some claim that the debate has been resolved and that most professionals agree on a balanced approach including both code breaking and meaning. However, the war is still raging. In the book *Understanding and Resisting Systematic Direct Intense Phonics Instruction*, Meyer (2002) contended that systematic phonics instruction is rigid, direct phonics instruction involves little interaction between teacher and students, and intense phonics instruction means long periods of time devoted to phonics at the expense of students' other needs.

Today, a balanced approach combining both code-breaking and meaning-based instruction is most frequently advocated (Carlisle & Rice, 2002). Despite this call for a balanced approach, advocacy of the phonics approach is on the upswing at the federal, state, and local levels for all students, including struggling learners. The Reading First Initiative that is part of the No Child Left Behind (NCLB) Act of 2001 (PL 107-110) (see The Partnership for Reading, 2001) advocates systematic, explicit phonics instruction for students from kindergarten to third grade. The state of California went from requiring whole language reading instruction to phonics reading instruction for all students in public schools (California Department of Education, 1995). The dominance of the code-breaking approach in education today is also demonstrated by the inclusion of phonics skills in statewide assessments for all students. For example, in the Virginia Standards of Learning, first-grade students are expected to use beginning and ending consonants and vowels in decoding single-syllable words (*Standards of Learning Currently in Effect*, n.d.). In addition, the academic achievement tests that are frequently used nationwide to assess students with disabilities in special education include subtests for phonics.

The great debate on how to teach beginning reading to all students is less pronounced when applied to the issue of how to teach reading to struggling learners, especially students with dyslexia and those who are educationally disadvantaged. Most special educators agree that students classified as having phonologic dyslexia need remedial instruction in phonics (Lerner, 2003). Many educators who work with students who are educationally disadvantaged advocate the use of phonics based on the extensive research on the effectiveness of this method for such children (Carnine et al., 2004). However, not all ELLs react positively to phonics instruction. ELLs whose native language uses an alphabetic principle in which there are sound–symbol associations (e.g., Spanish) will learn phonics more easily than students whose native language uses a logographic system of symbols without sound–symbol associations (e.g., Chinese) (Tompkins, 2003). Therefore, decisions as to whether to teach phonics or how much phonics to teach should be based on the type of language ELLs use and whether they can already read in their native language. If students' native language uses an alphabetic principle and the students know how to read in their language, then phonics should be used to teach English. If, however, students' native language uses a logographic system and the students know how to read in this language, then perhaps phonics should be minimized and visual methods emphasized.

DIFFERENT APPROACHES TO PHONICS INSTRUCTION

It is important to differentiate *direct* phonics instruction from *embedded* phonics instruction. Direct phonics instruction devotes certain time periods to teaching specific sound–symbol associations. Embedded phonics teaches sound–symbol associations when children have difficulty reading or writing words with specific sounds. If, while engaged in classroom reading and writing tasks, it becomes apparent to the teacher that the students do not know a particular sound, then instruction is diverted to teach the sound at that time. Phonics is embedded in overall reading instruction. Although typically developing readers may learn by embedded phonics, many struggling students do not. They need the structure provided by explicit phonics instruction.

Direct phonics methods can be *synthetic* or *analytic*. With synthetic phonics methods, students learn sounds in isolation and then learn to decode words with these sounds. The students cannot read these words before phonics instruction but are able to read them after learning the target sounds. Analytic phonics methods start with words that the students can already read and use these as the basis for analyzing the sounds in them. Synthetic phonics is advocated in this book.

Synthetic phonics methods can also be contrasted on the basis of whether a *sound-by-sound* approach or an *onset-rime* approach is used. With sound-by-sound synthetic phonics, the word *cat* is taught with three separate sounds (/k-a-t/). The sound-by-sound approach does not mean letter-by-letter because in some cases two letters have one sound. In the word *check*, there are five letters but three sounds (/ch-e-k/). With the onset-rime approach, different beginning consonant sounds (onsets) are added to a rime (or a rhyming group of letters). For example, to teach the word *cat* using this approach, the rime /at/ is presented as a unit, not as two separate sounds. Then, different consonants, or onsets, are added to create words (e.g., /k-at/, /h-at/). The term *onset-rime* is new and may be confusing because of the similarity of the words *rime* and *rhyme*; however, this type of phonics instruction is not new. It was called the linguistic approach for many years and was successfully incorporated in the Merrill Linguist Reading Program (1975) and Let's Read (Bloomfield & Barnhart, 1961). Both of these methods of phonics instruction are advocated in this book. The sound-by-sound phonics method is used to teach most sounds; however, the onset-rime method is used for word parts that cannot be easily separated into distinct sounds (e.g., it is not possible to separate the sounds represented by *ng* in /ing/, so /ing/ is taught as a rime for words such as *ring* and *wing*). It is important not to mix these two methods when teaching the same sound. For example, you would not want to teach the word *cat* using the sound-by-sound method (/k-a-t/) and also using the onset-rime method (/k-at/) because that would be confusing. When the onset-rime method is used, students should be explicitly told that this is a different approach from what they have been using and that it is used to sound out words in which the sounds cannot be easily separated.

Phonics methods can be contrasted on the basis of whether they can be used with *individuals, small groups,* or *classrooms.* Phonics programs have been successful with all three types of groupings. However, small-group or individual instruction has been shown to be more effective for struggling students (Swanson, 1999). The unique needs of each student can be taken into account when planning instruction for individuals and small groups.

In summary, the phonics approach described in this book is

- Direct: sounds are taught intentionally
- Synthetic: sounds are taught as the basis for decoding unknown words
- Sound-by-sound based: individual sounds in words are analyzed
- Onset–rime based: word families are taught for sounds that cannot be easily separated
- Designed for individuals or small groups

A number of published phonics programs have been successfully used with struggling students. However, these programs can only be successful if they are used by a teacher who knows how to teach phonics with or without a published program. A knowledgeable teacher is the most important ingredient in successful phonics instruction. The objective of this book is to make you knowledgeable so that you can teach phonics with or without the assistance of a published program.

Three published programs are anchored to a long history of demonstrated effectiveness with struggling learners:

1. The *Phonic Remedial Reading Lessons* by Kirk, Kirk, and Minskoff (1985; based on *Remedial Reading Drills,* written in 1936 by Hegge, Kirk, & Kirk) has been successfully used with students with mental retardation and learning disabilities. It provides a framework for teaching sounds using a specific instructional approach based on principles of learning and presents the sounds to be taught in an easy-to-difficult order. However, it does not provide materials and requires the teacher to create activities following the suggested format. Figure 2 shows a page from the *Phonic Remedial Reading Lessons* exemplifying how spatial cues and the principle of minimal change are used to facilitate mastery of the sounds. The spaces between the letters in the words in the first three sections are visual signals that the words are to be sounded out. The principle of minimal change is used as the basis for the sequence of words taught. The first section of words differs only in the first sound, the second section of words differs only in the last sound, and the third section differs in the first and last sounds. Figure 3 shows an example of the story reading that is used to transition students from reading words with target sounds in isolation to reading these words in passages.

Lesson 4

i

s i t	f i t	h i t	b i t	k i t
h i m	r i m	d i m	T i m	J i m
h i d	l i d	d i d	k i d	r i d
w i n	t i n	s i n	f i n	b i n
w i ll	f i ll	p i ll	t i ll	h i ll

h i t	h i m	h i d	h i p
s i n	s i t	s i p	s i x
r i b	r i m	r i p	r i g
p i g	p i n	p i t	p i g

r i g	l i d	t i n	r i m	f i t
s i p	p i g	r i b	s i t	h i t
h i m	s i n	l i p	p i n	h i d
f i x	p i g	h i p	s i x	f i ll
i n	• t i p	r i m	d i g	z i p

kit	Bill	fin	nip	dim	it	miss
Tim	rid	lip	sin	hit	hip	if
dip	win	Jim	pig	zip	him	fit
dig	big	fill	rib	six	bit	in
kid	six	tip	rim	sit	bid	fib

Figure 2. Sample page from the *Phonic Remedial Reading Lessons.* (From Kirk, S.A., Kirk, W.D., & Minskoff, E.H. [1985]. *Phonic remedial reading lessons* [p. 29]. Novato, CA: Academic Therapy Publications; reprinted by permission.)

The Pig Got Hit

A kid had a fat pig.

The pig got hit.

A cab hit the pig.

The cab hit the pig in the rib.

The cab did not kill the pig.

Figure 3. Sample story from the *Phonic Remedial Reading Lessons.* (From Kirk, S.A., Kirk, W.D., & Minskoff, E.H. [1985]. *Phonic remedial reading lessons* [p. 30]. Novato, CA: Academic Therapy Publications; reprinted by permission.)

2. The *Wilson Reading System* (Wilson, 1988) is based on the Orton-Gillingham approach that has been used successfully with students with dyslexia for many years. The Orton-Gillingham approach is difficult to use because it is not structured into easy-to-use lessons. The *Wilson Reading System* includes well-sequenced lessons and teaching materials and is user friendly. Figure 4 shows the format of the lesson plans to be used to teach all sounds with the program.

3. *Reading Mastery* is based on DISTAR, a reading program developed in the 1960s by Siegfried Engelmann, to meet the unique reading needs of students who are educationally disadvantaged. Research has shown this method to be effective with this group (Carnine et al., 2004). *Reading Mastery* uses a different orthography (i.e., some of the letters have different shapes to show their different sounds; see Figure 5). *Reading Mastery* (Engelmann & Bruner, 1988) is a scripted program that some view as an asset because it ensures that everyone who uses the program will use it as the authors intended. However, others view it as a limitation because it is rigid.

Other phonics programs that incorporate systematic, explicit phonics instruction are presented in Appendix D. All published programs have assets and limitations. If they are to be used effectively, then they have to be shaped to the unique needs of the students and used by teachers who are knowledgeable about teaching all areas of reading, especially phonics.

GUIDELINES FOR EFFECTIVE PHONICS INSTRUCTION

Whether you design your own phonics instruction, adapt a published phonics program to your students' needs, or closely follow a published phonics program, you need to provide phonics instruction that incorporates guidelines that have been found effective for teaching struggling students (see Table 7).

1. Provide systematic, explicit phonics instruction: When teaching struggling students to decode words phonetically, it is imperative that you use S.E.T. to provide daily instruction using a clearly defined path from the students' current level of mastery of specific sounds to the final goal of mastery of all sounds necessary for word identification. You must use explicit instruction that starts with advanced organizers, which show the students the target sound they are learning and how it relates to other sounds they have learned. Next, you model the strategies the students must master to acquire this sound. Modeling should focus on how to:

- Produce the target sound in isolation (e.g., "The /a/ sound goes with this letter: *a*.")

- Produce the target sound embedded in an isolated word (e.g., "We sound out this word as /k-a-t/: *cat*.")

Wilson Reading System® Lesson Plan

Lesson Block	Step		Activity	Approx. Minutes on Task	Block Emphasis
Word Study	**1**	`a`	**Sound Cards Quick Drill**	2-3	Phonemic Awareness Decoding Vocabulary Single Word Accuracy/ Automaticity Phrasing / Prosody
	2		**Teach & Review Concepts for Reading**	5	
	3	`b a t`	**Wordcards**	3-5	
	4		**Wordlist Reading**	5	
	5		**Sentence Reading**	5	
Spelling	**6**	`/a/?`	**Quick Drill (in reverse)**	1-2	Spelling Proofreading Vocabulary Irregular Words
	7		**Teach & Review Concepts for Spelling**	5	
	8		**Written Work Dictation (Sound, Words, Sentences)**	15-20	
Fluency / Comprehension	**9**		**Controlled Text Passage Reading**	10-15	Guided Reading Fluency Vocabulary Comprehension Visualization Oral Language Skills
	10		**Listening Comprehension / Applied Skills**	10-30	

Figure 4. Lesson plan from the *Wilson Reading Program*. (From Wilson, B.A. [1988]. *Wilson Reading System* [p. 35]. Millbury, MA; Wilson Language Training Corp.; reprinted by permission.)

the cow on the r̄oad

lots of men went down the

r̄oad in a little car.

a cow was sitting on the

r̄oad. s̄o the men ran to the cow.

"w̄e will lift this cow," they said.

but the men did not lift the

cow. "this cow is s̄o fat w̄e can

not lift it."

the cow said, "I am not s̄o

fat. I can lift m̄e." then the cow

got in the car.

the men said, "now w̄e can

not get in the car." s̄o the men

sat on the r̄oad and the cow

went h̄ome in the car.

the end

Figure 5. Sample page from *Reading Mastery.* (Engelmann, S., & Bruner, E. [1988]. *Reading Mastery I* [Story 1, p. 1]. Columbus, OH: Science Research Associates. Reproduced with permission of the McGraw-Hill Companies.)

- Produce the target sound embedded in a word in text (e.g., "Here is the word *cat* in a sentence. The cat is big.")

After the students can imitate your use of the strategies at the modeling stage, move to the guided practice stage in which the students practice using the strategies you modeled to correctly decode the target sound. Gradually remove all supports, prompts, and cues until the students are independently using the

Table 7. Guidelines for effective phonics instruction

Provide systematic, explicit phonics instruction.

Use a pretest-teach-posttest format to determine level of instruction and pacing.

Present phonics instruction as part of a three-stage process of phonological awareness, phonics, and structural analysis.

Teach the scope and sequence of sounds based on an easy-to-difficult progression.

Decide what phonics rules to make explicit based on student characteristics.

Always teach spelling as well as reading of target sounds.

Use a variety of strategies to help students master target sounds.
    Key word associations
    Think-alouds
    Visual cues
    VAKT (visual, auditory, kinesthetic, and tactile) methods
    Educated guessing
    Monitoring for meaning

Make phonics instruction fun.

Provide success—the best motivator for learning to read.

strategies to correctly decode the target sound. Then, move to the independent practice stage in which the students practice reading words and text with the target sound. Students do not have mastery of a target sound if they can only read it in isolation or in an isolated word; they have mastery when they can read words with this sound in authentic materials (i.e., their classroom reading materials). A model lesson demonstrating how to use S.E.T. to teach the short /o/ sound is at the end of this chapter.

2. Use a pretest-teach-posttest format to determine level of instruction and pacing: If you are teaching phonics to students who have no mastery of any sounds, then start with the first sound in the scope and sequence of sounds presented later in this chapter or included in the phonics program that you are using. If you are teaching remedially to struggling learners who have been exposed to some phonics instruction, then they may be at different levels of prior knowledge of different sounds. For example, you may be working with third graders with dyslexia who have been exposed to 2 previous years of classroom reading instruction. You need to pretest to determine what sounds they know and what sounds they do not know. Some students may already know consonant sounds and not need instruction on these. They can start with the short vowel sounds. Others may know the short vowel sounds but not the long vowel sounds. Instruction for these students starts with the long vowel sounds. Use the scope and sequence of sounds to pretest your students to find which sounds they know, and only teach those that they do not know. It is not recommended that you devote precious instructional time to skills that students already have when there are so many skills that they need to learn. However, you should review these sounds so that the students are at a 90%–100% level of mastery and can readily retrieve these sounds when necessary.

After teaching a new skill, posttest to determine if the students have mastered the skill. Posttesting should include assessing whether the students can read the target sound in isolation, in isolated words with the target sound, and in words with the target sound embedded in text. If they have mastered the target sound at these three levels, then move to the next harder sound that they do not know. If they have not mastered the target sound, then try different strategies until they achieve mastery. Continuously review previously learned sounds so that the students maintain 90%–100% level of mastery. Use the Reading Skills Record Form in Appendix E to chart student progress.

3. Present phonics instruction as part of a three-stage process of learning phonological awareness, phonics, and structural analysis: Phonics cannot be mastered unless students have a foundation of phonological awareness skills; therefore, phonological awareness training should lead directly into phonics instruction. Phonics helps students decode single-syllable words. After they can decode these words, they must learn structural analysis skills for decoding multisyllabic words. When they have analyzed a word into syllables, they need to apply phonics to decode each of the syllables and then blend them together. Therefore, phonics instruction should lead directly into structural analysis instruction.

Phonological awareness $\longrightarrow$ phonics $\longrightarrow$ structural analysis

4. Teach the scope and sequence of sounds based on an easy-to-difficult progression: Most phonics programs present similar, but not exact, scopes and sequences of sounds to be taught. A phonics scope and sequence is a description of all the sounds to be taught (scope) and the order in which they are to be taught (sequence). All programs start with teaching consonant sounds first because there is only one sound associated with most consonants and because these are the most frequently used sounds. Short vowels are taught next so that students can start to sound out the easiest pattern of words—CVC. Vowels are harder to learn than consonants because they have more than one sound associated with them. For the letter *a*, it is possible to say different sounds, such as the short or long sound. The scope and sequence of sounds presented in the next section is in an easy-to-difficult progression, so follow it to ensure that you are establishing a cumulative foundation. However, if you are using a published program, use the scope and sequence provided in the program.

It is advisable to teach one sound at a time when teaching sounds to struggling learners. For example, if students do not know any of the short vowel sounds, then start by teaching the /a/ sound. After this is mastered, teach the /o/ sound. Do not teach /a/ and /o/ at the same time. The demands of learning two vowel sounds at once are taxing in terms of the students' discrimination and retrieval of these similar sounds. Once this second sound is learned, activities should be presented in which the students have to read both /a/ and /o/ words to help them integrate the newly learned /o/ with the previously learned /a/.

5. Decide what phonics rules to make explicit based on student characteristics: Most phonics programs teach students to apply rules; however, almost all phonics rules have many exceptions, which is confusing when students try to generalize to the exceptions. For example, most phonics programs teach the rule that "when two vowels go walking, the first one does the talking" (e.g., vowel pairs such as *ai* in *pail* or *oa* in *goat*). However, this rule only applies 45% of the time (Lerner, 2003). For instance, when students apply this rule to the word *thief*, they are incorrect. During instruction on rules, make sure you only include words that follow the rule. Teach exceptions only after a rule has been mastered, and explain that the rule does not always work. For students who have memory problems or are concrete thinkers and have difficulty applying generalizations, memorization of rules should be kept to a minimum. Teaching words that are rule breakers using a jail theme is fun for students. Write a rule on an envelope with bars on it to make it look like a jail, and place exceptions to the rule in the envelope showing that these words break the rules, just like people who go to jail.

6. Always teach spelling as well as reading of target sounds: All phonics instruction should require students to both read words with the target sound being taught as well as spell the words. This will result in greater mastery of reading the target sound as well as improve the students' spelling. For example, when teaching students to decode words with the target sound of the short /a/, require them to not only read the words but also to spell the words from dictation. This "writing for sounds" method allows students to induce the multitude of spelling–sound correspondences that are required to read (Juel & Minden-Cupp, 2002).

7. Use a variety of strategies to help students master target sounds: Use as many of the following types of strategies as possible to build in phonics skills.

Key Word Associations

Most students have difficulty learning sound–symbol associations because of the abstractness of the sounds. Say the five short vowel sounds to yourself and listen to how difficult it is to differentiate them. To make it easier for students to recall sounds, use key word associations with pictures and verbal labels. For example, to help students recall the short /a/ sound, present a picture of an apple and say the word *apple*. Always use key words that begin with the target sound. Using the word *cat* as a key word for the short /a/ sound would be difficult because the students would have to segment the word and pull out the middle sound, which is the hardest to do. Segmenting a word using the first sound is easier. Model segmenting the first sound and using it in isolation to represent the short /a/ sound. Then have the students repeat what you have modeled. "The sound of the letter *a* is /a/. To help us remember how to make this sound, we'll use the picture of an apple. *Apple* starts with the /a/ sound. /aaa-pple/. /a/. Say the word *apple*. Say the first sound in *apple*. What sound is that?"

Keep the pictures for these key word associations available for the students to use when they have difficulty recalling a target sound. As they master the sound, remove the pictures, and have them recall the key word when they have difficulty with a sound. Obviously, the students must have the phonological awareness preskill of sound segmentation to use the key word association strategy.

Think-Alouds

Whenever you model sounding out a word, use think-alouds to verbalize the strategies you are using so that they can be imitated by the students. For example, when modeling decoding of words with the long /a/ sound, say, "Here is the word *cake* that has the pattern of an *e* at the end of the word and a vowel in the middle of two consonants. I know that I'm supposed to use the long vowel and silent *e* at the end when I see this pattern. /k-a-k/. Cake. Now you look at the word and tell me how you're going to sound it out."

Visual Cues

Spelling patterns, not individual letters, are important for phonics because the sound a particular letter makes is determined by its location (e.g., the adjacent letters in the words *can* and *cane* determine if the short or long sounds are used). These spelling patterns should be emphasized visually. For example, to stress the final *e* in the word *cane*, put a slash through it or write it in a smaller size to show that it is silent.

The visual aspects of words provide important cues for sounding out words, so emphasize them by using spacing of the letters, color coding, bolding, different fonts, marking letters out, and diacritical marks. Spacing cues can be used as a signal that the students are to sound words out. The spacing cues used with the *Phonic Remedial Reading Lessons* (Kirk, Kirk, & Minskoff, 1985) are shown in Figure 2. When students see letter cards or tiles presented with spaces between them (e.g., c a t), they are to sound the word out. When they see the word written without spaces (e.g., *cat*), they are to say the complete word. Spacing can also be used to help students associate the correct sound with a particular letter or group of letters. For example, for the conso-nant digraph /ch/, write the *c* and *h* together to signal that they have one sound (e.g., /ch-a-t/).

Color coding, bolding, fonts, and marking out also provide helpful visual cues. For example, when teaching students to decide whether a short sound should be used, teach them to look for the CVC pattern. Make the consonants one color and vowels another. Lead them to discover that they should use the short vowel sound if they find this color pattern. When teaching use of the long vowel with the final silent *e*, write the final *e* in a smaller size or mark it out to signal that it is silent.

Use of the visual cues provided by diacritical marks varies with phonics programs. Some programs use these marks and others do not. Many phonics approaches teach students to mark short vowel sounds with breves (c ă t) and long vowel sounds with macrons (c ā ke). Diacritical marks should not be used with students who find it difficult to memorize their meanings. It is unwise to devote extensive instructional time to a task unless it is necessary for the de-coding of a target sound. Students can learn to read phonetically without use of diacritical marks.

VAKT Methods

Whenever possible, use VAKT methods in which you integrate visual cues (looking at the letter or word with a target sound), auditory cues (saying the target sound or word with it), kinesthetic cues (writing letters or words or using movements related to them), and tactile cues (tracing letters or words with target sounds). Students often trace over letters, say their sounds, and then write them from memory when they use VAKT methods. Or, students write the letters in the air with their eyes open or closed after they have traced over visual copies. The more cues used, the more likely the students will mas-ter the target sound.

Use varied kinesthetic cues such as having the students write the letters for sounds using scented magic markers, sidewalk chalk, or finger paint. Stu-dents can also receive kinesthetic cues by placing their bodies in configurations to represent different letters. For example, students can stand sideways and put one arm up at an angle and the other down at an angle to represent the letter *k*, say the letter name, and then the letter sound. Tactile cues can be provided by having students trace letters using sandpaper, cotton balls, or beans while saying the letter names and their sounds.

Educated Guessing

Teach students to use an experimental approach in which they make educated guesses as to what a word might be to help them decode phonetically irregu-lar words. For example, when learning to read a word such as *thief*, demonstrate reading it with the long /i/ sound to use the rule that should apply. Then, demonstrate trying the long /e/ sound and conclude that this sound "works." "This word should be *thief* (say with long /i/ sound) if we use our rule that says when there are two vowels, we say the name of the first one. But there is no word like *thief*. Let's try some other vowel sounds. Let's try the long /e/ sound. *Thief* (say with long /e/ sound). That's a real word, so my guess to use the long /e/ sound worked." Have the students systematically try using different sounds to decode irregular words.

Monitoring for Meaning

Code breaking using phonics should *not* be separated from a meaning-based approach. Students must be taught to always ask themselves whether their decoding of words makes sense. Students must learn to monitor for meaning with all reading tasks in which they are engaged and not just comprehension tasks. When students transition from reading words with target sounds and words in isolation to words in text, they must learn to always ask themselves if the way they have decoded the word produces a word that fits the overall meaning of the text. If not, then they must continue trying to decode the word until they can produce a word that fits the meaning of the passage. If they do not learn to monitor for meaning, then they will not learn how to self-correct.

8. Make phonics instruction fun: Learning sounds is abstract and involves fleeting auditory stimuli that are difficult for children to hold on to. Many students find learning sounds boring, especially in relation to the fast-paced visual presentations they experience on television and with video games.

Use a variety of teaching activities to increase student interest. Do not use the same format for all phonics lessons. Phonics instruction can be made appealing to students by being embedded in games, high-interest materials, and computer-assisted instruction.

9. Provide success—the best motivator for learning to read: Most struggling learners have experienced or are experiencing school failure and have developed low academic self-concepts and learned helplessness. They do not believe that they can learn to read and rely on others to read for them. You have to show them that they can learn to read. This is best done by promoting errorless learning. Create instructional activities in which students achieve success because they are only required to use skills that they have mastered. Use controlled readers that only include words that the students have learned to decode. Some of these materials are boring or "babyish" because of the limited number of words that can be used. However, they have their place in the reading curriculum because they clearly demonstrate to students that they can read.

Keep explicit records of student progress using charts, public recognition, grades, and so forth. As your students start to achieve success with reading, they will become more motivated to learn to read. You will be able to break the vicious cycle in which students do not try to learn to read because they think that they cannot learn.

TECHNIQUES FOR TEACHING THE DIFFERENT
SOUNDS IN THE PHONICS SCOPE AND SEQUENCE

This section presents the scope and sequence of sounds that should be included in phonics instruction along with techniques for teaching specific types of sounds (see Tables 8 and 9). You must know how to decode words using each of the sounds in the scope and sequence if you are to successfully teach them to your students. Take the phonics test in Appendix C. If you have difficulty with any type of sound, then get instruction from your teacher, classmates, or colleagues and learn them to the 100% mastery level.

There are two excellent resources to help you plan instructional activities for phonics. *Words Their Way* by Bear, Invernizzi, Templeton, and Johnston (2004) and *Word Journeys* by Ganske (2000) include lists of words for each type of sound as well as activities for teaching them.

Consonant Sounds

Make sure that the students know the names of the letters before teaching consonant sounds. To prevent confusion between the two possible responses (the letter name and the letter sound) that can be made to the same stimulus (i.e., the grapheme), explain that letters have names and sounds that they make.

Table 8.   Scope of sounds in phonics instruction

Consonant sounds	Start with continuous sounds
	Teach the two sounds for *c*
	Teach the two sounds for *g*
	Teach the two sounds for *s*
Vowel sounds	Short vowels
	Long vowels with the silent final *e*
	Vowel digraphs
	Diphthongs
	R-controlled vowels
	Vowel combinations
	Schwa
Consonant digraphs	Beginning consonant digraphs
	Ending consonant digraphs
Consonant blends	Initial two-letter consonant blends
	Initial three-letter consonant blends
	Ending consonant blends
Onset-rimes	Complete phonics program using onset-rimes
	Partial use of onset-rimes in combination with sound-by-sound approach
Silent letters	

Table 9.   Sequence of sounds to be taught by levels of difficulty

Easy level	Advanced level
Consonant sounds	Vowel digraphs
Short vowel sounds	Onset-rimes
Long vowel sounds	R-controlled vowels
Consonant digraphs	Diphthongs
Two-letter consonant blends	Vowel combinations
	Schwa
	Silent letters
	Three-letter consonant blends

Present the analogy of a dog that has a name (e.g., Spot) and a sound that it makes (e.g., arf). Then teach that the letter *s* has the name *s* and makes the sound /s/.

In general education, consonant sounds are often taught in alphabetical order starting with /b/ and ending with /z/. However, it is more effective to teach consonant sounds in order based on whether they have continuous sounds and can be elongated for emphasis. For example, start with teaching the sound /s/ because it can be drawn out and because the shape of the letter can be compared with a snake and the sound a snake makes: /sss/. Other continuous consonants are *f, h, l, m, n, r,* and *sh*. Noncontinuous sounds are called stops because they cannot be drawn out (e.g., try drawing out the /b/ sound and you will find that the sound stops).

The sounds for *q* and *x* are unusual. The letter *q* has the /kw/ sound and is always followed by the letter *u*; therefore, this sound can be taught after students have mastery of short vowels, or *qu* words can be taught visually as whole words. Always color code the letters *q* and *u* or write them together to show that they are always linked. The letter *x* is sounded as /ks/. Because making the *x* sound in isolation is difficult, you may want to teach words with the /ks/ sound using the onset-rime method. You would separately teach the rimes of *ax, ex, ix,* and *ox* and add onsets to form word families such as *tax, tex, fix,* and *fox*. It is also possible to teach word families with the letter *x* using a visual approach. Because the *q* and *x* letters and sounds do not frequently appear in words at low reading levels, teaching their sounds can be delayed until other sounds have been learned.

The letters *c, g,* and *s* are unique because they have two sounds associated with them. The letter *c* has the /k/ sound, as in the word *cat* (the hard *c* sound), and the /s/ sound, as in the word *city* (the soft *c* sound). Do not teach both sounds at the same time. First, teach the letter *c* as the /k/ sound, and after this is mastered, teach it with the /s/ sound, explaining that the letter *c* can make two different sounds. When the hard *c* sound is taught, it is usually taught with the rule that the hard *c* sound is followed by the letters *a* (*cake*), *o* (*cone*), and *u* (*cut*), and the soft *c* is followed by the letters *e* (*cement*), *i* (*city*), and *y* (*cycle*). Do the same with the two sounds for the letter *g*. First, teach it with the /g/ sound, as in the word *girl* (the hard *g* sound), and then teach the /j/ sound, as in the word *giant* (the soft *g* sound). Another consonant that has two sounds when it is at the end of the word is the /s/. At the beginning of the word, the letter *s* has the /s/ sound, but at the end of a word, it may have the /s/ sound (*bus*) or the /z/ sound (*rose*). After the /s/ sound for the letter *s* has been fully mastered, teach the /z/ sound.

Use the key word association strategy when teaching all consonant sounds. Teach students to look at the picture of the key word, say it, segment the first sound, and use it to decode words with the target consonant. Then, phase out use of the picture, and have the students recall the key word when they have difficulty recalling the sound of the consonant. For example, say, "The sound for the letter *b* is /b/. To help us remember the sound, we use the picture of a ball, we say ball, and then we say the first sound in the word *ball*. Say ball. Say the first sound in ball." Remember to only use key words that start with the target sound so that it is easier for the students to segment the sound from the word.

A kinesthetic strategy that is helpful for recalling consonants is having the students act out words that go with each of the sounds (Richek, Caldwell, Jennings, & Lerner, 2002). For example, they can bounce a ball for /b/, catch a ball for /k/, dance for /d/, fall for /f/, gallop for /g/, hop for /h/, jump for /j/, kick for /k/, laugh for /l/, march for /m/, nod for /n/, paint for /p/, run for /r/, sit for /s/, talk for /t/, vacuum for /v/, walk for /w/, yawn for /y/, and zip for /z/.

Vowel Sounds

Short Vowels

After most consonant sounds have been mastered, students are ready to learn short vowel sounds so that they can put sounds together to form words. Introduce vowels by labeling letters as consonants or vowels. Tell the students that the sounds that they have learned so far are called consonants, and now they are going to learn sounds that are called vowels. Color code the consonants to differentiate them from the vowels. First teach the /a/ sound using the word *apple* as a key word association. Initially, teach the sound in isolation. When presenting the sound in isolation, draw it out for emphasis. "The sound for this letter is /aaa/. The word *apple* starts with the /a/ sound. /aaa-pple/. /aaa/. Say *aaapple*. Say /aaa/." Then, demonstrate how words can be formed by modeling how to analyze each of the sounds in the word *cat* and then blend them together to form the complete word. "We know the sounds for the *c* and the *t*, and now we know the sound for the *a*. I'm going to sound this word out and then blend it. *(Point to each letter and say the corresponding sound.)* /k-a-t/. Cat.

Now you say each sound as you point to the letter, and then say the whole word." Be sure to have the students point to each letter as they make its sound so that you are sure that they are associating the correct letter with the correct sound. Always have them say the complete word after sounding it out.

After the students can read isolated words with the target sound, have them read these words embedded in sentences. Make sure that the students know the other words in the sentence. For example, teach the words *this, is,* and *a* as sight words in a basic sentence such as "This is a _____." Fill in the last word with words having the target sound (e.g., *cat, hat, man*). Teach the students to visually attend to the CVC pattern by having them label whether letters are consonants or vowels before decoding the words. Use controlled reading materials that have only words with the consonant and short vowel sounds that have been taught, or create your own sentences (e.g., *Pat had a fat cat*).

Once a student has 90% mastery of the short /a/ sound, move on to the short /o/ sound using the same procedure. Use a key word such as *octopus*. Once the short /o/ sound is mastered, provide review activities with words having both the short /a/ and /o/ sounds. Then, teach the short /i/ sound with the key word *itch*, the short /u/ with the key word *umbrella*, and the short /e/ sound with the key word *egg*. As each new vowel sound is mastered, provide activities integrating it with the previously learned vowels. Be sure to provide activities requiring students to read words that differ only in the medial vowels (e.g., *pin, pan, pen; cup, cap, cop*). These are the most difficult words to decode at this level because the students must retrieve which of the five short vowel sounds is called for in a particular word.

It is necessary to teach the change in the final consonants for the letters *l, s,* and *f* when teaching decoding of words with short vowels. When these letters appear at the ends of words, they are usually, but not always, doubled (e.g., *hill, mess, puff*). Tell the students that when the letters *f, l,* or *s* are at the beginning of a word, only one letter is used for the sound. When they are at the end of a word, they may appear as twins, but they still have one sound. When teaching the final *s*, indicate that some CVC words end in one *s* (*bus*) and some end in two (*fuss*). This will help with both reading and spelling of CVC words ending in *ll, ss,* and *ff*.

Make sure that the words you use to teach a particular sound actually contain the target sound. Do not just attend to the written letter; attend to the sound. For example, the word *dog* looks like it would be a CVC word for the short /o/ sound, but most Americans say it with the /au/ sound, not the short /o/ sound. Always say words to yourself subvocally before teaching them to make sure that they have the target sound you are teaching.

After all the short vowel sounds have been mastered, and before moving on to long vowel sounds, teach the rule for the CVC pattern (i.e., when a vowel is between two consonants, the short sound is used). However, make sure you only use words that follow this pattern at the early stages of instruction because it only applies 67% of the time (Tompkins, 2003).

Long Vowel Sounds

After students have fully mastered short vowel sounds, introduce the long vowel sounds associated with the silent *e* rule. Demonstrate by saying, "Some words have a different pattern from the CVC pattern. They have the consonant, vowel, consonant, and an *e* at the end. When we see this pattern, we use different vowel sounds. We use vowel sounds that are called long vowel sounds. Here's the word *cape*. When I sound it out, I say /k-a-p/. I don't say the *e* at the end. It's called a silent *e* because it doesn't say anything. I'm going to put a line through it to show that we don't sound it out. When we see this pattern with the CVCE, we use the letter name for the vowel sound. The letter name for this is *a*, so we say the *a* sound. Long vowels say their names."

When teaching the long vowel sounds in isolation, present them using the CVCE pattern. Use a small *e* or a marked out *e* at the end to show that it is silent. First, teach the long *a* sound (*cape*), then the long *i* (*kite*), long *o* (*poke*), and long *u* (*cute*). The long *e* rarely appears with the CVCE pattern. Use key word associations to help the students recall the sounds if the cue of saying their names is not adequate. Use the key word *ape* for the long *a*, *eagle* for the long *e*, *ice* for the long *i*, and *unicorn* for the long *u*. Teach the students to use the rule of the long vowel sounds for the CVCE pattern but to watch for exceptions such as the words *come* and *have*, which should be taught as sight words.

At a later point in instruction, teach patterns of words ending with vowels that are long (e.g., *he*, *go*), and introduce the *y* as a vowel as in the words *fly* and *baby*. Explain that *y* can be a consonant or a vowel. When *y* is used as a vowel at the end of a word, it can have the long *i* sound (*fly*) or the long *e* sound (*baby*).

Vowel Digraphs

When two adjacent vowels appear together, they are sometimes called vowel digraphs because they have one sound. The sound that they usually, but not always, make is the sound of the first vowel. The rule "when two vowels go walking, the first one does the talking" applies to decoding vowel digraphs. Introduce this rule, but make sure that you use words that follow the rule. First, teach the vowel digraphs *ai* (*rain*) and *ay* (*say*). Write the two letters together, or color code them to show that they make one sound. Then, teach the vowel digraphs *ee* (*feet*) and *ea* (*seat*). Words with the *ea* vowel combination have many exceptions to this rule. For example, *ea* can be sounded as the long *e* (*seat*), the short *e* (*bread*), and the *r*-controlled vowel /er/ (*heard*), so be careful with the words that you use to exemplify the long /e/ sound for *ea*. Lastly, teach the vowel digraph *oa* (*boat*). Also, teach vowel digraphs that appear at the ends of words, such as *ie* (*pie*) and *oe* (*toe*).

Diphthongs

Some vowel combinations have unique sounds that are not associated with either of the two vowels making up the combinations. These are called diphthongs and include *oi* (*boil*), *oy* (*boy*), *ou* (*out*), and *ow* (*cow*). Use the key words of *oil* to aid in recall of the /oi/ and /oy/ sounds and *ouch* for the *ou* and *ow* diphthongs.

R-Controlled Vowels

In most cases, when the letter *r* follows a vowel, the vowel sounds are unique; therefore, this class of vowels is referred to as *r*-controlled sounds. The /ar/ vowel combination (*car*) is taught first with *art* as the key word. Then, teach /or/ (*corn*) using the key word *orange*. The *r*-controlled vowels of /er/ (*fern*), /ir/ (*sir*), and /ur/ (*turn*) have the same sound. Use the key word *earth* as an aid to recalling this sound. Be sure to color code the vowel and the *r* that follows it to indicate that these are *r*-controlled vowels. First, teach the /er/ combination. Then, tell the students that /ir/ makes the same sound and teach words with it. Finally, explain that the /ur/ is the third *r*-controlled vowel that has the same sound. Then, teach them together, and use many dictation tasks in which you give a word with /er/, /ir/, or /ur/. This will help the students recall which of the three vowels goes with which words (e.g., "Write these words: *sir, turn, her, fur, girl*").

Other Vowel Combinations

Other vowel combinations that are often taught in phonics programs include /aw/ (*paw*) and /au/ (*haul*), /ew/ (*new*), and /oo/ (*moon*) and /oo/ (*book*). These may be best taught to some struggling students using the onset-rime approach or visual methods because it is difficult for some students to recall these sounds in isolation.

Schwa

One of the sounds that some phonics programs teach is the schwa, which is the sound that you hear at the beginning of the word *about* (/uh/). It is an unaccented sound that is harder to isolate than other vowel sounds and should be taught at a later time. It is also difficult because it is represented by different graphemes (e.g., the letter *a* in the word *about*, the letter *o* in the word *love*, the letter *u* in the word *medium*). When teaching the schwa, use the upside down *e* (ə) to represent it. Also, to recall the sound of the schwa, use the analogy of what people say when they are hit in the stomach, and have students push in their stomachs as they say the schwa sound. Because the schwa is so hard to learn, some phonics programs do not systematically teach this sound and use visual methods to teach words with it. If you do not teach the schwa, then use the educated guess strategy to have the students guess what a word is when they know all the sounds, except for the schwa sound.

Consonant Digraphs

When some combinations of two adjacent consonants appear together, they are spoken with one sound and are called consonant digraphs. These are usually taught after consonants and short vowel sounds are learned. They are harder to learn because of the change from one-to-one correspondence of one letter to one sound to the association of two letters and one sound. Consonant digraphs include the beginning combinations of *sh* (*ship*), *ch* (*chin*), *th* (*thin*), *wh* (*white*), and *ph* (*phone*) and the ending combinations of *sh* (*rush*), *ch* (*rich*), *ck* (*tack*), and *tch* (*catch*). Some phonics programs teach the voiced *th* as in *they* and the unvoiced *th* as in *thin*, and other programs do not differentiate these two *th* sounds. Many words with the voiced *th* are taught as sight words (e.g., *the*, *they*, *there*, *these*). Spatially separate the digraphs or write them in a different color to show that they have one sound. When teaching *sh*, use the motor cue of putting your finger over your lips to represent the sign for quiet. After the students can produce the *sh* sound in isolation, have them read words starting with *sh* (ship) in isolation and in text. After these are learned, teach words ending with the consonant digraph *sh* (push). Use words with the CVC short vowel patterns that the students previously learned, and substitute consonant digraphs for consonants (e.g., *sip*, *ship*). Use the association of a train sound for the *ch* consonant digraph. The consonant digraph *ch* can be at the beginning of words as in *chip* and also at the end of words as in *rich*. First, teach words ending in *ch* and later teach *tch*, which is harder because there are three letters in this consonant combination. Include many dictation tasks to help students correctly spell words ending in *ch* and *tch*. Use the key word association of *thumb* for the *th* consonant digraph, and use the key word association of *wheel* for *wh*. Make clear to the students that the *ph* combination goes with the /f/ sound, and use the key word association of *phone*.

Consonant Blends

Consonant blends are two (or three) letters that retain their sounds and are blended together. They differ from consonant digraphs because they have two or more sounds; consonant digraphs have only one sound. First, teach consonant blends that appear at the beginning of words (e.g., <u>st</u>ick) and then teach those at the ends of words (e.g., fa<u>st</u>). Teach consonant blends in groups that share the same initial letters.

- The *s* group with *st* (*stop*), *sm* (*smell*), *sn* (*snap*), *sp* (*spell*), *sl* (*slip*), *sc* (*scat*), *sk* (*skull*), and *sw* (*swim*).

- The *b* group with *bl* (*block*) and *br* (*broom*)

- The *c* group with *cl* (*clock*) and *cr* (*crack*)

- The *f* group with *fl* (flag) and *fr* (free)
- The *g* group with *gl* (glass) and *gr* (grass)
- The *p* group with *pl* (*plant*) and *pr* (*press*)
- The *t* group with *tr* (*tree*) and *tw* (*twin*)
- The *d* group with *dr* (*drum*) and *dw* (*dwarf*)

Demonstrate the separate sounds of each consonant and how they are blended together when you model blends. "This is the letter *s* that has the /s/ sound, and this is the letter *t* that has the /t/ sound. Some words have these two letters together, and when they're together we blend them. We say /st/." Use letter tiles, and point to each of the letters as you say them separately, then bring the tiles together and blend the sounds together. Use the CVC words the students have previously learned and insert initial consonant blends (e.g., *top, stop*). At a later time, introduce three letter consonant blends (e.g., /spl/ [*splash*], /spr/ [*spray*], /scr/ [*scream*], /str/ [*street*]).

Also at a later time, teach ending consonant blends such as /st/ (*must*). Some ending consonant blends are best taught using the onset-rime method because of the difficulty separating the consonants. For example, /mp/, /ld/, /nk/, and /ng/ are difficult to separate and are more effectively taught using onsets and rimes such as /amp/ (*lamp*), /old/ (*cold*), /ink/ (*pink*), and /ing/ (*sing*).

Onsets and Rimes

You can use the onset-rime method in two ways. You can teach decoding primarily using onsets and rimes and not emphasize the sound-by-sound method. This is also called the word family method and has been used to successfully improve word recognition (Wanzek & Haager, 2003). You can also use the onset-rime method for sounds that are hard to say in isolation. This is the method advocated in this book because it has been found to be more effective with students who already have some decoding skills, whereas the sound-by-sound method has been found more effective with students with lower level decoding skills (Juel & Minden-Cupp, 2002). The sound-by-sound approach should be used at the initial stages of phonics instruction. The onset-rime method should be used at more advanced levels of phonics instruction for sounds that are hard to pronounce separately. Table 10 shows onsets and rimes that should be taught at more advanced levels of phonics instruction after a solid foundation of phonics mastery has been established using a sound-by-sound approach.

When teaching with the onset-rime method, explain that some sounds cannot be separated and students will be learning these as word parts. Present a basic rime such as /ing/, and have the students say it after you. "This says /ing/. Say /ing/." Then, demonstrate how the rime can be paired with different onsets to form words. Use cards with different consonants written in a color different

Table 10. Onsets and rimes to be taught in conjunction with a sound-by-sound method

ang (sang)	ing (sing)	ong (song)	ung (rung)
ank (sank)	ink (sink)	unk (sunk)	
and (sand)	end (send)	ind (mind)	ound (round)
ant (pant)	ent (sent)	int (mint)	unt (punt)
anch (ranch)	ench (bench)	inch (pinch)	unch (lunch)
old (gold)	olt (bolt)	elt (belt)	ilt (tilt)
all (ball)	alt (salt)	ight (light)	
amp (lamp)	imp (limp)	ump (lump)	

than the rime. "Here is the letter *s*. Let's add that to /ing/ to make a word. /s/. /ing/. Sing. Say the first sound, then the main part of the word, and then the whole word." Then, demonstrate words that have different consonants, consonant digraphs, and consonant blends (e.g., *king, thing, sling*).

Silent Letters

Students already know about silent letters from instruction on the silent *e* and CVCE pattern words. Teach the following silent letters with these letter combinations: *kn* (*know*), *gn* (*sign*), *wr* (*write*), *alk* (*talk*), *gh* (*high*), and *mb* (*lamb*). Write the silent letter in a lighter color or strike it out.

Sequencing the Teaching of Sounds

It is impossible to teach the 500 different spelling–sound rules or the 80,000 different words that students are exposed to by the end of the third grade (Juel & Minden-Cupp, 2002). The real purpose of phonics instruction is to get the students to the level at which they can read enough words to enter the world of books and learn words based on repeatedly seeing them in print—the level at which they can teach themselves to read. You need to determine if some of your students reach this point before all sounds in the phonics scope and sequence have been taught. For example, the *Wilson Reading System* takes at least 3 years to complete. If you are using this program or any program that entails a long period of time devoted to decoding skills, then you need to ask yourself: 1) Are the students ready to move ahead before the completion of the program? 2) Is their reading progress being held back because they can teach themselves new words? 3) Are they ready to learn the advanced comprehension skills that are necessary for meeting their classroom reading demands? As students enter higher grades, they need more comprehension skills for classroom reading, so it is important to take them to the stage at which comprehension skills are taught as soon as possible. There is no one rule for all students. Some students need systematic instruction on all sounds in the scope and sequence of phonics, even if it takes 3 years or more. Other students "catch on" and become independent readers and no longer need intensive phonics instruction.

How do you make the difficult decision about how much phonics to provide to individual students? When do you stop phonics instruction? You can divide phonics skills into two levels (easy and advanced) to help you make this decision (see Table 9). As students master each of the skills at these levels, ask yourself if they are ready to move to a more comprehension, text-based instructional emphasis or whether a decoding-skill instructional emphasis is still needed. If you make this move, it does not mean that phonics is no longer taught, but rather, phonics instruction becomes less important than comprehension instruction.

Model Lesson for Teaching Phonics
Octopus Opera

OBJECTIVE
Students will read CVC words with the short /o/ sound in isolation with 90% accuracy.

ADVANCED ORGANIZER
At this stage, the short /a/ sound is reviewed to ensure that the students are ready to make the step up to learning the short /o/ sound.

Link
Link to previous lessons on the short /a/ sound. Use the picture cue cards for /a/ and /o/ and cards with CVC words with /a/ sounds.

"What is this a picture of? . . . Right, an apple. /ă/. Apple. /ă/. That's the sound we have learned for the letter *a*. If this is /ă/, then what is this word? . . . Right, it's *cat*: /k-a-t/." *(Continue reviewing the /a/ sound with several words.)*

Identify
Identify the goal of the lesson.

"Today we're going to learn a new vowel sound. We're going to learn to read words with the short *o* sound, /ŏ/."

Provide Rationale

Explain the importance of the lesson.

"By learning another sound, you'll be able to read a lot more words."

MODELING

Use octopus puppets (laminated pictures of octopuses on tongue depressors) to emphasize the short o sound. Use a picture card of an octopus to provide visual cues. Use letter tiles to provide kinesthetic cues on how to sound out each separate letter in CVC words and how to blend them together. For additional visual and kinesthetic cues, use mirrors to help students focus on both your lips and their lips as the short o sound is spoken. Use the association of the short o sound to the sound a doctor asks the students to make when examining their throats.

"I've given each of you a puppet. What is it? . . . Right, an oooctopus. Octopus starts with the /o/ sound. Oooctopus. /ooo/. Say octopus . . . Say /o/ . . . Great. Have you ever been to a doctor? . . . What does the doctor ask you to do when she looks down your throat? . . . Right! You say /ooo/. That's the /o/ sound. It's just like the /o/ sound in the word *octopus*. Look at my mouth when I say /o/. What does it look like? . . . Pick up your mirrors and say the /o/ sound with me. What does your mouth look like? . . . When we say oooctopus, /o/, we make a circle with our mouth and our jaw drops. It sounds a little like we are singing. We're having an octopus opera! *(Sing the sound and the word* octopus.) /ooo/. Oooctopus. /ooo/." *(Review the sound and cue word several more times if needed.)*

"Now we're going to read some words with the /o/ sound. We know how to sound out all the consonants in these words and we're going to add the /o/ sound to them, just like we did with our /a/ sound words. Let's do this first one. *(Present the letters on tiles with spaces between each. Point to each letter tile as you say the corresponding sound, then bring the tiles together and say the complete word.)* Remember, we're going to use the /o/ sound, like in the word *octopus*. /p-o-t/. This word is *pot*. Now you sound it out after me and then say the whole word. /p-o-t/. Pot . . . Great." *(Continue to demonstrate with words such as* mop *and* cop.)

GUIDED PRACTICE

Octopus Building

Each student should have a cutout of an octopus that has Velcro on each of its tentacles, a set of letter tiles, and word cards with Velcro backing. As you call out a CVC word with the short o sound (e.g., *pot*), the students spell the word using letter tiles, find the corresponding word in their word card bank, and then Velcro the word on an octopus tentacle. When all words are done, the students read the words back before removing them from the octopus. After the students are able to do this, show a picture of a short *o* word, and have the students build the word using the letter tiles, find the matching word card, and place it on the octopus. Once the octopus is built again, the process can be reversed, with students taking off the word cards as you call out the words.

Octopus Shuffle

Post pictures for words with the short *o* sound (e.g., *mop*, *top*) around the room. Give each student an octopus puppet that has a short *o* word on it. Play music, and have the students walk around the room. When the music stops, have the students find the picture corresponding to the word on their puppet. Each student reads her word, then puppets are redistributed, and the game is played again.

INDEPENDENT PRACTICE

Have students practice the skill without assistance. Record the accuracy of the students' responses so you can evaluate their mastery of the objective.

Octopus Search

Students are given a packet of laminated short *o* words and a set of colored dots, markers, or stamps. Show a picture of a word with the short *o* sound that is numbered, colored, or stamped (e.g., a picture of a mop with the number 1). Students find the matching word card in their packets and mark it with the corresponding number, color, or stamp. Students then read the word cards aloud at the end of the activity.

Octopus Match

This is a version of the game Concentration. Have students lay out pictures and corresponding word cards face down. Students find matches of pictures and words as they turn the cards face up.

GENERALIZATION

Present controlled readers with short *o* words, and record the number of words the students read correctly. Also, use trade books or basals and point out CVC words with short *o*, and have the students read them.

5

Reading the Big Words

Teaching Structural Analysis Skills

CONCEPTS EXPLORED

- Role of structural analysis in the overall model of reading
- Types of structural analysis skills
- Guidelines for teaching structural analysis skills
- Techniques for teaching different types of structural analysis skills
- Model lesson for teaching structural analysis

Structural analysis is an advanced decoding skill that involves the ability to analyze words based on their parts, or their structure. These word parts include 1) affixes (both prefixes and suffixes), 2) compound words, 3) contractions, 4) syllables, and 5) roots. Structural analysis is often neglected in reading programs because of the erroneous assumption that if students master all areas of phonics, then they have attained an independent level in word decoding. Mastery of phonics leads to independent decoding of only one-syllable words. Students need to learn to decode longer words using structural analysis so that they can read complex content area words (e.g., the multisyllabic word *ecologically* for science). It is not possible to read lengthy multisyllabic words sound by sound. Such words must be broken down into more manageable parts that can be decoded. It cannot be assumed that because students can decode single-syllable words, they can decode these same syllables when they are parts of multisyllabic words. Students must be taught rules for analyzing the sounds of the letters in one part of a word based on the relationship among all the parts in the word. For example, to decode the word *kitten*, students must first separate the word into two parts and then use the CVC pattern to sound out each part.

The fourth-grade slump in reading achievement reported by many researchers (Sweet & Snow, 2002) may be related, in part, to the limited instruction directed at structural analysis skills. Some believe that reading skills can be fully developed by third grade and that students are ready to learn additional reading skills on their own. Students do not have adequate mastery of all word identification skills until they reach the reading to learn stage, which extends from grades 4 to 8. Throughout this stage, students need systematic instruction to develop structural analysis skills to decode the lengthy, complex words in their content area readings.

Although there is limited emphasis on systematic teaching of structural analysis skills past third grade, there is considerable emphasis on testing of structural analysis with standardized academic achievement tests and assessments of state standards. Knowledge of root words, prefixes, and suffixes is one Virginia Standard of Learning assessed at both fourth- and fifth-grade levels (*Standards of Learning Currently in Effect*, n.d.). The following item assesses this standard in the fourth- and fifth-grade 2000 statewide assessment of English.

"The dogs bark to warn the sheepherders."
In which word does <u>ers</u> mean the same as it does in sheepherders?
A. St<u>eers</u>
B. Feath<u>ers</u>
C. P<u>ers</u>on
D. Teach<u>ers</u>

ROLE OF STRUCTURAL ANALYSIS
IN THE OVERALL MODEL OF READING

Structural analysis is a word identification skill that must be rooted in a solid foundation of phonics, phonological awareness for syllables, visual methods of word identification, and morphological aspects of language. Students must have mastered phonetic skills so they can apply them to decoding the word parts that they identify using structural analysis. For example, they must use structural analysis to separate the word *rabbit* into the two syllables of *rab* and *bit*. Then they apply the phonics rule of short vowel sounds to decode each syllable with the CVC pattern. Three prerequisite phonological awareness skills for developing structural analysis skills are: identification of the small words in orally presented compound words, syllable blending of orally presented syllables, and segmentation of orally presented syllables. Students need to identify the two small words in compound words that they hear before they can analyze small words in written compound words. They need to be able to blend syllables into complete words when they hear them so that they can apply this skill to blending syllables that they have decoded while reading. Likewise, they need to segment words they hear into syllables so that they can do the same with words that they are attempting to read.

Visual skills are important for learning structural analysis skills because students must learn to attend to certain visual patterns that are related to analyzing the parts of a word. For example, students must have good skills for seeing the small words embedded in larger words so that they can decode compound words as well as base words with prefixes and suffixes. They must be able to see that the word *lock* appears in the word *unlock*. They must be able to spot visual patterns such as the doubling of the consonant in CVC pattern words when suffixes are added (e.g., the two *n*'s in the word *running*).

Students need to have mastered morphological oral language skills so that they can use these as the basis for using structural analysis cues for reading. The word parts that they are analyzing are morphemes, the smallest units of meaning in language. For example, there are two morphemes in the word *jumped*, the word *jump* and the *ed* ending, which represents past action. Students need to understand and use the past tense in their oral language so that they can eventually read and understand written words with the *ed* ending. Students who speak nonstandard dialects and ELLs have difficulty with this aspect of reading because they often do not understand or use these morphological structures in their oral language. For example, for Spanish speakers, it would be useful to explicitly teach that the English suffix *ty* is the same as the Spanish suffix *dad* using base words that are the same in Spanish and English (the English word *variety* equals the Spanish word *variedad*).

Structural analysis skills are important not only for word identification but also for comprehension. Analyzing words based on the meaning of the parts helps in understanding the meaning of the whole word. For example, when teaching students to decode words with the prefix *dis*, instruct them that this prefix means *not*. They can understand the meaning of a word by analyzing the meaning of the prefix and the base word (e.g., the meaning of the word *dislike* is to *not like*). Phonics only aids students in word identification, but some structural analysis skills aid students in both word identification and word comprehension. This dual purpose of structural analysis makes instruction in this area of reading especially important.

TYPES OF STRUCTURAL ANALYSIS SKILLS

Structural analysis skills involve the ability to read compound words, affixes (which include both prefixes and suffixes), contractions, syllables, and root words. Compound words and affixes are taught first. Start instruction on compound words using compound words in which the students know how to read and understand the two small words. For example, if the students already know how to read and understand the words *fire* and *man*, then teach the compound word *fireman*. Affixes are relatively easy to learn if the students can already read the base words to which the affixes are added. For example, if students are being taught the prefix *un*, and they already know how to read and understand the word *lock*, then learning the word *unlock* is easy for most students.

Contractions are introduced next. Very often, contractions are not explicitly taught. It is assumed that the students will know how to read them because they use them in their oral language; however, for many students, this assumption may not be correct. Contractions are hard to understand because of the absence of some of the letters needed to decode the complete word and because they involve verbs that are abstract (e.g., *is* as in *isn't*). Therefore, they are more difficult to understand than words for concrete nouns (e.g., the word *dog*).

Instruction on syllables is taught next. It should be noted that there is some disagreement as to where to include syllable instruction—in phonics or in structural analysis (Mercer & Mercer, 2001). The *Wilson Reading System* (Wilson, 1988) and the *Phonic Remedial Reading Lessons* (Kirk, Kirk, & Minskoff, 1985) include it under phonics instruction. However, syllable instruction is best taught with structural analysis because separating words into parts is the single focus of instruction. If syllables are included in phonics instruction, then students have to focus on two aspects of reading—learning to decode sounds and learning to separate words in parts.

Syllable instruction differs from other instruction on structural analysis skills because it uses explicit rules and the relationship of these rules to phonetic decisions. For example, students are taught the rule for open syllables (i.e., if the syllable ends in a vowel, then the vowel is long, as in the word *lady*). Therefore, there is a close relationship between syllabication and phonics.

Roots are taught at the highest levels. Roots involve word parts based on Latin and Greek derivatives (e.g., the root *bio* means life and is in the word *biology*). Teaching this skill is recommended only for students who are exposed to advanced content area instruction and who will most likely enter post-secondary education. Instruction on roots must focus on how to read the word part as well as its meaning (e.g., learning that the root *man* means hand makes reading and understanding of words such as *manicure* and *manual* easier). Although some struggling students may not reach the advanced level of learning root words, it should not be assumed that this level is too high for all students. The decision as to whether to teach roots should be based on the students' need to read high-level vocabulary in their advanced content area classes.

GUIDELINES FOR TEACHING STRUCTURAL ANALYSIS SKILLS

The following guidelines for teaching compound words, affixes, contractions, syllables, and roots are presented in Table 11.

1. Teach analyzing of meaning as well as decoding of word parts. Structural analysis assists students with identifying how to decode a word and in some cases how to analyze its meaning, unlike phonics, which only helps with the decoding of a word. Whenever possible, relate the meaning of the word part to the meaning of the entire word. For example, when teaching the meaning of the prefix *re*, emphasize that this prefix means to do something again, so the meaning of the word *retype* is to type something again.

2. Teach structural analysis skills for both reading and spelling. For all structural analysis skills, assess if students can read words using a particular structural analysis skill. If they cannot, then teach both reading and spelling of the word part being taught. If students can read a word using the skill but can-

Table 11. Guidelines for teaching structural analysis skills

Teach analyzing of meaning as well as decoding of word parts.
Teach structural analysis skills for both reading and spelling.
Teach one word part at a time.
Teach easiest to hardest word parts based on frequency of use, linguistic complexity, and the number of words parts in a word.
Teach words that follow rules, and then teach words that are exceptions.
Use VAKT (visual, auditory, kinesthetic, and tactile) methods to emphasize significant structural cues.
Start instruction using words in the students' oral vocabulary.
Integrate instruction on structural analysis with dictionary use.
Make instruction on structural analysis fun.

not spell it, then teach spelling using this structural analysis skill. For example, if students can read words with two syllables in which the middle consonant is doubled (e.g., *kitten*) but cannot spell such words, then provide instruction on spelling.

3. Teach one word part at a time. To prevent overloading, do not teach multiple word parts at the same time. For example, if students do not know the prefixes *un*, *re*, *pre*, and *dis*, then do not teach all four at one time. Teach the *un* prefix first, and after this is mastered, teach *re*. As a new word part is mastered, integrate it with previously learned parts by providing frequent review.

4. Teach easiest to hardest word parts based on frequency of use, linguistic complexity, and the number of word parts in a word. Tables 12 through 16 include items for teaching various structural analysis skills, and they are arranged in order of difficulty based on the frequency of use of the item. For example, the prefix *un* is the most frequently used prefix, and the prefix *hemi* is less commonly used (Vacca, Vacca, & Gove, 1995), so *un* is taught before *hemi*. Linguistic complexity is determined by the abstractness of the meaning of the word part. For example, the root *auto*, which means *self* as in *autobiography*, is less abstract that the root *dict*, which means *say* as in *predict*, so the root *auto* is taught before the root *dict*. The number of the word parts is also a factor in sequencing instruction. When teaching syllabication, words with two syllables are taught first, then three, and so forth. When teaching affixes, present words with one affix (e.g., the prefix *un* as in *unlock*) and then two affixes (e.g., the prefix *un* and the suffix *ed* as in *unlocked*).

5. Teach words that follow rules, and then teach words that are exceptions. It is important that you first teach consistent patterns so that students can generalize the underlying rule, and then teach irregular forms. For example, when teaching suffixes, first teach the rule that *s* is added to form the plural using base words that do not change (e.g., *cat—cats*), and then teach exceptions to this rule (e.g., *dress—dresses*).

6. Use VAKT methods to emphasize significant structural cues. Structural analysis skills involve visual attention to the order and arrangement of letters in words. Use color, spatial, and movement cues to emphasize these visual features. For example, when teaching students the structural analysis rule of doubling the consonant in words such as *hopping*, color code the two *p*'s.

7. Start instruction using words in the students' oral vocabulary. Using words in the student's oral vocabulary helps them use meaning cues to master structural analysis skills. Once they master a specific structural analysis skill with words that they know, move on to words that they do not know.

This will be more difficult because the students will not be able to associate the word with a corresponding word in their oral language repertoire, and they will have to solely rely on their decoding skills. It is especially important to apply this principle with ELLs, students who speak nonstandard dialects, and students with language-based learning disabilities.

8. Integrate instruction on structural analysis with dictionary use. Once students master a specific structural analysis skill, teach them to apply it to using a dictionary. For example, when teaching students to analyze syllables following a certain pattern, have them look words up in the dictionary that follow the pattern (e.g., identifying words that start with *ma* that follow the open syllable rule and those that do not: *major* versus *mature*).

9. Make instruction on structural analysis fun. Activities for teaching structural analysis can be boring and difficult because of the metalinguistic nature of the task of analyzing word parts. There is little semantic content to make instruction in this area interesting as there is in comprehension instruction. Use games, movement-oriented activities, and computer-assisted instruction to motivate students to work on these critically important, but dry, activities.

TECHNIQUES FOR TEACHING DIFFERENT TYPES OF STRUCTURAL ANALYSIS SKILLS

Two excellent sources that provide lists of words and teaching activities for teaching the following structural analysis skills are *Words Their Way* (Bear et al., 2004) and *Word Journeys* (Ganske, 2000).

Compound Words

Analysis of the small words in compound words is an effective means for learning to both decode and understand the meaning of such words. Table 12 presents lists of words to be taught, arranged in order of difficulty, so assess and teach them in the order listed. Compound words that have concrete semantic meaning (e.g., *mailbox*) are taught first, followed by compound words with abstract meaning (e.g., *anyhow*). It is not possible to analyze the meaning of the compound words with abstract meanings based on the meanings of the two small words. Review the phonemic awareness skill of word segmentation of orally presented compound words before teaching reading of compound words.

Use color coding to emphasize the two words that comprise the compound word. When teaching groups of compound words that share one of the small words (e.g., *fireman, firehouse, fireplace*), use the same color for the shared word. Use of spatial and physical cues provides additional support. For ex-

Table 12.   Compound words

Concrete compound words	Abstract compound words
Mailman, mailbox	Anyone, anybody, anytime, anywhere, anyhow
Fireman, firehouse, fireplace, fireworks	Someone, somebody, sometime, somewhere, somehow, someday
Policeman	
Bookbag, bookcase	Everyone, everybody, everywhere, everyday
Basketball, baseball, football, softball	Nobody, nowhere
Bedroom, bathroom, playroom, sunroom	Whichever, whenever, however
Newspaper, newscast	Another, otherwise
Workbook, cookbook	Myself, herself, himself, itself
Footprint, footstep	Into, inside, indoors
Daylight, daytime, daydream	Outside, outdoors, outline
Sunburn, suntan, sunlight, sunshine	Within, without
Grandmother, grandfather, grandson, granddaughter	Backward, forward
Playroom, playground, playtime	
Upstairs, downstairs	
Teaspoon, tablespoon	
Blackboard, chalkboard, keyboard	
Snowball, snowflake, snowstorm	
Rainbow, raindrop, raincoat	
Eyeball, eyelash, eyebrow	

ample, write each of the small words on separate cards and physically bring them together to emphasize the motor aspect of VAKT. To include motor activities by the students, have each student in a group hold a card with a small word and then stand next to other students and decide if the word that they created is a compound word or not. For example, have one student hold a card with the word *fire*, stand next to someone with the word *mail*, and decide that *firemail* is not a compound word. Then, have the student holding the card with the word *fire* stand next to a student with the word *man* and decide that *fireman* is a compound word.

Use pictures to help students analyze the meanings of the compound words. For example, have the students match the words *fireman*, *policeman*, and *mailman* with corresponding pictures.

Affixes

Teach the prefixes and suffixes in Tables 13 and 14 in the order listed. First, teach suffixes, which include word endings representing verb tenses (*jumped*), comparisons (*smaller*), plurals (*shoes*), and possessives (*girl's*). These are easiest to learn because they occur frequently and because the student sees the base word first and then the suffix. When teaching other suffixes and prefixes, teach them in the order listed because their order is based on their frequency of use

Table 13.   Prefixes

Easy, most frequently used prefixes

Prefix	Meaning[a]	Example
Un	Not	Unhappy
Re	Again	Retype
In		Inform
Im	Not	Impossible
Ir	Not	Irregular
Il	Not	Illogical
Dis	Not	Disagree
En		Engulf
Em		Empower
Over		Overrule
Mis	Wrong	Misspell
Sub	Under	Substandard
Pre	Before	Preseason
Inter	Between	Interlock
De		Defuse
Trans	Across	Transatlantic

Intermediate level prefixes

Prefix	Meaning[a]	Example
Anti	Against	Antisocial
Bi	Two	Biped
Co	With	Copresident
Com		Combine
Con		Converge
En		Encircle
Equa (equi)	Equal	Equator (equilateral)
Ex		Extend
Hemi	Half	Hemisphere
Hyper	Too much	Hyperactive
Micro	Small	Microphone
Mid	Middle	Midnight
Milli	One thousandth	Milligram
Mis	Not	Misread
Mono	One	Monograph
Multi	Many	Multivitamin
Non	Not	Nonfat
Poly	Many	Polygraph
Post	After	Postseason
Semi	Partly	Semicolon
Tri	Three	Triangle
Uni	One	Unilateral

From Graves, M.F., Juel, C., & Graves, B.B. *Teaching reading in the 21st century* (p. 206). Published by Allyn and Bacon, Boston, MA. Copyright © 1998 by Pearson Education. Adapted by permission of the publisher; and from Gunning, T.G. *Assessing and correcting reading and writing difficulties* (p. 273). Published by Allyn and Bacon, Boston, MA. Copyright © 1998 by Pearson Education. Adapted by permission of the publisher.

[a]Some prefixes have abstract or multiple meanings that are hard to teach. Therefore, emphasize the decoding aspects and not the meanings for these prefixes.

Table 14. Suffixes

Easy, frequently used suffixes	Example
s	Jumps
es	Dresses
's	Girl's
ed	Jumped, hoped, hopped
ing	Jumping, hoping, hopping
er	Lighter, nicer, bigger, prettier
est	Lightest, nicest, biggest, prettiest
ly	Friendly
er	Teacher
or	Advisor
en	Redden
ion, tion, ation, ition	Education
ible,	Visible
able	Valuable
al, ial	Accidental
y	Windy
ness	Wellness
ful	Helpful
Intermediate level suffixes	**Example**
age	Postage
an	Mexican
ian	Canadian
ance	Importance
ary	Ordinary
ence	Independence
ian	Historian
ic	Periodic
ify	Modify
ish	Foolish
ist	Typist
ity	Activity
ize	Memorize
ive	Cooperative
less	Helpless
ly	Likely
ment	Employment
ous	Humorous
ster	Mobster

From Gunning, T.G. *Assessing and correcting reading and writing difficulties* (p. 276). Published by Allyn and Bacon, Boston, MA. Copyright © 1998 by Pearson Education. Adapted by permission of the publisher.

(e.g., *un* is the most frequently used prefix and is taught first) and ease of understanding (e.g., *re* is easy to demonstrate and therefore easy to understand because it means to do something again). First, teach words containing one affix (e.g., *misspell*) and gradually move to more difficult words containing multiple affixes (e.g., *misspelling*).

Explicitly teach rules underlying the use of a particular class of affixes. First, teach rules that do not require structural changes in the word parts. For example, first teach the *ed* past tense suffix with base words that do not change (*jump<u>ed</u>*). Then, add the *ed* suffix to base words that change (e.g., dropping the final *e* for CVCE pattern words [*hoped*], doubling the final consonant in CVC pattern words [*hopped*]). Obviously, the students need to have mastered the prerequisite phonetic decoding of CVCE and CVC pattern words. Finally, teach the rule for changing the final *y* to *i* (e.g., *worr<u>y</u>* to *worr<u>ied</u>*).

Use color coding cues to emphasize the prefix or suffix. Color the base word and the affix in different colors. Also, color code structural changes in words (e.g., for analysis of the word *education*, write *educa* and the word *educate* in the same color and then write *tion* in another color). Use color coding or bolding to emphasize suffixes. These are often ignored by struggling readers because they are at the end of the word and because they are short. In addition, have students who tend to drop the suffixes when reading point to each word part as they read it.

Use spatial and physical cues to emphasize the affix. Write the affix and main word on separate cards and physically bring them together to emphasize the motor aspect of VAKT. To demonstrate the dropping of the *e* for CVCE pattern words, present letter cards for each letter (e.g., *h o p e*). Then, have the students drop the *e* letter card on the floor to show that it is dropped when the /ed/ suffix is added.

Whenever possible, emphasize the meaning of words based on their affixes. Demonstrate and explain the change in meaning of the base word with and without the affix (e.g., *happy* versus *unhappy*). Use visual cues to correspond to the meaning of the affixes (e.g., pictures of a happy and unhappy face to correspond to the words *happy* and *unhappy*). Also, use demonstrations (e.g., demonstrate zipping and unzipping a coat for the words *zip* and *unzip*). Use of visual cues to support the meaning of the written words is especially important for ELLs.

Use nonexamples and have the students evaluate whether these are real words. For example, give the students cards with different affixes and base words, and have them pair up with each other to form words. Have the students move around and practice matching up their cards with cards held by other students and describing whether the words they formed are real words. For example, have students hold cards with these prefixes and base words: *un*, *mis*, *dis*, *like*, *type*, *lock*. Have them stand next to each other and read the resulting word and decide if it is a real word (e.g., *distype*, *likemis*, *unlock*).

Teach the students to attend to affixes quickly to improve their fluency in using these cues. Use activities in which the students must find all words with a particular affix (e.g., all words with *tion*), and highlight these on a printed page with a color highlighter. Also to increase speed, have the students write as many words as possible with a base word and various affixes as quickly as they can (e.g., have them add the affixes *s*, *ed*, and *ing* to the words *run*, *hop*, and *skip* in a 1-minute period).

Contractions

Make sure that students can visually discriminate apostrophes and commas before teaching contractions. Some students with visually based problems confuse these similar marks and do not attend to their up and down position. In addition, clearly differentiate between the use of apostrophes for possession (which is taught as a suffix) and contractions. Tell the students that the marks used are the same, but they have different meanings.

Teach contractions in groups that share the same word (e.g., teach all the words that have the word *not* contracted as *n't*). The contractions listed in Table 15 are grouped into words that have the same contracted words. Teaching in groups helps the student generalize from one item in a group (e.g., *isn't*) to another item in the group (e.g., *can't*).

Visually contrast the letters in a word with its corresponding contraction (e.g., *I am*, *I'm*). Color code the *a* to show that it is missing from *I'm*. Use the same color for the apostrophe to show that it represents the omitted letter or letters. Also, have students visually discriminate between contractions and visually similar words (e.g., *we're*, *were*; *she'd*, *shed*).

Use spatial and physical cues as part of a VAKT approach. Use letter cards to form a complete word, and then have the students produce the corresponding contraction using letter cards. Have them use the apostrophe to represent the omitted letters. This can also be done by having the students place an *X* over the letters that are omitted from the complete word.

Also, use activities with nonexamples in which you present contractions with the apostrophes in the correct or incorrect positions in the words, and have the students decide if the contractions are correct. For example, present the contraction *is'nt*, and have the students correct it.

Syllables

Review the phonological awareness skills of syllable blending and syllable segmentation before teaching students to decode words using syllabication. Introduce syllables by explaining that some words are long and hard to sound out. Demonstrate how you can read long words by separating them into parts. Tell the students that each word part is called a *syllable*. First, demonstrate with compound words and words with affixes to show that the students already know how to read longer words, and use these to demonstrate use of syllables. Show them that there are two syllables in the compound word *mailman* and the word *unlock*. Then, use new words such as *kitten*. Write the word *kitten* on the board and show how it can be separated into two parts or syllables—*kit* and *ten*.

Table 15.   Contractions

Not			You		
Aren't	Are not		You'd	You had	
Can't	Cannot		You'll	You will	
Couldn't	Could not		You're	You are	
Didn't	Did not		You've	You have	
Don't	Do not		**They**		
Hadn't	Had not		They'd	They had, they would	
Hasn't	Has not		They'll	They will	
Haven't	Have not		They've	They have	
Isn't	Is not		They're	They are	
Shouldn't	Should not		**It**		
Wasn't	Was not		It'll	It will	
Weren't	Were not		It's	It is	
Wouldn't	Would not		**Who**		
I			Who's	Who is	
I'd	I had, I would		Who'd	Who would	
I'll	I will		Who'll	Who will	
I'm	I am		Who've	Who have	
I've	I have		**Others**		
He			Let's	Let us	
He'd	He had, he would		That's	That is	
He'll	He will		There's	There is	
He's	He is		What's	What is	
She			Where's	Where is	
She'd	She had, she would		How's	How is	
She'll	She will		Won't	Will not[a]	
She's	She is				
We					
We'd	We would				
We'll	We will				
We're	We are				
We've	We have				

From Ganske, K. (2000). *Word journeys: Assessment-guided phonics, spelling, and vocabulary instruction* (p. 226). New York: Guilford Press; adapted by permission.

[a]*Won't* differs from other contractions because the base word *will* does not appear in the contraction.

Present a number of demonstrations to make the students feel more confident about decoding longer words. This is necessary because many struggling readers are poor decoders and are discouraged by the length of multisyllabic words, so they need instruction to build their confidence in attacking such words (Gunning, 1998). Many poor readers look at the first syllable, sound it out, and guess the remaining syllables. It is important to have them focus on each of the syllables by using their fingers to make sure that they are attending to all parts of words. Teach students to decode words using syllabication by applying the following rules.

1. Each syllable must have one vowel *sound* (not one vowel grapheme or written letter) when breaking a word up into syllables. Be sure to demonstrate that vowel digraphs (e.g., *rain*) and diphthongs (e.g., *foil*) have one vowel sound even though they have two vowel graphemes. Also, demonstrate that silent vowels are not counted (e.g., there is only one vowel sound in the word *lake* because the final *e* is silent). To demonstrate this rule, present words such as *rabbit* and *radio* and count the number of vowel sounds and the resulting number of syllables. Use this cue: Hold your hand under your chin and count the number of times your chin drops to help identify the number of vowels in a word. Tell the students that their mouths open and their chins drop when they say vowel sounds.

2. Words with two middle consonants are usually divided between the consonants (e.g., *bas ket*, *pub lic*). Be sure to demonstrate that words with consonant digraphs are not separated (e.g., *rushed* is not *rus hed*).

3. Syllables that end in vowels take the long vowel sounds (open syllable rule). Start with one-syllable words (e.g., *no*), and then move to two-syllable words (e.g., *do nate*). Start with prefixes that students already know that end in long vowels (e.g., *re paint*), and then move to words that they do not know.

4. Syllables that end in consonants take the short vowel sounds (closed syllable rule). Start with one-syllable words (e.g., *cat*), and then move to two-syllable words (e.g., *nap kin*). Start with prefixes that they already know that end in consonants (e.g., *mis type*), and then move to words that they do not know.

5. Words ending with the *le* consonant pattern are divided so that the consonant before *le* is included (e.g., *fum ble*, *gig gle*).

Teach the strategy of educated guessing. Encourage the students to experiment with breaking words into different syllable arrangements and finding the analysis that leads to the correct pronunciation of the word. Gunning (1998) stated that it is *not* important for students to break words at the syllable's exact boundaries as long as they are able to pronounce each of the syllables and blend them to correctly pronounce the whole word. Teach the students to use a trial-and-error approach in which they say each syllable and then blend them together to form the complete word. If the syllables were incorrectly pronounced, then indicate that it is not a word, and have them try again. To demonstrate the rule for closed syllables, say the syllables *rab* and *bit* with long vowels and the blended word, and explain that this is not a word. Then, try it again with the short vowels.

Use color coding cues to emphasize rules and important visual features. Color code the different types of syllables. For example, open syllables may be written in one color and closed syllables may be written in another color as a prompt for long and short vowels.

Use spatial and physical cues to provide multisensory support. Present syllables on different cards and then physically combine the syllables to emphasize how syllables are combined to form words.

Use completion activities in which you present an incomplete word and the students have to select syllables to complete the word (e.g., present the syllable *pen* and then the following choices: *cil, der,* and *get*). Also, present cards with syllables in random order, and have the students combine the syllables to make a word (e.g., present cards with the syllables *nec, tion,* and *con,* and have the students form the word *connection*).

Clearly state the rule that you are using, sound out the syllables, and say the blended word when you model breaking a word into syllables. Have the students follow your example when practicing syllabication.

Roots

Roots are parts of words that contain the basic meaning. For example, the root *man* means hand and can be used to understand the word *manicure*. Teaching students to decode and understand roots is appropriate for students at the highest level of functioning in word identification and should be taught after syllabication is mastered. You may decide that instruction in syllabication is enough for many of your students and you may choose *not* to provide instruction on root words. Analysis of Latin and Greek roots involves highly abstract words used in advanced content area classes and should only be taught if students are being exposed to such words. A list of some common roots is in Table 16.

Present a root and explain its meaning using pictures or symbols, if appropriate. For example, for the root *man,* use a picture of a hand next to the word *man.* Then, present words with the root *man* and use color coding or bold to pull it out of the word (e.g., **man**ual). Present words with particular roots in sentences so you can demonstrate how to integrate the use of context clues and analysis of the meaning of the root word. For example, present the following sentence: She went to the beauty salon to get a manicure. Explain how the sentence content along with the meaning of the root are useful in understanding the sentence.

Table 16.   Roots

Root	Meaning	Examples
Amb	Walk	Amble, ambulatory
Arch	Ruler	Anarchy, monarch,
Aster/astr	Star	Asterisk, astronaut,
Auto	Self	Autobiography, automobile
Audi	Hear	Auditory, auditorium
Bio	Life	Biography, biology
Cent	Hundred	Century, percent
Circ	Around	Circle, circumference
Cosm	Universe	Cosmic, microcosm
Cycl	Wheel	Bicycle, cycle
Dict	Speak	Dictate, predict
Fract	Break	Fraction, fracture
Graph	Write	Autograph, paragraph
Gram	Letter	Diagram, grammar
Ject	Throw	Trajectory, inject
Logy (ology)	Study of	Biology, geology
Man	Hand	Manicure, manual
Mar, mer	Sea	Marine, mariner
Meter	Measure	Diameter, speedometer
Micro	Small	Microscope, microbe
Mini	Small	Miniature, minimize
Nym	Name	Anonymous, synonym
Ped	Foot	Biped, pedal
Phono	Sound	Phonics, microphone
Photo	Light	Photograph, photosynthesis
Port	Carry	Export, porter
Rupt	Break	Rupture, bankrupt
Scope	See	Microscope, periscope
Scribe, script	Write	Transcribe, scripture
Sect, sec	Cut	Bisect, section
Spec, spect	Look	Spectator, inspect
Sphere	Ball	Hemisphere, atmosphere
Struct	Build	Construct, structure
Tact	Touch	Tactual, contact
Tech	Skill	Technology, technique
Tele	Far	Telephone, television
Terr	Land	Territory, terrain
Therm	Heat	Thermostat, isotherm
Trac, tract	Pull	Tractor, contract
Vis, vid	See	Visit, video
Viv, vit	Live	Survive, vitamin
Volv	Roll	Revolve, evolve

From TOMPKINS, GAIL E., LITERACY FOR THE 21ST CENTURY, 3rd Edition © 2002. Adapted by permission of Pearson Education, Inc., Upper Saddle River, NJ; and from Harris, R. (2002). *Word roots and prefixes*. Retrieved March 5, 2003, from http://virtualsalt.com/roots.htm; adapted by permission.

Model Lesson for Teaching Structural Analysis
Prefix Puzzles

OBJECTIVE

Students will be able to read and identify the meaning of words with the /re/ prefix with 90% accuracy.

ADVANCED ORGANIZER

Link to the previous lessons on the *un* prefix. Present a puzzle with the pieces unassembled and then assemble them. Have a card with *un* written in red, and have various base word cards written in blue. Cut the edges of the cards so the *un* cards fit into the front of the base word cards.

Link

Link to the previous lessons on the *un* prefix.

"How many of you have ever done a puzzle? Now, when you do a puzzle, can you put just any pieces together? . . . No, of course not. You have to put the pieces together that fit. *(Demonstrate putting together a puzzle with matching and nonmatching pieces.)* When we look at longer words, we sometimes have to break them into pieces and then put them back together. We have to think of reading long words like doing puzzles. We have been working on reading words that have the prefix *un*. *(Show the color coded /un/ card that is shaped like a puzzle piece.)* I have a base word. What is it? . . . *(Show the color coded base word* lock.*)* Right. This word is *lock*. What does it mean? . . . Sure, it means to close something with a key. Now, if I fit the *un* to this word, I've made a new word. What is my new word? . . . Super. It's *unlock*. What does my new word mean? Yep, it means to open something with a key. How is the meaning of my new word different from the meaning of my base word? . . . Great. It means the opposite because *un* means not or the opposite. That is why working with prefixes is like doing a puzzle. When you put two pieces together, your puzzle changes. Well, when you put a prefix in front of a base word, the meaning of the base word changes."

Identify

Identify the goal of the lesson.

"Today we're going continue to work on a new prefix. We're going to learn to read and understand the meaning of words with the prefix *re*." *(Show a card with* re *written in red.)*

Provide Rationale

Explain the importance of the lesson.

"Remember that trying to find if long words have prefixes is a way to help read long words."

MODELING

Use a set of cards with the prefix *re* written in red and with one edge cut to fit the edge of the other cards with base words written in blue. Also, have another set of cards with the base word written in black and other cards having the prefix *re* with a Velcro backing so that the prefix can be attached to the front of a base word.

"I'm going to color this picture. Wow, I didn't color within the lines. It's pretty messy coloring. I'm going to color this picture again, and I'm going to do a better job. Now, I'm going to read a sentence about what I did. I colored the picture. Now, I'm going to read another sentence about what I did. I colored the picture again. I **re**colored the picture. We use the prefix *re* to mean we do something **again.** Read this word. . . .Yes, *colored.* Now read this word. . . .Yes, *recolored."*

(Use the color coded, puzzle edged cards to demonstrate forming words with prefixes using base words such as type, paint, write, *and* pack.*)* "Let's form words with the *re* prefix using these cards. Here is the word *type.* I'm going to put *re* in front of it, and now I have the word *retype.* What word is this? . . . Yes, *type.* Now what word is this? . . . Sure, it's *retype.* What does retype mean? . . . Absolutely, it means to type something again. What color is the prefix written in? . . . Right, red. What color is the base word written in? . . . Yes, blue. See how the edges of the cards fit together like a puzzle."

GUIDED PRACTICE

Provide activities and games in which students read words with prefixes and analyze their meaning.

Prefix Puzzle Activity

Use a high-interest puzzle that is within the students' ability to assemble (e.g., 18–24 pieces). Present word cards that have the prefix *re* correctly added (e.g., reread) and other cards that have *re* incorrectly added (e.g., rehappy). Turn the cards face down, and have the students pick a card, read it, and then determine if it is a real word. If they are correct, then they can put one piece in the puzzle. Continue this until the puzzle is completed.

"This is a puzzle of Scooby Doo. We're going to play a game, and every time you get a right answer, you can put one of the puzzle pieces in the puzzle until you finish it. Pick a card, read it, and then tell me if it you can add the prefix *re* to that word. Okay, what word did you pick? . . . Yes, the word is *renose.* Can you add *re* to the word *nose*? . . . No way. Okay, you got the answer right. Pick any two pieces of the puzzle and put them together. Now pick another card. What does that say? Yes, it says *repaint.* Can you add *re* to the word *paint*? . . . Sure. Okay, put another piece in the puzzle."

INDEPENDENT PRACTICE

Have students practice the skill without assistance. Record the accuracy of their responses so you can evaluate their mastery of the objective.

Fill in the Blanks

Give the students a worksheet with a series of sentences with missing words. Have them use a word bank at the top of the page that can be used to fill in the blanks. All missing words have the *re* prefix. For example, the students should pick the choice *reset* from the word bank for the sentence: The clock stopped, so Pam had to _____ it.

GENERALIZATION

Have students find all words with the prefix *re* in their science book and read the sentences with these words into a tape recorder.

6

Teaching Words by Using Visual Cues

CONCEPTS EXPLORED

- Visual skills and meaning-based approaches to teaching reading
- Relationship of visual skills to dyslexia
- Visual skills needed for reading
- Guidelines for teaching visual skills
- Techniques for teaching different types of visual skills
- The LEA method
- Model lesson for teaching sight words

Students need visual skills to become competent readers. These skills are required for visual methods of reading instruction, just as auditory skills are required for phonics methods of reading instruction. Visual methods differ from phonics because phonics methods focus on the association of one sound with one or more graphemes (written letters), whereas visual methods focus on the association of a spoken word with all the graphemes in a written word. For example, it is not possible to phonetically decode the word *onion* (/unyun/) because it does not follow phonetic rules. Students must memorize that the spoken word *onion* goes with the graphemes *o n i o n*.

VISUAL SKILLS AND MEANING-BASED APPROACHES TO TEACHING READING

Chapter 4 discussed the great debate over how to best teach reading to all children—the code-breaking approach versus the meaning-based approach. The code-breaking approach is represented by phonics methods, whereas the meaning-based approach is represented by whole language, basal series, and LEA methods. These methods make strong demands for both comprehension and visual skills.

Whole language has been the most prominent and most controversial meaning-based approach. The basic premise underlying whole language is that students *naturally* learn to read based on exposure to print and immersion in language and books (Goodman, 1986). It is assumed that children learn to read and write naturally, just like they learn to speak naturally by being exposed to oral language in their environment. As the term implies, whole language instruction is focused on all aspects of language arts (i.e., listening, speaking, reading, writing). Equal emphasis is placed on reading and writing starting from kindergarten. Reading is taught as a meaning-oriented activity with emphasis on children's literature and authentic reading materials (e.g., recipes for making cookies for the class). From the whole language perspective, it is not possible to break reading into separate reading skills. Students learn to read through self-directed experiences, with limited teacher direction (Leu & Kinzer, 2003). When students cannot read a particular word using context and/or picture cues, the teacher may use the look-and-say or the whole word method. With this method, the teacher tells the students a particular word, and the students repeat it as they look at the word. It is assumed that the students will recall the word by hearing it and looking at it. Another approach teachers may use when students cannot read a word is embedded phonics, in which they teach the specific sounds in the word so that the word can be decoded. With whole language, primary emphasis is on comprehension and secondary emphasis is on visual skills.

Whole language has been one of the most popular methods of reading instruction in general education. Most general education teachers and special education teachers who are identified as being effective reading teachers reported that they used whole language to some degree in their classes (Rankin-Erickson & Pressley, 2000). So, the different types of struggling students in general education are exposed to this approach. Almost all students with learning disabilities are included in general education classes and, therefore, are likely to receive whole language instruction even though research has demonstrated that the whole language approach has not been effective for students with learning disabilities or students who are economically disadvantaged (Rankin-Erickson & Pressley, 2000).

The basic premise of whole language is not supported when applied to struggling learners. They do not learn to read naturally. If they did, they would learn by the whole language approach when they are exposed to it in general education classrooms, and research shows that they do not. The whole language approach does not match their instructional needs because of three factors:

1. It does not break reading into teachable skills.

2. It does not use strategic, explicit instruction.

3. It does not include strong teacher direction.

However, it is important to recognize there are some positive aspects of whole language (e.g., the emphasis on literature, the linking of reading and writing), and these have been incorporated into guidelines for teaching narrative comprehension skills presented in Chapter 11.

The basal series, the oldest approach to teaching reading that dates back to the McGuffey readers in 1836, is another popular approach to reading instruction in general education. Vacca et al. (2003) estimated that this approach is used in 90% of elementary schools across the nation. With this approach, instruction is provided from the pre–first-grade level through the sixth- or eighth-grade level using sequential books with stories and supportive skills materials. Illustrations are important for determining meaning and providing attractiveness. A teacher's guide gives directions on how to teach reading with the stories and skill materials. There has been much criticism of basal readers because of uninteresting stories, stereotyping of cultural groups, and insufficient attention to skill development. In response to these criticisms, publishers have produced basals that include children's literature, a multicultural emphasis, and instruction on phonics. At the present time, it is really not possible to characterize all basal series as using the same instructional approach; however, most continue to emphasize meaning and visual skills.

The LEA (Lee & Allen, 1963), another meaning-based approach that uses the look-and-say method, is a well-accepted method for teaching reading. This is a popular approach for beginning reading instruction at the kindergarten and early first-grade levels and is often included with the whole language approach. The LEA is an effective method for teaching certain skills to struggling students, especially ELLs.

RELATIONSHIP OF VISUAL SKILLS TO DYSLEXIA

Although visual skills are necessary for learning to read, they have been ignored because of overemphasis on phonics. This lack of recognition of the importance of visual problems is apparent in The International Dyslexia Association's definition of dyslexia, which only focuses on phonological dyslexia (i.e., reading problems associated with phonological awareness and phonics; Lyon, Shaywitz, & Shaywitz, 2003). This definition excludes a group of students who have significant reading problems; namely, students with orthographic dyslexia (i.e., visually based reading problems). These students confuse similar looking graphemes, reverse letters, have difficulty mastering high-frequency sight words, read slowly, and are nonfluent readers (Roberts & Mather, 1997).

The following example shows the devastating effects of orthographic dyslexia when the author observed a third grader reading a four-sentence passage with the short *a* sound. The word *the* appeared six times in the passage. Each time the word appeared, the student could not read it, so the teacher said the word for him and he repeated it. Although he could read all the short *a* words in the passage, he could not read the word *the*, the most frequently used word in the English language. When he completed reading the passage, the student was visibly upset and called himself "dumb" because he could not read a "baby" word such as *the*. The positive reinforcement that the teacher gave him for reading the short *a* words correctly had no effect on him.

For a while, phonological awareness deficits were viewed as the only cause of dyslexia. Then, the dual deficit theory was put forth with a second cause of dyslexia—problems with RAN (Wolf & Bowers, 1999). Now, there is support for a triple deficit theory for the cause of dyslexia (Carlisle & Rice, 2002)—orthographic processing (or visual skills). This reflects a growing recognition that dyslexia is a complex condition that includes students with different types of reading problems resulting from different causes.

Reversals (e.g., confusing the graphemes *b* and *d*) have long been considered as the defining characteristic of dyslexia by the general public. Most students diagnosed with dyslexia do not have significant problems with reversals, but some do, and these are individuals with visually based reading problems.

ELLs who learned to read with a different symbol system (e.g., a logographic system such as Chinese) or a different alphabet (e.g., the Cyrillic alphabet of Russian) may also have difficulty with the visual aspects of learning to read. In addition, students who have a superficial learning style and do not attend to details may struggle to meet the demands for attention to visual details that are required to become a competent reader.

VISUAL SKILLS NEEDED FOR READING

Auditory and visual pre-reading skills are necessary ingredients for a foundation on which to build reading (see Chapter 3). Pre-reading visual skills that are important for learning to read are visual discrimination of letters and words based on shape, length, order, and detail; directionality (i.e., attention to left–right aspects of letters, words, and text); and visual memory (i.e., recall of sequences of letters). Struggling learners must be taught to focus on these critical visual aspects involved in learning to read.

Four visual skills necessary for becoming a competent reader are described in this chapter: 1) learning the names of graphemes; 2) identifying visual details of words; 3) attending to directionality; and 4) mastering sight words. To learn the names for upper- and lowercase graphemes, students must associate the visually presented grapheme with the name. Letter names need to be taught before letter sounds because they are more frequently used. In addition, reading of upper- and lowercase letters should be taught in conjunction with writing these letters. Learning the names of the graphemes may be problematic for some students because they do not attend to the visual characteristics of letters (e.g., one hump in the letter *n* and two humps in the letter *m*). Other students may have difficulty learning letter names because of directionality problems. They may make left–right reversals, such as confusing *b* and *d*, and up–down reversals, such as confusing *u* and *n*.

Students with difficulties attending to the visual details of words may not focus on the length of words (e.g., *us* versus *use*), the shape or configuration of words (e.g., the four tall letters in the word *bubble*), or letter sequences (e.g., *leak* versus *lake*). Some struggling students have special problems attending to word endings. They may read the word *jumped* as *jumper*, or they may totally omit the end of words and read the word *jumped* as *jump*.

Directionality is not only important for learning to differentiate similar graphemes, such as *b* and *d*, but it is also important for attending to the order of letters in words (e.g., confusing the words *was* and *saw*) and attending to the order of words in sentences (e.g., confusing the sentence, "The boy saw the girl first." and "The boy saw the first girl."). Skipping of lines and then getting lost in the text is also a difficulty some students with directionality problems experience when reading text.

It is impossible to phonetically decode all words in the English language. Some words must be taught by sight (i.e., they must be visually recalled). The term *sight word* is used in two ways in the field of reading, which leads to confusion. In this book, the term *sight words* refer to words that are learned visually. Some writers in the field of reading refer to sight words as words that students can read automatically and do not have to decode. In this book, the term *automatic words* is used to refer to such words.

There are four types of sight words: high-frequency words; content area words; functional words; and unphonetic, irregular words. High-frequency sight words are included on lists of words that are most frequently found in reading materials for young children. The Dolch list is the most frequently cited list of 220 sight words that are commonly used in basals. Other lists have been generated based on the Dolch list (e.g., the Kucera-Francis list; see Table 17). Many of these words cannot be learned phonetically and can only be learned by sight (e.g., *was*). Other sight words come from the students' subject matter content classes and must be learned by sight because they are too difficult to be learned phonetically (e.g., *photosynthesis*) or are unphonetic (e.g., *chlorophyll*). Functional sight words include survival words such as *poison*, *exit*, and *police* and words that are needed for meeting the demands of everyday life (e.g., directions for microwaving a TV dinner). These words are especially important for students who will not attain functional literacy—the reading level necessary for meeting the demands of everyday life. Students with mild mental retardation do not usually attain functional literacy. Finally, unphonetic irregular words must be taught by sight. It is necessary for students to use visual memory to recall the letters in a word in association with the spoken word for all types of sight words.

It is exceedingly difficult to learn to read using only visual methods. Competent readers combine visual skills with the other word identification skills they have acquired through phonics and structural analysis. For example, to decode a word such as *work*, students might use phonics to decode the first and last sounds and recall that the *or* has a different sound in this word. In addition, students might also recall that when they saw the word *work*, the teacher told them that the word was *work*. We need to teach *all* word identification skills so struggling students can combine visual, phonic, and structural analysis skills to successfully identify the many types of words that they meet.

GUIDELINES FOR TEACHING VISUAL SKILLS

Four guidelines should be followed when designing instruction for visual skills.

1. Emphasize the special visual details of letters and words to be learned. One of the most important strategies for helping students recall letters and words is to highlight what is special about them. For example, bold the second hump in the letter *m* to help students recall that the letter *m* has two humps and the letter *n* has one hump. Or, to help students recall that *girl* is not read or spelled *gril* (one of the most frequent errors of students with learning disabilities), color code the letter *i* using green and the letter *r* using red. Green is often used to represent a starting point and red is used as a stopping point. Use color coding, bolding, spacing, drawings, pictures, or other visual cues to focus student attention on critical details. For example, to help students recall the word *look*, make eyes out of the two *o*'s in the middle of the word and associate the meaning of the word *look* with the eyes.

2. Use the VAKT method to provide varied sensory input for recall of letters and words. Use as many visual, auditory, kinesthetic, and tactile cues as possible to highlight critical visual details so that the students can re-

Table 17. Kucera-Francis list of high-frequency sight words

Preprimer	Primer	First	Second	Third
1. The	45. When	89. Many	133. Know	177. Don't
2. Of	46. Who	90. Before	134. While	178. Does
3. And	47. Will	91. Must	135. Last	179. Got
4. To	48. More	92. Through	136. Might	180. United
5. A	49. No	93. Back	137. Us	181. Left
6. In	50. If	94. Years	138. Great	182. Number
7. That	51. Out	95. Where	139. Old	183. Course
8. Is	52. So	96. Much	140. Year	184. War
9. Was	53. Said	97. Your	141. Off	185. Until
10. He	54. What	98. May	142. Come	186. Always
11. For	55. Up	99. Well	143. Since	187. Away
12. It	56. Its	100. Down	144. Against	188. Something
13. With	57. About	101. Should	145. Go	189. Fact
14. As	58. Into	102. Because	146. Came	190. Through
15. His	59. Than	103. Each	147. Right	191. Water
16. On	60. Them	104. Just	148. Used	192. Less
17. Be	61. Can	105. Those	149. Take	193. Public
18. At	62. Only	106. People	150. Three	194. Put
19. By	63. Other	107. Mr.	151. States	195. Thing
20. I	64. New	108. How	152. Himself	196. Almost
21. This	65. Some	109. Too	153. Few	197. Hand
22. Had	66. Could	110. Little	154. House	198. Enough
23. Not	67. Time	111. State	155. Use	199. Far
24. Are	68. These	112. Good	156. During	200. Took
25. But	69. Two	113. Very	157. Without	201. Head
26. From	70. May	114. Make	158. Again	202. Yet
27. Or	71. Then	115. Would	159. Place	203. Government
28. Have	72. Do	116. Still	160. American	204. System
29. An	73. First	117. Own	161. Around	205. Better
30. They	74. Any	118. See	162. However	206. Set
31. Which	75. My	119. Men	163. Home	207. Told
32. One	76. Now	120. Work	164. Small	208. Nothing
33. You	77. Such	121. Long	165. Found	209. Night
34. Were	78. Like	122. Get	166. Mrs.	210. End
35. Her	79. Our	123. Here	167. Thought	211. Why
36. All	80. Over	124. Between	168. Went	212. Called
37. She	81. Man	125. Both	169. Say	213. Didn't
38. There	82. Me	126. Life	170. Part	214. Eyes
39. Would	83. Even	127. Being	171. Once	215. Find
40. Their	84. Most	128. Under	172. General	216. Going
41. We	85. Made	129. Never	173. High	217. Look
42. Him	86. After	130. Day	174. Upon	218. Asked
43. Been	87. Also	131. Same	175. School	219. Later
44. Has	88. Did	132. Another	176. Every	220. Knew

From Johnson, D.D. (1971, February). The Dolch list re-examined. *The Reading Teacher, 24*(5), 455–456. Copyright © 1971 by the International Reading Association. Adapted by permission.

member them when identifying letters and words. Visual cues come from emphasizing visual details as described in the previous guideline and visual imagery described in the next guideline. Auditory cues come from saying the word or the letter names. It is important to emphasize that when students attack words with visual methods, they do *not* say the letter sounds but, rather, the letter names. By saying the letter names aloud while looking at them, students are mutually reinforcing the auditory and visual memory needed to recall the letters in sequence. Using music and rhythm (e.g., singing the alphabet song, using raps) also helps provide auditory cues. Kinesthetic cues come from body movement and can be provided by writing on paper or in the air as well as tracing. Tactile cues come from tracing over raised surfaces, such as sandpaper or cotton.

3. Use visual imagery, or visualization, to help students recall what they have seen. Many of us can visualize words to help recall how to read or spell them. Look at the first word in this sentence (*Look*), and then shut your eyes and picture it written in red letters. Are you seeing it with the uppercase *L*? Are you seeing red letters? If so, you are using visual imagery. Although this technique is helpful to some students, others find it exceedingly difficult to use. If students can visualize words, then use this as a cue to help them recall letter sequences in words.

4. Whenever possible, associate words to be learned visually with objects, pictures, and demonstrations. To help students read words that have meaning, pair the written word with the corresponding object, picture, or demonstration. This is frequently done in preschool and early childhood classes where a card with the word *door* is on the door and a card with the word *window* is on the window. When teaching reading of color words, write the letters in the word in that color (e.g., use purple ink to write the letters in the word *purple*). When teaching reading of shape words, write the words on cards with that shape (e.g., write the word *circle* on a circular card, draw a circle around the word). When teaching a sight word such as *down*, present the word written in a downward fashion (see Figure 6). If you are teaching sight words for a story that the students will be reading, then present these words with the associated pictures (e.g., use a word card containing the word *elephant* and a picture of an elephant for a story about Babar the elephant).

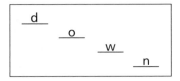

Figure 6.   When teaching a sight word such as *down,* present the word written in a downward fashion.

TECHNIQUES FOR TEACHING VISUAL SKILLS

Letter Identification

Students are taught upper- and lowercase letters together when they learn the alphabet in a general education class. This is too difficult for some struggling students with problems learning visually. Instead, teach lowercase letters first because they are more frequently used in print. Then, teach uppercase letters (except for the first letter in a student's name, which should be capitalized as soon as the students learn to read and write their names). To facilitate the transition from lower- to uppercase letters, first teach uppercase letters that have the same shape in both the lower- and uppercase forms (e.g., *c* and *C*).

Teach letter naming and letter writing together so that the motor responses provide cues to aid in letter name recall. Use different materials for tracing the letters (e.g., cotton balls) and different media for writing the letters (e.g., magic markers, glitter glue). Always have the students say the letter names as they trace or write them. To provide gross motor cues, make a large outline of a new letter to be learned, and have the students crawl along the outline to get a feel for the shape of the letter. Also, to draw students' attention to the details of various letters, have them group letters into stick letters (e.g., *l*, *t*, *x*), curves (e.g., *c*, *e*, *s*), and combinations (e.g., *a*, *b*, *d*).

Teach the alphabet song to provide rhythm cues. Provide auditory cues by describing how the letters are made (e.g., for the letter *a*, say that we first make a ball and then a stick on the side). Have the students repeat these descriptions as they write the letters. Visually emphasize letter details to aid students in reading and writing them correctly (e.g., color code the first *v* in the letter *w* to differentiate it from *v*). Do *not* provide pictures of words starting with the letter (e.g., /a/ for *apple*) because you are not teaching the sound, you are teaching the name of the letter.

Use games to provide variety and fun. For example, place cut-outs of several letters in a bag, and have the students put their hands in the bag, feel the letters without looking at them, and tell their names. Or, play concentration in which the students have to get matching cards with the same letters. Also, provide activities in which the students identify letters embedded in words. For example, after they have learned to read the letter *e*, have them circle all the *e*'s in words on a printed page.

Attention to Visual Details

Provide instruction on attending to word details for students who are not analyzing visual cues to read text. An effective way of finding out if students are using visual cues when reading text is to use miscue analysis, a method where you mark the types of errors, or miscues, that a student makes as she reads aloud. This analysis may be part of an informal reading inventory (IRI), which is an individualized comprehensive assessment designed to provide extensive information on students' reading levels and the types of errors that they make when reading aloud (see Chapter 12).

Color coding or bolding helps students focus on troublesome word parts. For example, if a student does not attend to word beginnings, then bold these. Finger pointing also helps students who are not attending to parts of a word, making omissions, or reversing words. Another effective strategy is for you to read a passage making errors, and have the students silently read the passage along with you and identify the errors.

Activities for teaching attention to visual details include worksheet activities in which students mark words that differ on the basis of visual characteristics (e.g., mark the one that is different from the following: jumped, jumped, jumper, jumped). Present words that students frequently misread or misspell, and have the students correct them (e.g., present the word *receive* spelled with *ie* instead of *ei*, and have the students correct it; spell the word *girl* as *gril*, and have the students correct it). Another activity is to have students put words of varying lengths in order from shortest to longest to draw their attention to word length (e.g., ordering the following words: *a, am, amp, ample*).

Directionality

Some students continue to show consistent letter reversals into second grade. Up to that time, reversals are found in typically developing children and may not be a sign of directionality problems. Letter reversals involving the letters *b* and *d* are most frequent. Three strategies might be helpful to help students overcome this when they read and write these letters. One strategy is to teach them to write the cursive *b* and *d* and write them over the manuscript *b* and *d* when they are having trouble recalling the letters. The cursive *b* and *d* are not reversed because of the continuous flow of motion when writing. Another strategy that helps some students is to write the word *bed*, point out the *b* and *d*, and make your hands in the shape of a bed. Make two fists and have them touch at the knuckles with your palms facing you. Then, put your thumbs up. Tell the students that your left hand represents a *b*, like the beginning of the word *bed*, and your right hand represents a *d*, like the end of the word *bed*. Whenever they have to identify whether a letter is a *b* or *d*, have them put their hands into the bed formation. Another strategy is to associate the stick in the *b* with the number 1 and to tell the students that *b* comes first because it has the number 1 in it.

For directionality problems in which students reverse letters in words (e.g., *eat* versus *ate*), use worksheet activities in which students identify the word that is different from several words (e.g., mark the word that is different: *was, saw, was*, and *was*). When students reverse letters in words when reading text, have them focus on the first letter, sound it out, and determine that it does not match the written letter. For example, if a student read the word *was* for the word *saw*, have the student identify the /s/ sound as the first sound in *saw* and then match that to the first letter in the word *was*. If students consistently reverse specific words, such as *was* and *saw*, bold these when they appear in text so that the students know to pay special attention to them.

When students reverse the order of words in sentences that they read, have them use their fingers to point to each word. Also, provide worksheets in which students have to mark words that are in a different order in similar sentences (e.g., connect the word *girl* with where it is in the first and second sentences: The girl gave the boy a present. The boy gave the girl a present).

To help students overcome problems skipping lines when reading passages, have them use their fingers or a card to track from one line to the next. Also, teach them to self-monitor for meaning when they skip a line, asking themselves if what they read makes sense and finding why it does not make sense.

Sight Words

Two guidelines should be used to design instruction for teaching sight words. First, sight words must be taught in isolation and in text. It is important to teach sight words in isolation so that you can highlight the visual characteristics to be used to recall the word and to use VAKT methods. After students can read words in isolation, they must learn to read these words embedded in sentences. It is much easier to recall words in isolation because there are a limited number of words that they are working on. However, reading words in text is a more complex task because students must identify all of the words in the sentences, not just the sight word being taught, and then interpret the meanings of all the words. To facilitate the move from reading a sight word in isolation to reading it embedded in text, bold the word to draw the student's attention to it. Gradually, fade out the bolding cue.

A second guideline for designing sight word instruction is to teach the reading of sight words along with the spelling of the words. The methods for teaching students to read high-frequency sight words (especially VAKT) are the same as the methods for teaching students to spell these words. Provide activities in which students first read sight words being taught and then spell them. The VAKT method effectively trains students' visual memory for the sequence of letters in a word that is important for both reading and spelling.

High-Frequency Words

High-frequency words are the most frequently appearing words in early reading materials and are the sight words that should be taught first. Many of these words are difficult to learn because they do not have semantic content, but they have syntactic meaning (i.e., they have a role in determining the meaning of a sentence). For example, the word *are* has no semantic meaning. You cannot see an *are* or perform an action involving *are*. The abstractness of these words makes it difficult for students to master them, especially students who have difficulties with English syntax, such as ELLs, students who speak a non-standard dialect, and students with language learning disabilities. In addition, many high-frequency words are visually similar (e.g., *is, in, it, if*), requiring that students pay close visual attention to details. These words have the same configuration or shape, are of the same length, and start with the same first letter, all of which make it hard for them to be learned visually.

To teach high-frequency sight words, use the Kucera-Francis list of words in Table 17. These words are based on the original Dolch list of the most frequently appearing words in early reading materials. They are arranged in order of difficulty with the first 40 words at the preprimer level and 40 at the primer level (these levels are equivalent to the kindergarten/early first-grade level), followed by words at the first-, second-, and third-grade levels. Individually pretest a student on each of these words. Do *not* test for all 220 words at one time. This would be overwhelming to any child but especially to one who is struggling. Put each of the words on a laminated card and present them in the order listed. Record the words the student knows and does not know. Stop testing when you have identified 10–15 words that the student does not know. You will teach these words. Once the student masters them, you will go back to the list and continue testing until you identify the next 10–15 words that the student cannot read.

Decide how many sight words you want to teach the student weekly. This will depend on the student's instructional level, the other reading skills being taught, and the amount of instructional time you can devote to sight word development. For most students, teaching 5–10 words weekly is advisable. Have each student keep a word box in which he keeps the sight words that he masters weekly. If a word has not been mastered at the end of the week, then keep working on it for a second week. Review the words in the word box frequently so that the student retains a high level of mastery.

One of the most effective VAKT methods for teaching sight words, especially high-frequency sight words, is the Fernald Kinesthetic Method. This method was developed by Grace Fernald in 1943 as a means for teaching students to visualize whole words (Lerner, 2003). The author used the Fernald Kinesthetic Method as the basis for her master's thesis more than 40 years ago and found that the method significantly improved mastery of sight words in students with mild mental retardation. A modification of the Fernald Kinesthetic Method is recommended as a highly effective means for teaching sight words. With this modification, the steps of saying a word, tracing it, and writing it are retained, but other strategies are added. A modified Fernald Kinesthetic Method includes

- Presenting a word on a card and telling what the word is. Have the student repeat the word.

- Having the student say the word, copy it as she says each letter name, and then say the word again

- Having the student say the word, trace each letter as she says its name, and then say the word again

- Having the student look at the word, say it, shut her eyes, and picture the letters in her mind as she writes the letters in the air and says their names

- Having the student look at the word, say it, cover the word, and write it from memory

- Having the student compare the word she wrote with the model. If the word is incorrect, then have her mark where the error was and copy the word again.

- Repeating these steps until the student can correctly write the word from memory

- Having the student read the word without cues. When she can read it successfully five times, put it in the word box. Put a sticker, star, or other visual reinforcer on the card every time the student reads it correctly so that the student can see the progress that she is making.

After students can read sight words in isolation, have them read these words in text. Have them track and circle all the target sight words in a passage. Then, present the target sight words written in bold or color in a passage to help the student make the transfer from reading the word in isolation to reading the word in text. Finally, fade out these cues, and have the students read the sight word in text.

Content Area Sight Words

Content area sight words are easier to teach than high-frequency sight words because they usually have semantic meaning and usually have distinctive visual characteristics (e.g., *chlorophyll* has two *l*'s at the end, which is distinctive). Select words that students must learn to read for their content area classes. Do not overwhelm the students with learning all the words that they need. Try to pick only those that are most essential. Do not teach the spelling of these words unless the spelling is a classroom requirement. Emphasize meaning when teaching these words. For example, write the word *chlorophyll* in green, or draw the shape of an amoeba around the word *amoeba*. Students may recall content area words for short periods of time when they are reading them in their texts. They may not maintain these words in their reading vocabulary when they no longer see them. Therefore, you may have to reteach them at the end of marking periods or the school year when they will be used for testing.

Functional Sight Words

Functional sight words include survival words and phrases as well as words needed for everyday living. Students with disabilities who will probably not attain functional literacy need to be taught these words. Table 18 presents the 50 most important survival words identified by teachers, and Table 19 presents the 50 most important survival phrases identified by teachers (Polloway, Patton, & Serna, 2001). Survival words and phrases need to be taught embedded in the setting in which they usually appear and not on word cards. Students will not be reading these words in isolation or in passages but, rather, they will be reading them in their environment. For example, the word *flammable* would be found on a spray can so present it written on a can. Likewise, the phrase *do not enter* would be found on a door so place this phrase on a picture of a door or on the classroom door. When teaching everyday functional words, such as

Table 18.   List of the 50 most important survival words

1.	Poison	26.	Ambulance
2.	Danger	27.	Girls
3.	Police	28.	Open
4.	Emergency	29.	Out
5.	Stop	30.	Combustible
6.	Not	31.	Closed
7.	Walk	32.	Condemned
8.	Caution	33.	Up
9.	Exit	34.	Blasting
10.	Men	35.	Gentlemen
11.	Women	36.	Pull
12.	Warning	37.	Down
13.	Entrance	38.	Detour
14.	Help	39.	Gasoline
15.	Off	40.	Inflammable
16.	On	41.	In
17.	Explosives	42.	Push
18.	Flammable	43.	Nurse
19.	Doctor	44.	Information
20.	Go	45.	Lifeguard
21.	Telephone	46.	Listen
22.	Boys	47.	Private
23.	Contaminated	48.	Quiet
24.	Ladies	49.	Look
25.	Dynamite	50.	Wanted

Table 19.   List of the 50 most important survival phrases

1.	Don't walk	26.	Wrong way
2.	Fire escape	27.	No fires
3.	Fire extinguisher	28.	No swimming
4.	Do not enter	29.	Watch your step
5.	First aid	30.	Watch for children
6.	Deep water	31.	No diving
7.	External use only	32.	Stop for pedestrians
8.	High voltage	33.	Post office
9.	No trespassing	34.	Slippery when wet
10.	Railroad crossing	35.	Help wanted
11.	Rest rooms[a]	36.	Slow down
12.	Do not touch	37.	Smoking prohibited
13.	Do not use near open flame	38.	No admittance
14.	Do not inhale fumes	39.	Proceed at your own risk
15.	One way	40.	Step down
16.	Do not cross	41.	No parking
17.	Do not use near heat	42.	Keep closed
18.	Keep out	43.	No turns
19.	Keep off	44.	Beware of dog
20.	Exit only	45.	School zone
21.	No right turn	46.	Dangerous curve
22.	Keep away	47.	Hospital zone
23.	Thin ice	48.	Out of order
24.	Bus stop	49.	No smoking
25.	No passing	50.	Go slow

[a]This can be taught as one word (*restrooms*) as well.

reading labels on medicines, write the words on a medicine bottle so that students will realize that this is where these words will be found.

Irregular Words

When teaching unphonetic, irregular words as sight words, you need to provide an explanation of why a word does not fit the phonetic pattern that the students have learned. Make sure that the students have fully mastered the phonic pattern so that they understand that the word that you are teaching is an exception. For example, when teaching the word *bread*, explain that *ea* usually follows the vowel digraph rule in which the first vowel sound is used in its long form. However, for the word *bread*, the /br/ and /d/ sounds can be sounded, but *ea* is different and says short /e/ rather than the long /e/. Be sure to color code letters that represent exceptions to phonetic rules (e.g., the *ea* in *bread*).

Use the modified Fernald Kinesthetic Method to teach all four types of sight words. In addition, use games such as Wheel of Fortune and Hangman. Crossword puzzles and word searches are especially good for helping students read and write sight words. Use the Discovery Channel web site to download templates for constructing crossword puzzles and word searches (http://school .discovery.com/teachingtools/teachingtools.html).

THE LEA METHOD

The LEA, a well-established reading method that has been used since the turn of the 20th century (Edelsky, Altwerger, & Flores, 1991), is frequently used at the kindergarten and first-grade levels and with ELLs. With this approach, students use their own language and experiences as the basis for creating reading material. Students dictate their experiences to the teacher, who writes these down so they can be used as reading material. This method is effective for three groups of struggling students: ELLs, students who are economically disadvantaged, and students who are reading at very low levels and have limited word identification skills. For ELLs who are in the process of learning English, the LEA method constitutes an effective means for using their newly acquired language skills as a link to learning how to read in English. For students who are economically disadvantaged and have limited experiences to use as prior knowledge for conventional reading material, the LEA approach provides a means for ensuring that the students have the prior knowledge for reading the material. Finally, the LEA provides a basis for text reading for students who are at reading levels below trade books or basals. It is effective in teaching students how oral language is graphically presented in sentences and how sentences are segmented into words.

When used with populations who are hard to teach, the LEA method should be used on an individual or small-group basis. The students discuss an experience and, through carefully planned questioning, the teacher elicits a story as she writes it down. Do not have the students copy the story because they often make errors. After the story has been written, the teacher reads it with the students. Then, over a number of days, the teacher guides the students in reading each of the sentences in the story and then reading each of the words in the sentences. The purpose of this instruction is to go from the whole to the part (i.e., memorize the complete story, use this as the basis for analyzing the sentences, and then use the sentences as the basis for analyzing the words). The purpose of the LEA is to build sentence reading and sight recall of high-frequency words. It also is helpful in training students at very low reading levels to learn the concept of a word in text (i.e., that a written word goes with a spoken word).

When using the LEA method, sequence instruction from easy to difficult by controlling the number of sentences and the length of each of sentence in a story. You can control the story by the nature of the questions that you ask. Have the students produce a sentence corresponding to each question that you ask. The construction of the sentence should match the construction of the question. For example, if you asked the question, "What kind of cookies did we make yesterday?" you would get a sentence from the student such as, "We made chocolate chip cookies yesterday." If you asked a question such as,

"What were all the things that we put in the cookies?" you would get a sentence such as, "We put flour, sugar, eggs, chocolate chips, and butter in our cookies." This second sentence is longer and more complex than the first. If students give one-word responses to your questions, then teach them to expand their responses to sentences. For example, if you asked, "What kind of cookies did we make yesterday?" and a student responds, "chocolate chip," then you would ask the student to say that in a complete sentence. If he could not, then you would start the sentence and have the student complete the sentence (e.g., "We made . . . ").

The following is a day-by-day description of how the LEA method might be used with a group of struggling students. The group is made up of three students with severe learning disabilities who are ages 8 and 9 but read at the early first-grade level. They are writing an LEA story based on a classroom visit by a fireman who discussed fire safety.

Day 1

The teacher and the students fully discuss the fireman's visit. After the oral discussion, the teacher asks questions to elicit a story. She asks two questions of each of the three students to create a six-sentence story. The students have written previous stories with four and five sentences, and the teacher decides that the students are ready to move to a six-sentence story.

"Now, let's write a story about our classroom visitor. Who came to our class yesterday? . . . What did the fireman talk about? . . . What did he say about playing with matches? . . . What did he tell us to do if we saw a fire? . . . What did he give us? . . . What did he drive when he left school?"

Based on these questions, the students wrote the following story. Each sentence produced by the students is written on a separate line.

A fireman came to our class.
The fireman talked about fire safety.
He said that we should never play with matches.
He told us to call 911 if we see a fire.
He gave us a sticker with 911 on it.
The fireman drove his fire truck when he left school.

Day 2

The teacher presents a wall chart with the story as well as individual sheets with the story for each student. The students discuss the visit again and then read the story with the teacher as the teacher points to each word in each sentence. Then, they tape record the story, and the teacher plays the tape recording as she points to each word in each sentence. Each student practices reading the two sentences that he wrote and reads them when called on by the teacher.

Day 3

The students practice reading the whole story and then each other's sentences. Next, the teacher presents the six sentence strips corresponding to each sentence in the story. The students have to match the sentence strips to corresponding sentences in the story. Then, each student practices reading each sentence strip.

Day 4

The students practice reading each of the sentence strips to each other and reading them into a tape recorder. Then, each student reads the story to kindergarten children.

Day 5

The teacher presents selected words from the story to teach as sight vocabulary. There are too many words to teach, so the teacher selects five words that she wants the students to learn by sight. Some of the words in the story are difficult for this level, so the teacher uses rebuses (i.e., pictures corresponding to the meanings of the words) for words such as *matches* and *sticker.* She places the rebus above the corresponding word to enable the students to read these difficult words. Now the students will not be overwhelmed by difficult words and will still be able to read their stories. The teacher selected these five sight words to teach from the story: *fire, came, told, gave,* and *saw.* The students match word cards with these sight words to sentences in which they appear. They first read the sentence and then the word. The students use the Fernald Kinesthetic Method to learn these sight words so that they can read them apart from the story when they see them in isolation or another passage. They continue working on the sight words over the next week.

There are variations of the LEA method that are also effective. You can have the students create biographies with separate stories or chapters about each member of their families as well as information about themselves. They can create stories about their special interests or favorite games or sports. Older students with low reading levels can create stories about their interests or plans after graduation. For example, a 16-year-old who reads at the first-grade level might create a story about his interest in NASCAR racing or his interest in becoming a long-distance truck driver. Have the student fully discuss his ideas first, and then ask controlled questions to create a story at his instructional level.

The LEA makes strong demands on both auditory and visual memory skills. The students must use auditory memory to recall the story. They can only do this through repeated readings by you and them. They need visual memory to recall the sight words, so use the strategies described previously to enhance their mastery of these words.

A frequent criticism of the LEA method is that it does not lead to the systematic development of reading skills; however, it is not designed for this purpose. It is designed for entry-level reading of text and mastery of sight words. This approach has also been criticized because it is slow and tedious. Despite its limitations, the LEA method may be the best method for providing opportunities for students at low reading levels. This approach is effective when there are no other options. It is especially useful for ELLs who do not have adequate mastery of English to read texts. The LEA can be effectively integrated with other instruction. For example, while students are learning the consonant sounds, the LEA method can be used to build in mastery of sight words. As the students learn the various consonant sounds, they can use them as an aid to decoding the words in the LEA stories that they write.

One frequent issue is what should be done when students use incorrect or nonstandard English in their LEA sentences. You need to correct such language so that you are not reinforcing incorrect school language. Use the concept of "school talk" to represent Standard American English, which should be used in school, and "home talk" to represent students' dialects, which should be used outside of school. You can also use terms such as *dress-up talk* and *jeans talk*. Present the analogy that dressing formally in certain settings (e.g., church, a wedding) is like using "school talk," and dressing informally to play is like using "home talk." It is important that you treat the students' dialects with respect and not speak of them negatively.

Model Lesson for Teaching Sight Words
Treasure Chest

OBJECTIVE

Students will read the sight words *who, what, when,* and *where* with 100% accuracy.

ADVANCED ORGANIZER

Students have individual treasure chests where they keep the sight words that they have mastered each week. They have decorated these boxes, and they have keys to the boxes that they use to take the cards in and out. Reading of new sight words is introduced on Mondays, followed by guided practice Tuesday through Thursday. Independent practice evaluating whether the objective has been achieved is done on Friday.

Link

Make a link to previous lessons.

"You have been learning new sight words every week and putting them in your treasure chest. Unlock your treasure chest, and take out the words that you learned last week. Let's review them. . . . Fabulous!! You remembered all of them."

Identify

Identify the goal of the lesson.

"Today you're going to learn four new words. You're going to learn words that are used to ask questions. You're going to learn the words *who, what, when,* and *where.*"

Provide Rationale

Explain the importance of the lesson.

"These are important words to read because you can read questions on your own, and you won't need me to help you with them."

MODELING

Use color coded cards in which the *wh* is written in the same color in each word and the remaining letters are in another color. To the right of each word, there is a question mark. Each card also has a picture cue for meaning. There is a picture of a boy on the *who* card, there is a picture of a dog on the *what* card, there is a picture of a clock on the *when* card, and there is a picture of a map on the *where* card.

"Each of you has a set of cards with your new words. There is a question mark at the end of each word. Do you know why? . . . Yes, it's a reminder that each of these words is used to ask a question. When you see these words at the beginning of sentences, you'll also see question marks at the end of the sentences. Look at the colors that the words are written in. They all start with the letters *wh* and these are written in green. The letters after the *wh* are different so they're written in different colors. There's also a picture to give you a clue about what the word means. Let's start with this one. This says *who.* It's the shortest question word. It only has three letters. I'm going to trace each of these letters and say their names. Who. *W h o.* Who. I'm going to use the word to ask a question. Who is wearing a blue shirt? . . . Yes, Billy is wearing a blue shirt. Now you make up a question with the word *who.* . . .Great question. Now you say the word, trace it, and say the word again. Super. Now let's write the word and spell it as we write it.

Who. *W h o*. Who. Now let's shut our eyes and write the word *who* in the air. Who. *W h o*. Who."

Provide the same modeling for the three other question words.

GUIDED PRACTICE

Picture/Word Matching
Play a game in which there are cards with the four question words and pictures representing who (a girl, a man), what (a bird, a fish), when (a watch, a calendar), and where (a globe, a street scene). Have the students match question words with corresponding pictures.

Scrambled Letters Game
Give the students tiles corresponding to each of the letters in a question word in a scrambled order. Say the word, and have them put the tiles in the correct order. They get a point for each letter placed in the correct order.

INDEPENDENT PRACTICE

Have the students practice reading these words without assistance. Record the accuracy of the students' responses so you can evaluate their mastery of the objective. Present word cues with no picture cues or color coding. Have the students read them aloud. If they can read all the words with 100% accuracy, then have them unlock their treasure chests and put the cards in them. Then, have them count all of the words in the box so that they can see how many words they have learned. If they cannot count that high, then you do so.

GENERALIZATION

Have the students read question words in their books and on their worksheets as you point to them.

7

Developing Speed and Accuracy

Teaching Fluency Skills

CONCEPTS EXPLORED

- Role of fluency in the overall model of reading
- Guidelines for developing fluency skills
- Techniques for developing automatic word identification
- Techniques for developing reading with expression
- Techniques for developing fluent oral reading
- Techniques for developing rapid silent reading
- Model lesson for teaching fluency

The term *fluency* refers to both a stage of learning to read and a distinct set of reading skills. The fluency stage in learning to read is when students learn to read smoothly and at a reasonable rate (Reutzel & Cooter, 2001). At this stage, which typically occurs around second and third grade, students develop automatic identification of words and comprehension skills that they mastered at the early reading stage. The fluency stage is when students transition from reading word by word to smooth, rapid reading with expression. The fluency stage is the bridge from focusing on word identification to focusing on comprehension. Most reading researchers (Kuhn & Stahl, 2000) believe that students have a limited amount of attention that they can pay to a cognitive task, such as reading. When students are learning to read, they must channel most of their attention to word recognition, and consequently, they have limited attention for comprehension. Once they can easily identify words phonetically and visually, they can shift most of their attention to comprehension. Many fluency skills are developed at the fluency stage; however, they continue to develop over subsequent stages.

Students who have difficulty with fluency skills may read too slowly or too fast, and their reading may be choppy and have little expression. These problems may be related to deficits in RAN, which is the second type of deficit involved in the double deficit theory of dyslexia (Wolf & Bowers, 1999). Students with dyslexia may have problems with phonological awareness and phonics, but they may also have difficulty with quickly retrieving information. They have difficulty on tasks involving timed naming of pictures, numbers, letters, or word reading leading to the hypothesis that their fluency problems result from deficits with rapid production of verbal responses.

ROLE OF FLUENCY IN THE OVERALL MODEL OF READING

Students need to first learn to read words accurately and then learn to read words quickly, or automatically. Accurate decoding of words is mastered at the word identification stage. Automatic word reading is mastered at the fluency stage. Accurate, automatic word identification can be understood by comparing it with accurate and automatic recall of addition facts. First, students must recall the answers to addition problems using whatever strategies and cues they need to arrive at the right answer. After they consistently get the right answer, they need to learn to do so quickly. Likewise, students must learn to accurately identify words that they read phonetically or by sight; then they must learn to do so quickly. The key to becoming proficient at a sport or playing a musical instrument is practice, practice, and more practice. The same is true for becoming proficient at reading.

Fluency encompasses more than reading words rapidly; it also includes reading sentences and connected text quickly. Reading text rapidly applies to both oral and silent reading. In addition, students must learn to read with expression when they read orally. Reading with expression involves attending to prosody, which has to do with pitch or intonation; stress or emphasis; and tempo or rate (Kuhn & Stahl, 2000). Prosodic aspects of oral language involve how we use our voice to send messages to supplement the messages sent by the meaning of the words. For example, saying the sentence, "What a great day I'm having," would be spoken differently if the speaker were saying the sentence literally or sarcastically. Knowing how to read material with proper inflection is dependent on the meaning of the words as well as the punctuation. Students who ignore periods, commas, and question marks read with inappropriate inflection. Prosodic reading also involves chunking words into meaningful phrases so that the students are no longer reading word by word. Skills in prosody may be related to the pragmatic area of language (i.e., how language is used). Students must know how to use *oral* language to express their ideas in different communication settings so that they can apply this to reading with expression. In addition, students must have mastered oral syntax, or the grammar of language, to read phrases.

Instruction must be provided to each of the following fluency skills.

1. Automatic or instant recognition of words
2. Oral reading with expression
3. Smooth oral reading
4. Rapid silent reading

Some reading professionals use the term *sight words* for words that are identified automatically. In this book, the term *sight words* is used for words that are learned visually. The term *automatic words* is used for words that are identified rapidly. Oral reading does not have to be fast, but it should not be word by word. Readers need to group words into meaningful phrases and read with expression. How much instructional emphasis to place on oral reading depends on how important oral and silent reading are to the students' overall educational program. Students need to use rapid reading when reading silently, not orally, to meet the demands of the stages after the fluency stage. Keeping students at the oral reading stage too long may hamper their transition to the more important skill of silent reading. Overemphasis on oral reading may make it more difficult for them to read all the materials that they need for their academic content classes.

GUIDELINES FOR DEVELOPING FLUENCY SKILLS

There are seven guidelines for designing instruction for developing fluency skills for automatic word reading, oral reading with expression, fluent oral reading, and rapid silent reading (see Table 20).

Table 20.   Guidelines for developing fluency skills

Provide explicit modeling of fluent reading of words and text.

Make sure that students have mastery of accuracy before teaching speed.

Tell students when they have to read for accuracy and for speed.

Chart student progress.

Provide massive amounts of practice.

Provide short, frequent periods of fluency instruction at different times.

Make practice varied and fun.

1. Provide explicit modeling of fluent reading of words and text. It is important to use S.E.T. and include explicit modeling of fluent reading. Research has shown that repeated reading with a model is more effective than repeated reading without a model (Chard, Vaughn, & Tyler, 2002). Modeling by the teacher is most effective, followed by audiotape or computer-modeled reading. Other adults who can assist with repeated reading are paraprofessionals, volunteers, and parents. In some cases, modeling by peers may be effective, especially if the peer is older and more proficient at reading.

2. Make sure that students have mastery of accuracy before teaching speed. Currently in the field of reading, there is a growing emphasis on the area of fluency (Chard et al., 2002). This is evidenced by the addition of the fluency subtests in reading, math, and writing on the most recent revision of the Woodcock-Johnson III (WJ III) Tests of Achievement (Woodcock, McGrew, & Mather, 2001a), a widely used tool for assessing learning disabilities. Overemphasis on fluency can lead to pushing students to perform quickly at the expense of performing accurately. In addition, overemphasis on fluency may lead to rote repetition of isolated words, which may lead to student boredom and lack of motivation to engage in more effective fluency activities. It is important to provide corrective feedback for fluency activities so that students are correctly repeating words or text.

3. Tell students when they have to read for accuracy and for speed. Make clear to students when they need to read for accuracy and/or automaticity. For example, when students are studying for a test, they should *not* read rapidly; they should read slowly for the purpose of identifying what they will need to learn for the test. They need to know why they are reading the material and how to adjust their speed accordingly.

4. Chart student progress. Chart student progress for accuracy first. When students attain 90%–100% accuracy for reading words following specific phonic rules or sight words, move to the automatic stage. Record student progress using the time taken to read words or text. Chart students' progress in terms of words read per minute to show their improved speed with oral and silent reading.

5. Provide massive amounts of practice. Research indicates that it is the increased exposure to print rather than the type of activities that is important for developing fluency skills (Kuhn & Stahl, 2001). There is no set number of times students need to repeat the reading of words or text. The number of repetitions needed depends on the students' progress. Some students may need five repetitions to achieve rapid recognition of a particular word, whereas others may need 50 repetitions. When reading text, most students will need to repeat the reading of the text at least three or four times. If students are reading text to an audience, then they may need 10 repetitions before achieving fluency.

6. Provide short, frequent periods of fluency instruction at different times. Because of the potential for boredom and overloading, provide short, frequent periods for repeated reading of words and text at different times. For example, you might have your students read a story twice with your modeling and guidance and return to it later in the reading period when the students read the story independently. Or, the students may read the story over the next few days. It is necessary to have students practice over a number of days for repeated reading of words. Automaticity of word identification cannot be achieved in one day.

7. Make practice varied and fun. The more exposure to print that students have, the more fluent they become; therefore, repetition is necessary. However, repeatedly reading the same words or text can be boring to the students and the teacher. It is necessary to provide varied practice that is fun and motivating to the students. Use materials that are of interest to the students so that they want to read them over. For example, if a student is interested in skateboarding, then get books, magazines, and web materials on this topic. Have the student read these repeatedly so that he can fluently read them when all of the students read articles related to their interests.

TECHNIQUES FOR DEVELOPING AUTOMATIC WORD IDENTIFICATION

Assessment data relative to students' grade level mastery of automatic word identification can be obtained from IRIs (see Chapter 12). The Qualitative Reading Inventory–3 (QRI-3; Leslie & Caldwell, 2001) provides information on automatic mastery of words from the pre-primer to the high school level. Students read lists of words from various grade levels. If they correctly read a word in 1 second, then the word is considered automatically identified. If they take longer to read the word, then it is concluded that they can read it accurately but not automatically. You should also use this same assessment technique to informally evaluate words that you have taught your students to decode phonetically and visually. After they can accurately read words with specific phonetic patterns or sight words, they need to be taught to read such words automatically. For example, once students can accurately decode words with the phonetic pattern /ar/, they should be informally tested to determine if they can read such words quickly. If not, instruction on rapid word identification of /ar/ words should be provided.

Fluency instruction is especially important for high-frequency sight words. Students need to learn to read them quickly so that they can attend to the words with semantic content that are important for determining meaning. For example, in the sentence, "The boy is throwing a ball," the words *the*, *is*, and *a* are not important to the meaning of the sentence and have to be decoded quickly so that the reader can attend to the words *boy*, *throwing*, and *ball*, which carry the meaning of the sentence.

Some activities for developing automatic word identification include a 1-minute drill at the beginning of the reading period. Students read the words that they are working on for automaticity as quickly as possible. Daily records should be kept to demonstrate the increased number of words read automatically in the 1-minute time frame. Another activity for developing automatic word identification involves making a tachistoscope, which is a blank card with a small opening. Behind the card, a list of words on another card is moved up and down so that one word appears in the opening. The students read the word as it appears in the opening. Gradually decrease the time the word appears in the opening.

TECHNIQUES FOR READING WITH EXPRESSION

It is difficult for some students to overcome reading word by word because they were taught to point to each word as they learned to read to overcome their problem of skipping words. Once students no longer skip words, present sentences with separated phrases as a strategy for overcoming word by word reading. For example, present the following phrases on separate cards: "The boy," "hit the ball." Model reading each of the phrases, then push the cards together and read the complete sentence. When presenting such separated sentences, use noun phrases and verb phrases. For longer sentences, add prepositional phrases (e.g., "The boy," "hit the ball," "over the wall"). Gradually move from sentences separated into phrases to modeling with complete sentences in which you scoop the phrases with your finger or a pencil (Reutzel & Cooter, 2001). Have the students read each of the words in a phrase together as they scoop it.

To model the prosodic features of pitch, stress, and tempo, orally read the same sentence in different ways and discuss which reading best fits the meaning of the sentence. For example, read the sentence, "The owl hooted in the dark barn," first using a low pitch and then a high pitch. Discuss why the low pitch is better suited for scary content. Demonstrate the importance of stress by modeling a sentence spoken with stress on different words. For example, contrast the differences in meaning for the sentence, "Mary found the money," spoken with the word *Mary* stressed versus the same sentence spoken with the word *found* stressed. Discuss how stressing these two words changes the meaning of the sentence. To demonstrate the importance of tempo, read a sentence such as, "The boy hit the ball over the wall," word by word versus reading it grouped by phrases. Another activity for training students to read with inflection is to use pictures of faces showing different emotions. Have the students read sentences using intonation to match different facial expressions. For example, show a picture of an excited face, and have the students read the sentence, "Our team won the soccer championship game." Then, show a picture of a sad face and have the students read the sentence, "Our team lost the soccer championship game."

Another effective technique for developing students' ability to read with expression is to have the students read along with you, another adult, or a peer who is a good reader. They can also read along with audiotapes of books or print-to-speech software for electronic same material. Echo reading in which you read the material followed by students reading the same material is also effective. Have students read to younger students to provide additional opportunities for reading with expression. Participating in reader's theatre in which students rehearse and perform reading the news, stories, plays, or poems to an audience is also effective.

TECHNIQUES FOR DEVELOPING FLUENT ORAL READING

Increasing speed for oral reading entails repeated reading of material. For some purposes, the reading level of the material used should be easy for the students so that they experience success and are motivated to repeat reading the material. In other situations, you may want to use repeated reading with material that is challenging and at the students' instructional level. You may read along with the students to ensure that they experience success with the repeated reading. When you are working with a student who is reading a book at her instructional level, you do not want her to read it only once. The first reading usually is labored and requires teacher assistance with decoding of words. Subsequent readings help the student to read each of the words fluently and start to concentrate on reading with expression and fluency.

IRIs are the best way to identify different levels of student reading. With this approach, three levels of oral reading are identified (Richek et al., 2002):

1. The *independent level*, at which the student attains 98%–100% accuracy for word recognition, 90%–100% accuracy for comprehension, and is the level at which she can read fluently with comprehension

2. The *instructional level*, at which the student attains 95%–98% accuracy for word recognition, 70%–89% accuracy for comprehension, and is the level at which she can progress with instructional guidance

3. The *frustration level*, at which the student attains less than 95% accuracy for word recognition, less than 70% accuracy for comprehension, and is the level at which she cannot understand the material

The percentages of accuracy at each level are arbitrary, and you may find different cut-off points used in various IRIs.

Once you have identified these three levels, you can select reading material to be used for different purposes for a specific student. Material at a student's independent level is easy to read and is best used for developing fluent oral reading, especially for students who have experienced much reading failure and need success to build their self-confidence in their ability to learn to read. You should use materials at a student's instructional level for teaching specific reading skills. Materials at this level are challenging, but you can guide the student in meeting the challenges. Materials at the frustration level are too difficult for the student and lead to failure and should be avoided.

The following example illustrates how you would use these three levels to plan instruction for Bob, an 11-year-old sixth grader with a reading disability. Bob's IRI showed that his independent level was at second grade, his instructional level was at third grade, and his frustration level was at fourth grade. For independent reading, the teacher uses high interest, controlled vocabulary materials (materials that are of interest to older students who read at low levels) at the second-grade level. Because Bob's instructional level is third grade, she uses third-grade level materials to develop his reading skills. He is expected to read sixth-grade textbooks, which are above his frustration level of fourth grade. Bob is presented with his textbooks on audiotape so that he is not expected to read at the sixth-grade level but is still provided with the academic content that he needs to learn.

Activities for increasing a student's speed of reading oral materials are the same as those recommended for teaching reading with expressions and include repeated reading aloud with adults (e.g., teacher, paraprofessional, volunteer), peers, and younger children and using audiotapes and dramatic presentations.

TECHNIQUES FOR DEVELOPING RAPID SILENT READING

Rapid silent reading becomes increasingly important as students enter higher grades because of the increased amount of reading that they are required to do for their academic classes. As soon as possible, students need to transition from oral to silent reading. For many students with reading disabilities, this is difficult, in part, because of the emphasis placed on fluent oral reading. To gradually move from oral to silent reading, have students go from reading aloud to whispering and from whispering to making no mouth movements. If they have difficulty transitioning from whispering to silent reading, then have them purse their lips so that they cannot form words.

The strategies for teaching rapid silent reading are different from those used for oral reading because students are taught *not* to read every word with silent reading, whereas they must read every word with oral reading. Teach students to attend to words with semantic content and skip function words during rapid silent reading. Present students with reading material in which words with semantic content are underlined or bold. Have the students read these silently and then ask themselves comprehension questions. Demonstrate how they can read material faster and still understand it if they focus on meaning words. Guide them in analyzing words on which they do not have to focus (e.g., articles, auxiliary verbs). Have them go through materials and underline words that have semantic meaning and read the passage by focusing on them only.

It is important that students learn to read at different speeds depending on the purpose of their reading. Fluency with silent reading at higher grade levels involves matching reading rate to the type of text. They should learn to read rapidly when they are reading for enjoyment at their independent level (e.g., sports magazines). They should read slowly if they are studying and need to identify important information (e.g., solving a word math problem, reading directions for an assignment). They should learn to read quickly to scan (rapidly search for information such as a date or name) or skim (preview or review of material to get key ideas; Reutzel & Cooter, 2001). Scanning is especially important for reading electronic text. You can use IRIs to obtain independent, instructional, and frustration levels for silent reading as well as oral reading.

Two frequently used activities for improving students' silent reading are sustained silent reading (SSR) and drop everything and read (DEAR), both of which involve silent reading over a fixed period of time with self-selected materials. For these activities to be successful, it is important that students select materials in which they are interested but are also at their independent silent reading levels. This approach also needs to be modified for students with ADHD who may have difficulty sustaining attention for lengthy periods. For such students, it may be necessary to break these time blocks into shorter periods and intersperse other types of activities involving more engagement (e.g., writing a summary of what the student read, speaking a summary into a tape recorder).

$$\frac{\text{Number of words} \times 60}{\text{Number of seconds to read}} = \text{Words per minute (wpm)}$$

Figure 7.   Formula for calculating words per minute. (From Richek, M.A., Caldwell, J.S., Jennings, J.H., & Lerner, J.W. *Reading problems: Assessment and teaching strategies* [4th ed., p. 78]. Published by Allyn and Bacon, Boston, MA. Copyright © 2002 by Pearson Education. Adapted by permission of the publisher.)

Table 21.   Acceptable reading rates at various instructional levels

Level	Oral reading words per minute	Silent reading words per minute
Pre-primer	13–35	N/A
Primer	28–68	N/A
First	31–87	N/A
Second	52–102	58–122
Third	85–139	96–168
Fourth/fifth	78–124	107–175
Sixth/seventh/eighth	113–165	135–231
High school	N/A	93–334

From Richek, M.A., Caldwell, J.S., Jennings, J.H., & Lerner, J.W. *Reading problems: Assessment and teaching strategies* (4th ed., p. 79). Boston: Published by Allyn and Bacon, Boston, MA. Copyright © 2002 by Pearson Education. Adapted by permission of the publisher.

It is necessary to calculate students' speed of reading to improve their rate of oral and silent reading. Use the formula given in Figure 7 to calculate the words per minute that students read. Acceptable reading rates for material at student's instructional levels are shown in Table 21. If they read slowly, then find out if they understand the material. If they understand it, then work on increasing their speed. If they do not understand the material, then work on comprehension because fluency is not important if students do not understand what they are reading.

Have students chart their reading speed. If they have difficulty improving their reading speed, then have them try using a card and move it line to line to hasten their speed. Also, they can run their finger down the center of a page and read the words that are near the center. Remember that the most important aspect of learning to read is comprehension. First, make sure that students can decode words and understand what they read. Then, work on improving their speed.

Model Lesson for Teaching Fluency
Horse Racing

OBJECTIVE

Students will read previously learned words within 1 second with 100% accuracy.

ADVANCED ORGANIZER

The purpose of the advanced organizer is to inform the students that they already know how to read accurately, and now they are going to learn to read quickly.

Link

Link to mastery of sight words previously learned.

"Yesterday we reviewed all of the sight words that you have learned in the past 4 weeks. You've learned 20 new words. You can read them perfectly."

Identify Purpose

Identify the goal of the lesson.

"It took you a little while to read the words, so we need to work on having you learn to read the words quickly."

Provide Rationale

Explain the importance of the lesson.

"Reading words quickly is important so that you can pay attention to what the words mean."

MODELING

Use a horse racing theme. Give each student a toy horse. Have the students name their horses. Present a race track with mile markers going up to 10 miles. Each time students read words faster, they can move their horse 1 mile. When they reach the end of the track, they can select a prize.

"We're going to have a horse race. You're going to read your 20 sight words. Every time you read the words faster, you can move your horse 1 mile. There are 10 miles on this race track. When you get to the end, you get a prize from the class store. I'm going to show you how to read these words quickly. I'm going to use this timer to time myself. *(Read the students' 20 words, and then record how many seconds it to took to read them.)* Now, I want to see if I can read them faster. *(Read them more quickly and record your new time.)* Now, let's read the words together. Try to keep up with me. . . .That was great. You kept up with me."

GUIDED PRACTICE

Sandglass Timer
Have the students use a 1-minute sandglass timer (or a kitchen timer) and see how many words they can read in 1 minute. Have students work in pairs, and have one student count the cards read by the other student and record the number. Have the students work toward improving their own performance, not compete against their partners. Make sure that only correctly read words are counted.

Flag Game

Play a game in which the students read the words quickly or slowly depending on the color of a flag you hold. When you hold up a blue flag, they are to read the words quickly. When you switch to a red flag, they are to read the words slowly. Alternate having them read quickly and slowly.

Daily Horse Race

Every day have the students read the cards as quickly as possible and record their time. Try to make sure that the students eventually cross the finish line so they can be rewarded.

INDEPENDENT PRACTICE

Have the students practice the skill without assistance. Record the accuracy of the students' responses so you can evaluate their mastery of the objective. Present one card at a time for a 1-second interval, and have the students read it.

GENERALIZATION

Observe the students' oral reading of text containing their sight words. Make sure that they read these words fluently. If not, provide more guided practice.

Teaching Reading Comprehension

The Basic Approach

CONCEPTS EXPLORED

- Comprehension skills at the different stages of learning to read
- Three factors for individualizing reading comprehension instruction
- Guidelines for effective reading comprehension instruction

Reading comprehension is one of the major areas of instruction in the model for teaching reading to struggling students that is used in this book. The need to systematically teach comprehension skills was emphasized in the report issued by the RAND Reading Study Group (2001), which was formed as a result of the federal government's commitment to improving educational research and practices. The report pointed out that many students are not able to meet the demands of middle and secondary academic classes and high stakes testing because of poor reading comprehension. In addition, it reported that reading comprehension instruction is minimal or ineffective in many schools. The authors of the report stated that no one method of teaching reading comprehension will meet the needs of every child. So, teachers must select a method that will work for a specific student if instruction is to be effective. A number of methods are presented in the next three chapters that will enable you to match methods to students.

Reading comprehension is best defined as a process for extracting and constructing meaning from text (Sweet & Snow, 2002) or thinking guided by print (Kamhi & Catts, 1999). Reading comprehension is not only understanding what has been decoded but also using what has been read for the purpose of thinking. This link of reading and thinking is the basis for student mastery of advanced academic knowledge as well as the development of higher order cognitive processes. In school, we learn to think, in large part, based on what we read.

The International Dyslexia Association defines *dyslexia* as difficulties with accurate and/or fluent word recognition and poor spelling and decoding, which result from deficits in phonological awareness (Lyon, Shaywitz, & Shaywitz, 2003). Reading comprehension problems are viewed as secondary results of word identification and phonological awareness deficits. The author views dyslexia as a disability in any of the major areas of the reading process (i.e., pre-reading, phonics, visual skills, fluency, reading comprehension), which results in students having difficulty meeting the literacy demands of school, work, or everyday life. Therefore, reading comprehension deficits are not just secondary to other problems.

Students may have reading comprehension difficulties for a number of reasons resulting from

- Language problems: difficulty understanding the words and sentences in reading material

- Cognitive processing deficits: difficulty applying thinking to mentally processing reading material

- Lack of knowledge of text structures: difficulty using strategies for understanding the unique organizational features of different types of reading materials such as stories, textbooks, technical material, and electronic material

- Lack of mastery of skills in the areas of pre-reading, word identification using phonics or visual skills, or reading fluently

Students with reading comprehension problems are often not identified until fourth grade and are labeled as having "late-emerging" reading disabilities. In a study of fourth graders with reading disabilities, Leach, Scarborough, and Rescorla (2003) found that 35% had poor word identification problems and adequate comprehension skills, 32% had weak comprehension skills and good word identification skills, and 32% had both poor word identification and weak comprehension skills. This indicated that early intervention programs may not prevent late-emerging reading problems or that these problems are undetected by the schools. Rather, students with late-emerging reading disabilities have problems in reading comprehension and decoding the multisyllabic, abstract words that abound in their content area textbooks.

Not only do reading comprehension problems constitute a significant disability for many children, but they are also more difficult to address than problems in pre-reading, word identification, and fluency. The latter skills are limited (i.e., specific number of sounds, specific number of high-frequency words, specific reading rate). However, reading comprehension skills are broad and ever-changing. They involve understanding all words and sentence types in printed material, mastery of higher order thinking processes necessary for understanding all types of reading material, and strategies for understanding the organization of different types of text structures. Consequently, there needs to be a constantly changing focus on reading comprehension disabilities until adult competency is reached.

COMPREHENSION SKILLS
AT DIFFERENT STAGES OF LEARNING TO READ

Comprehension skills differ at each of the six stages of the reading process. At the pre-reading stage, students develop skills in understanding orally presented material; they learn the meanings of words and sentences as well as literal and inferential comprehension skills for material that they hear. At later stages, they apply these skills to understanding material that they read. It is important that students at the pre-reading stage listen to books read aloud because this helps them understand book language, which contains formal sentence structures and abstract or unfamiliar words (Carlisle & Rice, 2002). Reading aloud to students is essential for them to master comprehension skills for orally presented material so that they can eventually apply these to written material. Reading by parents is especially important because it makes reading a key component of the parent–child bond. Family literacy programs that teach parents to read are important so that parents can provide the critical experiences of reading aloud to their children.

At the early reading stage, students learn to understand the words that they have decoded. Just being able to say a word aloud does not mean that students understand the word. You can say the word *kipper* aloud, but you may not know that it is a type of fish. Children learn to match words that they have de-coded with words in their oral vocabulary (e.g., matching the written word *ball* with the concept of an object that is thrown). When there is no match, the meaning of the word must be taught so that it can be associated with the writ-ten word. Also at this stage, students learn to understand simple sentences in-cluding words that they can decode. Emphasis at this stage is on literal com-prehension skills with narrative text (i.e., understanding the main ideas and details of stories).

The matching process between decoded words and their meanings, as well as processing the meaning of sentences, speeds up at the fluency stage. The comprehension skills that have been developed at the earlier stage are ap-plied to more difficult words and more complex sentences. Again, most of the reading material at this stage is narrative.

Comprehension skills take center stage at the reading to learn stage. Stu-dents can now fluently read words and sentences so they are ready to shift their primary attention to understanding what they read. Students learn words from their content area classes in science, social studies, and language arts. They de-velop literal, inferential, and evaluative comprehension skills for expository text, which they apply to learning academic content. In addition, they begin to master metacognitive skills for monitoring their reading. Researchers have re-ported a fourth-grade slump in many students because they are not able to read the expository material in their textbooks (Sweet & Snow, 2002). Part of this slump is due to lack of systematic instruction on the types of reading compre-hension skills needed to help students read expository material as they move through the grades.

Students apply comprehension skills to a wider variety of content areas (e.g., psychology, physics) at the advanced reading stage. They continue to broaden their vocabulary based on their classroom reading, and they develop higher order cognitive skills for understanding the concepts in these content areas. In addition, they develop metacognitive strategies involving reading for the purposes of studying and test-taking.

At the adult literacy stage, reading comprehension is used as the basis for lifelong learning, specifically for work and everyday purposes. Technical and electronic reading materials are especially important at this stage. Struggling students must be taught how to understand these materials before they leave school so that they are prepared for the literacy demands of adulthood.

THREE FACTORS FOR INDIVIDUALIZING
READING COMPREHENSION INSTRUCTION

Three factors must be considered when planning reading comprehension in-struction to meet the unique needs of struggling students:

1. The language demands of the reading material

2. The demands for using various cognitive processes to understand the material

3. The type of text structure of the reading material (i.e., how it is organized)

Comprehension of reading material requires that students use language skills in semantics, morphology, syntax, and pragmatics. Skills in phonology are needed for word identification, not reading comprehension. Students need semantic skills to understand the words that they read (e.g., the meaning of the word *ball* in a story about sports is different than the word *ball* used in Cinderella); they need morphological skills to understand the meanings of multisyllabic words (e.g., knowing the meaning of the prefix *dis* as the basis for understanding the meaning of the word *dislike*); they need syntactic skills to understand sentences that they read (e.g., discriminating the meanings of the sentences, "The boy saw the girl" and "The boy was seen by the girl"); and they need pragmatic skills to understand how language is being used to convey different meanings (e.g., knowing that when written dialogue in a conversation between a boy, his principal, and his classmate includes the word *sir*, the boy is speaking to the principal and not to his classmate). Students who have problems with semantics, morphology, syntax, and/or pragmatics (e.g., students with language learning disabilities, ELLs, or students who speak a nonstandard dialect of English) need to have specialized reading comprehension instruction that takes their special language needs into account.

There also needs to be a match between the demands for the cognitive processes needed to understand the reading material and the cognitive processes possessed by the students. Students need to have cognitive processes for three types of comprehension skills:

1. Literal comprehension of reading material for mastery of skills such as understanding main ideas

2. Inferential comprehension for mastery of skills such as determining cause and effect

3. Evaluative comprehension for mastery of skills such as differentiating fact from opinion

Some students do not have the required cognitive processes because of learning disabilities, differing learning styles, or lower cognitive skills (e.g., students who are classified as slow learners or as having mild mental retardation). These students need specialized reading comprehension instruction that takes into account strategies for building these cognitive processes along with reading comprehension.

Finally, reading comprehension instruction needs to encompass all types of text structures to which students are exposed. It cannot be assumed that because students can understand the main ideas of stories they can understand the main ideas of textbooks. Language and cognitive processing demands differ depending on the organization of the reading material. Narrative texts tell stories and have plots. Students must be taught to understand story features, such as characters, settings, and problems. Expository texts do not tell stories, they give information (e.g., a social studies textbook description of the three branches of the federal government). Electronic reading material may tell stories or give information. Electronic material is unique because it may not be linear (i.e., it may not be like a printed page with line after line of text); in turn, it requires understanding of the visual organization of material. For example, reading web sites often requires the reader to jump from box to box and to use evaluative comprehension skills to determine whether information is important for the purpose of continuing to read. Students need to be given reading comprehension instruction with all types of materials: narrative, expository, and electronic. This will enable students to meet the demands for reading at all stages in the process of reaching adult literacy.

Language, cognitive processes, and text structures must be considered when designing reading comprehension instruction for students. Basic guidelines for all types of reading comprehension instruction are presented in this chapter. The next chapter focuses on teaching the language aspects involved in reading comprehension (i.e., understanding words and sentences). Chapter 10 deals with the cognitive processing aspects of reading comprehension and focuses on literal, inferential, and evaluative comprehension skills. Finally, strategies for dealing with narrative, expository, and electronic text structures are presented in Chapter 11.

GUIDELINES FOR EFFECTIVE
READING COMPREHENSION INSTRUCTION

Before describing what effective reading comprehension instruction should be like, it is important to emphasize what reading comprehension instruction should *not* be. All too often, reading comprehension activities require students to read material once and then answer a few questions (usually for main idea and details) orally or in writing. There is no teaching before, during, or after the reading. The questions asked after the reading are not sufficient to develop the complex linguistic and cognitive skills involved in reading comprehension.

Designing effective reading comprehension needs to be anchored to the research findings on strategies that have been shown to improve reading comprehension. Chief among these strategies are teaching students to have a plan of action when reading, self-monitor, summarize, use graphic organizers, ask questions, use semantic organizers, identify story structures, relate reading material to prior knowledge, and use mental imagery (Duke & Pearson, n.d.; Gersten, Fuchs, & Williams, 2001; Swanson, 1999; Sweet & Snow, 2002; Vaughn,

Gersten, & Chard, 2000). These strategies have been incorporated into the guidelines presented in the following three chapters.

The following basic guidelines should be used for all reading comprehension instruction at all stages of the reading process:

1. Provide explicit instruction at the pre-reading, actual reading, and post-reading phases.

2. Teach students to use strategies to actively engage with the reading material.

3. Use a multisensory approach.

4. Use different formats for teacher questions and student responses.

5. Make reading comprehension fun and motivating.

Provide Explicit Instruction at the Pre-Reading, Actual Reading, and Post-Reading Phases

All reading instruction must have activities at each of these three phases, whether the students are being taught by you, working cooperatively with each other, or reading independently. Never have students read material without giving them preparation to guide their reading. Use the analogy of going on a trip to explain to students why they *must* go through these three phases. Explain that when you go on a trip, you must plan where you will go, what you will do, and what you will bring. When you are on the trip, you must do everything you planned to do, and when you return from your trip, you review everything that you did and evaluate the trip. This three-phase model of reading comprehension instruction is a long-established best practice and has been found effective with all types of learners (Carlisle & Rice, 2002; Tompkins, 2003). Two popular approaches using the three-phase model are reciprocal teaching and collaborative strategic reading in which there is previewing before reading with predicting and brainstorming, comprehension monitoring and clarifying during reading, and wrap-up with summarization (Bos & Vaughn, 2002).

Always provide explicit instruction during the three phases when teaching students in the early reading and fluency stages. Ask different types of questions at the three phases to guide the students to develop the various comprehension skills best suited for each phase. At the reading to learn and advanced stages, have the students ask themselves the questions at the three phases. Change the responsibility for the reading task by allowing the students to lead the questioning.

Instructional time devoted to the three phases varies. It may be possible to cover all three phases at one time in some lessons (e.g., a 40-minute lesson on reading a chapter from a health book). Or, one lesson may be devoted to a particular phase (e.g., a 30-minute lesson on post-reading activities of a chapter in the book *Matilda* [Dahl, 1990]). Also, one lesson may be devoted to two phases (e.g., a 30-minute lesson on pre-reading and actual reading of a chapter on the federal court system from a U.S. history textbook).

Table 22 presents activities that can be used during each of the three phases along with the types of comprehension questions that best fit each phase.

Pre-Reading Phase

The following activities are usually presented at the pre-reading phase:

- Giving the purpose of the reading
- Previewing the pages to be read
- Reviewing previously read material
- Activating prior knowledge
- Teaching the meaning of new vocabulary
- Teaching the decoding of new vocabulary
- Framing prediction questions to guide the reading

Give the purpose of the activity when starting a reading lesson (e.g., "Today we're going to read Chapter 11 on respiration so you can find out about the breathing process and can answer the questions on the end-of-the-unit quiz," "Today we're going to continue reading the chapter on how Harry Potter finds the train to get to Hogwarts," "Today we're going to learn how to read the list of entries in your Google search for your term papers"). Students and teachers need to be partners in learning to read, so students must know what they have to learn and why.

After discussing the purpose of the reading, preview the pages to be read. For narrative text, examine the title headings, pictures, and any dialogue. For expository text, examine the side headings, pictures, graphics, bold-faced words, study questions, and so forth.

Next, provide activities in which you discuss the meaning of the ideas that will be presented in the reading material. You can do this by reviewing previously read material and/or by discussing what the students know about a topic. To provide a review of previously read materials, ask questions to set the stage for understanding the material to be read in today's lesson (e.g., "What did we read about in yesterday's chapter on the heart?" "What did we read about in yesterday's chapter on what Harry had to bring to school?" "What did we learn about typing search words in Google?"). Use literal comprehension questions dealing with main ideas, relevant details, and sequences to ensure that the students recall the previously read material and can use it as the basis for understanding the material that they will be reading.

Table 22.   Teaching activities for the three phases of comprehension instruction

Pre-reading phase

1. Make the purpose of the reading activity clear.
2. Preview the material to be read. Analyze all organizational features of the material (e.g., side headings, bold-faced words).
3. Review previously read material related to the reading material. Ask literal comprehension questions dealing with main ideas and details relevant to understanding the material to be read.
4. Ask questions to activate prior knowledge about the topics in the reading material. Use brain-storming to elicit as many ideas as possible related to the topics. Use the KWL strategy to re-view what the students know about the topics, what they want to learn, and eventually what they learned (at the post-reading phase).
5. Teach the meanings of words that the students do not understand or are new. Show the print forms of the words and give comprehensive definitions using examples, visual aids, and so forth.
6. Teach the decoding of words that students will not be able to decode. Show the print forms of the words, and have the students apply whatever decoding skills they have to try to iden-tify the words and supply additional cues as needed.
7. Ask prediction questions to channel the students' attention to certain aspects of the reading material.

Actual reading phase

1. Ask literal comprehension questions periodically to ensure that the students understand the material. If necessary, clarify the material by guiding the students in analyzing different parts of the reading material.
2. Teach students to analyze the syntax of lengthy, complex sentences.
3. Integrate pre-reading instruction by having students identify words that were pretaught or answers to prediction questions when they meet them in the passage.
4. Teach the metacognitive skill of applying different cues to independently identify the mean-ing of the words students do not understand or cannot decode.
5. Teach the metacognitive skill of self-monitoring for understanding meaning.
6. Teach the metacognitive skill of self-monitoring for paying attention while reading.

Post-reading phase

1. Link pre-reading prediction questions to answers found while reading.
2. Relate pre-reading activities using the KWL strategy.
3. Relate pre-reading activities to brainstorming and prior knowledge.
4. Ask questions requiring summarization of the most important ideas.
5. Ask inferential and critical comprehension questions that require higher level thinking.
6. Teach use of story maps to aid understanding of narrative text.
7. Teach use of graphic organizers to aid understanding of expository text.
8. Teach the metacognitive skill of using look-backs to aid in understanding.

It is important to activate the students' prior knowledge about the ideas in the passage to be read. By discussing the topics before actually reading about them, the students are better equipped to integrate the new information with what they already know. Use brainstorming techniques in which you ask the students to give words and/or concepts associated with the topics in the read-ing material to elicit as much prior discussion about a topic as possible. After you write these down, have the students discuss each association. Use of webs (graphic representations showing the relationship of ideas) showing the inter-relations of the associations helps children see these ideas visually.

The KWL strategy is frequently used to teach students to activate their prior knowledge of a topic (Ogle, 1986). Students discuss what they already know about the topic of the reading material (activate prior knowledge), what they want to learn about the topic, and what they actually learned from their reading. This strategy is especially effective with expository material. The steps of the strategy are presented using a three-column format. In the first column (the **K** column), the students are guided to list what they **k**now about the topic in the reading material; in the second column (the **W** column), they list what they **w**ant to learn; and in the third column (the **L** column), they list what they **l**earned about the topic. The third column is completed at the post-reading phase.

It is also necessary to teach words in the reading material that you think the students will not understand or will not be able to decode. When the students are actually reading, you do not want their attention to be on decoding words when they should be focusing on understanding the ideas in the passage. When planning the lesson, select words that you think the students will not understand. Sometimes, you will mistakenly include words that the students actually know; you can quickly glide over these. Also, while reading, you may find words that you thought the students know but they do not. Just give the definition of the words so that the students can understand the passage. Write the words down so that you can give more intense instruction on their meanings at a later time. The vocabulary aspect of the preteaching phase is especially important for ELLs who need to have new oral vocabulary initially taught and then integrated into their reading vocabulary. A comprehensive description of how to teach reading vocabulary skills is in the next chapter on language-based reading comprehension skills.

Also, teach new words that may be difficult to decode because students have weak decoding skills or because the words have unusual sounding patterns (e.g., the word *tsar* in which the *ts* has the /z/ sound). Have the students apply their decoding skills to identify the word, and supply additional cues as needed. You may mistakenly select words that students can decode; in these cases, just quickly pass over them. If you did not include preteaching of a word that the students could not decode, then you have two choices. If you think that you can supply cues to help the students quickly decode the word, then do so. If you think that the students will not be able to decode the word, then say it and provide decoding instruction at a later time. You do not want to shift the students' focus from comprehension to decoding.

Preview the material to be read, and ask prediction questions to channel the students' attention to key aspects of the reading material. Always have the students look over all the pages that they will read. For expository text, use graphics, pictures, headings, bold-face words, and other organizational features as the basis for constructing prediction questions. For narrative text, use pictures and scan for key words that signal what will be included in the reading material (e.g., scan the pages of the chapter in *Harry Potter and the Sorcerer's Stone* [Rowling, 1997] to find the names of the characters who will appear).

Previewing the material is especially important for students with ADHD who need to know the limits of the reading that they will have to do. These students often believe that a reading assignment is endless and previewing the pages to be read helps set limits to the task. For such students, clearly show the beginning and end of the material to be read.

Actual Reading Phase

While the students are reading, ask literal comprehension questions periodically to make sure that the students understand the material. If they are reading aloud, then stop at certain points and ask questions to ensure that they are getting the main ideas, details, and sequence. If they are reading silently, then use sticky notes to place questions at important points in the material. Students can write the answers to these questions on the sticky notes, record their answers on a tape recorder, or say the answers aloud so that they can answer these questions when you ask them later at the post-reading phase. Therefore, you can evaluate their responses to make sure that they understood the ideas that they read silently. You can also use visual cues to signal the students that they should self-question or self-monitor their reading. For example, you can use a sticky note with a question mark or a light bulb to signal that the students should be mentally summarizing or monitoring their attention. You can also use sticky notes to allow the students to "talk" to the author. With this method, students place sticky notes with three messages—an exclamation point, a smiley face, and a question mark—in parts of the text as a way of expressing their feelings of surprise, agreement, or lack of understanding to the author (Richek et al., 2002).

The actual reading phase is the best time to analyze the meaning of lengthy, complex sentences for students who have difficulty with the syntax of language. This aspect of language-based comprehension is important for students with language learning disabilities, ELLs, or students who speak non-standard dialects. These sentences cannot be taught in the pre-reading stage because their meaning can only be interpreted in relationship to the text already read. When you take time to analyze the syntax of a lengthy sentence while students are reading, review the meaning of the passage read so far before having the students continue reading the rest of the passage. This shifts the focus from comprehension to analysis of the sentence syntax. Guidelines for providing instruction for syntax to aid reading comprehension of lengthy sentences are presented in Chapter 9.

It is important for students to integrate all aspects of the pre-reading phase of instruction at the actual reading phase. For example, have the students identify the new words that were taught in the pre-reading phase when they come across them when reading the passage. Likewise, have them identify answers to prediction questions that they find while reading by underlining or using sticky notes.

Three important metacognitive strategies should be developed in the actual reading phase:

1. Independent use of strategies to understand or decode unknown words

2. Self-monitoring for meaning

3. Self-monitoring for attention

All three require the creation of separate instructional activities using S.E.T. so that students can apply the strategies when reading passages. One of these metacognitive strategies involves teaching students to independently read words that they cannot understand or decode while reading. In the previous section on preteaching of vocabulary, it was suggested that you give the meanings or correct decoding when students have difficulty with certain words. This is true when the goal of the reading instruction is for the students to understand the meaning of the passage that they are reading. However, another reading comprehension goal is to have students learn strategies for understanding and/or decoding unknown words they find in their reading material. Create separate mini-lessons in which you teach the students to first identify words that they do not understand and then to find their meanings by analyzing the context. Directions for how to teach context clues are in Chapter 9. Also, create separate mini-lessons in which you teach the students to decode unknown words they come across in the reading material. Have them integrate use of phonics, visual, and meaning cues. For example, if they cannot read the word *angular* in the sentence, "The tiles were laid out in an angular pattern," then have them try to sound out the word based on their phonics knowledge, ask them what other words they know that look like this word, and ask them to try to figure out the meaning based on the context. Also, teach them that whenever they take time to analyze a word during reading, they need to mentally review what they have already read before they resume reading the remainder of the material.

A second metacognitive skill students must master is monitoring for understanding of the meaning of the material they are reading. To develop this skill using S.E.T., create separate mini-lessons in which students identify material containing information that does not belong (e.g., a paragraph with five sentences about paragliding and one sentence about the history of flight). Also, construct mini-lessons in which the reading material has missing or incomplete information (e.g., a three-paragraph passage on the assassination of Lincoln with no mention of John Wilkes Booth). Have students identify what information they need in order to understand the material.

It is also important to teach this strategy using the reading materials the students are using for their classes. They need to be taught to always ask themselves. "Does this make sense?" If the answer is no, then they need to be taught to use look-backs to find out why they are not understanding the material. They need to identify where the troubling information is located and re-analyze it.

The third metacognitive skill students must master involves self-monitoring to make sure that they are paying attention while reading. This strategy is especially important for students with attention problems. Create mini-lessons in which the students read short sections paragraph by paragraph and ask themselves questions before moving to the next section. Gradually increase the length of the sections to be read and summarized. Self-monitoring can be done by using a sticker or some visual cue to signal to the students where they are to self-question. They must also be taught to use look-backs to find the point in the reading material in which their attention lagged and start re-reading at this point.

Post-Reading Phase

It is important to link the activities used at the pre-reading phase to post-reading activities. Students are to answer the prediction questions that they asked by looking at the cues that were used as the basis for asking these questions (e.g., "Before we read this section, we asked how the geography of Mexico was related to Hispanics being the largest cultural group in the U.S. Now let's give the answer."). Students are also to complete the L column for the KWL strategy. Discussions relating prior knowledge and brainstorming to the knowledge presented in the reading material should lead the students to see what they have learned and how their knowledge base has broadened.

Differential questioning, in which you ask questions to elicit different types of thinking, is most important at the post-reading stage. Questions should emphasize summarizing the most important ideas of the material. All reading materials include information that is not necessary for understanding the main ideas, so students must learn to differentiate what is most important and not get overloaded with insignificant details. Students cannot store all the information from reading material; rather, they must store what is most important so that it can be incorporated into their knowledge base. You must always ask students to identify the main idea(s) of a sentence, paragraph, passage, chapter, or book. This sounds simple, but it is not. Students must use evaluative thinking skills to identify information as being essential or not.

The post-reading phase is the best time for asking questions requiring inferential and evaluative comprehension. These questions are important but only after you are sure that the students have literal comprehension and understand the meaning of the passage. Guidelines for framing literal, inferential and evaluative comprehension questions are in Chapter 10.

The use of visual aids, specifically graphic organizers and story webs, are helpful in teaching students to gain different comprehension skills. Graphic organizers aid students in mastering the different thinking skills developed with expository text (e.g., a Venn diagram for understanding the similarities and differences of fresh water and salt water). Story webs are useful for aiding students in understanding narrative texts because they visually emphasize the relationships between characters and actions in stories. Inspiration, a computer program with various templates for graphic organizers for older students, and Kidspiration, for kindergarten to fifth grade, are useful for providing such aids (http://www.inspiration.com).

Finally, the metacognitive skill of developing responsibility for independently finding answers in reading material is developed at this stage. When students cannot answer a comprehension question, they need to be taught to use look-backs to find the information in the passage that is related to the question that they cannot answer and re-read the information to try to answer the question. You must gradually withdraw your use of strategies to aid students in obtaining correct responses to comprehension tasks so that you can build student independence.

BCDE Strategy

The BCDE strategy (Minskoff & Allsopp, 2003) is designed to teach students at higher reading levels to ask themselves questions during the three stages (see Display 1). This strategy should be taught to students who are at the reading to learn and advanced reading stages. It is designed to facilitate the transition of instruction from being teacher led to student led. At the first step (**B**), students are taught to survey the reading material **b**efore they start reading expository text or to predict what will happen before reading narrative materials. At the **C** step, they are to **c**reate questions to ask themselves while reading and then answer the questions **d**uring their reading (**D**). Have the students make note cards for the questions that they create so they can use them to study for tests. At the **E** step, which is at the **e**nd of the reading, they are to summarize the main ideas, relate what they read to previous readings, and predict how this material will be related to future material that they will read.

Present students with Display 1, and describe each step as you model it. Then, have the students follow your modeling for the first step only. Once they can do this, have them follow your modeling of the first and second steps, then the third step, and finally the fourth step. It is too difficult for struggling readers to learn all of the steps in this strategy at one time. The BCDE strategy, along with graphics and examples, is included in the Learning Toolbox web site (http://coe.jmu.edu/learningtoolbox), which provides resources for helping struggling students become more effective learners.

BCDE strategy   (Display 1)

Purpose: To help me get the overall ideas when I read

Before reading, survey the material to be read.
- Always look over the pages you have to read before you actually start reading.
- If you are reading a textbook, read the title, side headings, paragraph headings, pictures, graphics, bold-faced words, and study questions. Think about how this chapter is related to previous chapters.
- If you are reading a story, look back at the previous section you read and predict what you think will happen in this section. Skim the paragraphs to get some ideas of what might be in the section you will be reading. Make predictions about the characters and the actions that you think will take place.

Create questions to ask yourself while you read the material.
- For textbooks, create questions about the material based on the title, side headings, paragraph headings, pictures, graphics, bold-faced words, and study questions. Have the teacher write these questions so that you can answer them later. If you can write them, then put them on the front of note cards.
- For stories, you or the teacher can write questions based on the predictions that you made. Make predictions about the characters and actions.

During reading of the material, answer the questions you wrote on the note cards.
- As you read the material, keep in mind the questions that you wrote.
- When you find the answers to the questions, write them on the back of the note cards, or have the teachers write them.

End of reading—summarize.
- After you have finished reading, look over all the questions you wrote. If you did not find an answer to a question, then go back and try to find it.
- Ask yourself the questions and try to answer them.
- Say a summary of the main ideas of what you just read aloud to yourself.
- Ask yourself how the material you just read is related to material that you read before this.
- Predict how the material you just read will be related to the material that you will read next.

Teach Students to Use Strategies to Actively Engage with the Reading Material

The first guideline concerning the three phases of reading comprehension instruction provides the framework for the remaining guidelines. Students must be actively engaged at each of the three stages of reading comprehension instruction. Reading should not be viewed as a passive act because students most often read silently. Both oral and silent reading must always be viewed as an activity in which the reader mentally interacts with the material. In the initial stages of teaching comprehension, students are taught to interact aloud with the material, but as they master the target comprehension skills, the interaction moves to the subvocal level in which they talk to themselves. To encourage students to always be actively engaged when reading, they must be taught to talk to the author and to themselves as they process the meaning of what they are reading.

Use of self-talk or think-alouds has been recognized as an effective strategy for developing this skill (Vaughn, Gersten, & Chard, 2000). You model talking to yourself as you read material, and you overtly describe the strategies you are using to help understand the material. For example, when reading a health textbook chapter on respiration, demonstrate asking yourself questions about the side headings and bold-faced words before starting to read. "First, I have to read the side headings so I know what topics are going to be covered in this chapter. I also have to look at the bold-faced words so I know what words are important." Have the students practice using think-alouds. As they gain mastery, have the students use these subvocally so that they do not attract attention to themselves when reading.

Use a Multisensory Approach

Multisensory instruction using the VAKT method to facilitate learning is a well-established best practice in education (Romeo, 2002). Although it is more difficult to use VAKT methods for reading comprehension than for word identification, these methods can and should be included in all reading comprehension instruction. Multisensory instruction includes the use of various sensory cues in the presentation of the reading material as well as mental imagery requiring the students to use their senses to create images to aid in understanding of reading material.

Visual cues can come from the printed page or from student visualization (visual images associated with the ideas in the reading materials). In early reading of narrative text, have students use pictures as aids to understand what they read. When students read content area textbooks, have them use the visual cues provided by pictures, graphs, maps, and diagrams. Also, story webs for narrative text and graphic organizers for expository text are invaluable sources to aid understanding of reading material.

Visualization can aid understanding with both narrative and expository text at all reading levels. Research has shown that representational imagery (or mentally constructing images) does improve memory for what has been read (Pressley, Symons, McGoldrick, & Snyder, 1995). When using these cues, have the students close their eyes and picture in their "mind's eye" ideas in the reading material. For example, when reading *The Diary of Anne Frank*, have them close their eyes and picture themselves living with all of their possessions in a closet in their home. The key word method (Mastropieri & Scruggs, 2000) is another good visual method to help students learn the meaning of words that they do not understand. It uses a key word that students do understand to recall the unknown word while mentally picturing an image relating the two words. For example, if students could not recall the meaning of the word *ziggurat* (a pyramid with steps), have them use the key word *zigzag* and visually picture the steps in the pyramid going in a zigzag pattern.

Auditory cues can be used as instructional aids by having students read aloud, listen to others read aloud, or listen to taped books. Auditory cues can also emanate from the students' imagery system by closing their eyes and hearing important sentences spoken by other voices. For example, they can summarize the main ideas of a passage that they read about Germany in the voice and accent of Arnold Schwarzenegger.

Kinesthetic and tactile cues include having the students use highlighters to identify important words or ideas when they come to them in reading passages. They can also air-write words and ideas or use pantomiming actions described in the reading material.

Use Different Formats for Teacher Questions and Student Responses

Teacher questions are the most important factors in developing reading comprehension skills. Therefore, you must carefully prepare the questions you will ask at each of the three reading phases. The questions you ask will determine the language and cognitive processes that the students use in their responses. For example, questions that ask for definitions will develop students' vocabulary, whereas questions that ask for causation will develop students' cognitive processing involving cause and effect.

It is important to first ask questions that require receptive responses from students (e.g., multiple choice, matching, true/false). These questions demonstrate whether students know the answers to the questions without the potential interference of problems that students may have in bringing forth their answers. Students may be able to recognize an answer when they see or hear it, but they may not be able to think of the response or call forth the words needed for the answer. Then, ask open-ended questions that require students to express the answers verbally or through motor movements (e.g., writing, pantomiming). It is especially important to use questions requiring receptive responses for ELLs because they can demonstrate their understanding of what they read without having to use their limited expressive language.

Assess student understanding of what they have read through a variety of methods. Do not just have students answer oral or written comprehension questions. Not only can this become boring but it can also become ineffective if it is the only response format used. When you do have students write answers to comprehension questions, make sure you separate the reading and writing aspects of the task. If you want the students to write their responses to comprehension questions using complete, grammatically correct sentences, then grade the correctness of the sentences separately from recall of the correct answers. If the sentence is grammatically incorrect, but the recall of the material is correct, then the students must be given positive reinforcement for the reading task and corrective feedback for the writing task.

Expressive measures of reading comprehension should allow students to demonstrate their understanding of materials in a variety of ways. In addition to traditional recall comprehension responses, students can respond expressively by acting out the ideas from the reading material, drawing their ideas, writing book reviews, orally presenting book reviews, journal writing, letter writing, creative writing, writing a newspaper article, presenting a mock television report, or creating a rap song describing the ideas in the material. These varied response formats are especially helpful when developing inferential and evaluative comprehension skills. Use of different response formats increases student interest and integrates reading with other language arts areas such as oral language and written expression.

Make Reading Comprehension Fun and Motivating

Kindergarten students are most motivated to read and high school students are least motivated to read (Gambrell, Block, & Pressley, 2002). This reduced motivation for reading is even more pronounced in struggling students because of the failure they experience whenever they try to read. Success is one of the best motivators for students with reading problems. We all want to do what we can do well, and we want to avoid what we cannot do well. As struggling students master new reading skills, you must make their progress visible to them so that they become aware of their success. They may be so focused on what they cannot do in reading that they do not recognize what they can do. Demonstrate their success through visual and formal recognition (e.g., awards). Create graphs to visually demonstrate student improvement in the number of comprehension tasks successfully completed. For example, chart a student's number of correct responses on comprehension tasks when using a particular strategy. Give the students certificates for mastering different reading skills (e.g., successful critical reading to identify faulty arguments in advertisements). Also, increase motivation by having students identify what they learned from reading that they did not know prior to the reading. Have the students ask themselves aloud, "What did I learn from this that I didn't know before?" When using the KWL strategy, emphasize what the students learned when completing the L column. In addition, have students show their new reading skills by reading to others, especially younger students. Reading to parents, siblings, and others at home also helps students gain confidence as they master text reading and comprehension skills.

Motivation can also be improved by making reading interesting. Have students select what they want to read, when appropriate. Obviously, selecting what to read from a required history book is not possible, but students can select what they want to read for recreational purposes or for two frequently used silent reading programs—sustained silent reading (SSR) or drop everything and read (DEAR). If a student likes wrestling, then use wrestling magazines for the student's recreational reading. However, be sure that the students apply the reading comprehension strategies that they are learning when they read these materials. Also, use timeless literature that children have loved over the years. For example, give a summary of books such as *A Wrinkle in Time* (L'Engle, 1998) and *Charlotte's Web* (White, 1974), and ask students to select one that they would like to read. Also, use videotapes of books made into movies; and have students read a chapter of the book and then view the corresponding part of the videotape and compare their visualization with the movie.

Make reading fun by showing your enthusiasm. For example, when introducing a Harry Potter book, come in wearing a cloak, a witch's hat, and a lightning bolt on your forehead. Or, bring in artifacts such as arrowheads and feather headdresses when reading a social studies chapter on Native Americans in Colonial America.

Struggling students find reading a daunting, fear-inducing activity. You must reduce the anxiety associated with reading by making it as interesting and as much fun as possible. Use games, whenever possible. For example, the formats of Candy Land and Monopoly are effective for young children, whereas the formats of Jeopardy! and Trivial Pursuit are good for older students. Appendix F lists games that can be used for teaching all reading skills, including various comprehension skills.

9

Teaching Reading Comprehension and Language Skills

CONCEPTS EXPLORED

- Importance of language for reading comprehension
- Language-based reading comprehension skills
- Guidelines for designing word comprehension instruction
- Techniques for teaching word comprehension skills
- Guidelines for designing sentence comprehension instruction
- Techniques for sentence comprehension instruction

IMPORTANCE OF LANGUAGE FOR READING COMPREHENSION

Reading is best viewed as a complex mental activity requiring simultaneous integration of rapid and accurate word identification, attaching meaning to words and sentences, and connecting text information to background knowledge (Carlisle & Rice, 2002). Word comprehension (or vocabulary) and sentence comprehension are necessary for reading comprehension. There has been increased attention to vocabulary instruction since its inclusion as one of the five areas of reading instruction in the Reading First initiative (see The Partnership for Reading, 2001). However, there has been little attention to the significant role of sentence comprehension for mastering reading comprehension.

To understand the role of oral language skills in the reading process, it is necessary to understand the sequential development of the four levels of communication skills children learn. At the first level, infants from birth to age 1 begin to master *receptive oral language*—understanding words and sentences they hear. When an infant cries after hearing her mother say that, "Daddy is coming home soon," this indicates that the infant understands the word *Daddy* and is reminded that he is not present. Once children have some receptive language skills, between the ages of 1 and 2, they enter the second level where they begin to develop *expressive oral language* skills. They start by saying words (e.g., "Daddy") and then string words together to form their first attempts at sentences (e.g., "Daddy go"). After children have a solid foundation in both receptive and expressive oral language, at about age 5 or 6, they enter the third level, at which they are ready to apply these oral language skills to print, and begin to master *receptive written language* skills, or reading. At this stage, they are able to understand language that is conveyed through print instead of voice. After they have mastered beginning reading skills, at about age 7, they enter the fourth level and are ready to master *expressive written language* skills, or writing. This communication sequence is used as the basis for teaching reading because it clearly shows that a strong foundation of oral language is required for effective reading instruction. It also clearly shows that instruction at both the receptive and expressive levels must be included.

To understand oral language and its role in the development of reading, it is necessary to analyze the five components that comprise oral language: phonology (the sounds or phonemes of language), morphology (the smallest units of meaning of language), semantics (the meaning of words), syntax (the grammar or rules for combining words), and pragmatics (the uses of language with different speakers and settings). Phonological and morphological skills (see Chapters 4 and 5) are necessary for word identification, and semantics and syntax are most essential for the development of reading comprehension. Students must first understand the meanings of words that they hear before they can understand the meanings of words that they read. Likewise, they must first understand the meanings of sentences that they hear before they can understand the meanings of sentences that they read. To a lesser extent than semantics and syntax, pragmatics is necessary for the development of reading comprehension and fluency.

The reciprocal relationship between vocabulary growth and reading is well established (Stanovich, 2000). Poor vocabulary is both the cause and effect of reading problems (Gunning, 1998). On the one hand, vocabulary knowledge facilitates reading comprehension. Children who have large oral vocabularies learn to understand what they read more readily than children with smaller vocabularies. On the other hand, reading of higher level materials leads to vocabulary growth. Children who are competent readers master the meanings of more abstract words than children who are poor readers. The vital role of vocabulary in the development of reading comprehension cannot be overestimated.

Vocabulary demands for reading change over time because words become increasingly abstract as students progress through school. In the early grades, the majority of words that children learn are based on their experiences and refer to concrete concepts (e.g., table, ball). By the third or fourth grade, students are expected to read all the words in their oral vocabularies (Graves, Juel, & Graves, 1998). After fourth grade, the words that students are expected to learn to read are abstract (e.g., economy, synthesize) and come from their textbooks and classroom discussions in their content area classes.

It is important to note that vocabulary is not only important for learning to read but also for the development of verbal intelligence. One of the subtests on the Wechsler Intelligence Scale for Children–Fourth Edition (WISC-IV; Wechsler, 2003), the major instrument used to measure intelligence in children, assesses vocabulary by requiring students to orally define words. Tests such as the SAT, used as a major criterion for college admission, and the GRE, used as a major criterion for graduate school admissions, also heavily emphasize vocabulary knowledge. Statewide assessments of reading frequently assess vocabulary. On the Virginia Standards of Learning fifth-grade language arts assessment, there are items to evaluate students' knowledge of word origins, synonyms, antonyms, homonyms, and multiple word meanings (*Standards of Learning Currently in Effect*, n.d.).

The complexity of the syntax demands involved in reading also change over time. In the early grades, the sentences in reading material are relatively short and easy to understand. However, even at these levels, the syntax is more difficult than the sentence structures that students hear in their everyday environment. Children are required to learn *book language*, a formal way of talking that is used in books and includes uncommon sentence structures (Carlisle & Rice, 2002). Consequently, students may encounter problems understanding syntax at the earliest stages of reading connected text. The syntactical complexity of books increases significantly when students start to read content area textbooks. Sentences become progressively longer and include many complex structures that are not used in oral language.

Sentence length is a significant variable in reading both narrative and expository text. The following is a 62-word sentence from the popular children's book, *James and the Giant Peach* (Dahl, 1961). To understand such a lengthy sentence, readers must break the total sentence into smaller, more manageable parts so that each part can be understood.

> And sometimes, if you were very lucky, you would find the Old-Green-Grasshopper, in there as well, resting peacefully in a chair before the fire, or perhaps it would be the Ladybug who had dropped in for a cup of tea and gossip, or the Centipede to show off a new batch of particularly elegant boots that he had just acquired. (p. 144)

The importance of vocabulary and syntax is reflected in their inclusion in readability formulas, which are used to estimate the reading level of print material. The Fry readability formula is the most popular and the easiest to use (Gunning, 1998; see Appendix G). It uses sentence length as a measure of grammatical complexity and number of syllables as a measure of word length, based on the premise that longer words are more difficult. The Flesch-Kincaid formula, increasingly popular because it is available through Microsoft Word and is automatically calculated, also uses word and sentence length as the basis of determining reading level of material. Another approach for estimating the difficulty level of reading material is the Reading Recovery approach. Books are analyzed based on seven factors, two of which are vocabulary and sentence complexity (Tompkins, 2003). No matter what the specific approach for identifying difficulty level of reading material, all use vocabulary and syntax as major determinants.

Four groups of students who have language difficulties also have correlated reading problems: ELLs, students who speak dialects different than Standard American English, students who are economically disadvantaged, and students with language learning disabilities. ELLs do not have the vocabulary and syntax skills in English necessary to meet the demands for these two language areas as they progress through the grades. It takes about 2 years for ELLs to master Basic Interpersonal Communication Skills (BICS). These skills are learned through face-to-face interactions and involve the concrete everyday words that are needed for oral communication and early reading. They develop Cognitive Academic Language Proficiency (CALP), which is needed to understand the abstract vocabulary and complex syntax of textbooks, in 5–7 years (Cummins, n.d.). It is critically important to bombard ELLs with oral vocabulary and syntax instruction so that they can apply these skills to reading as soon as possible. Instruction in oral language skills should be linked to applying these skills to reading and writing. When students learn the meaning of a word orally, they need to also learn to read the word.

Students who speak different dialects have difficulty with syntax when reading. They use their "home talk" for situations in which "school talk" is needed. They need to become bidialectal and learn Standard American English for school purposes. These students have difficulty understanding what they read because they bring the structure of their dialect to reading textbook sentences that are written using the dialect of formal Standard American English. For example, students who speak AAVE use the word *be* instead of the auxiliary verbs *am* and *is* (Salient Features of AAVE, 2004). When they read the sentence, "The president is elected," they have to translate it into their own dialect to understand the sentence as, "The president be elected." Students who speak the Appalachian dialect may use two auxiliary verbs, such as *might could*, and have difficulty understanding and using Standard American English written syntax (Humphries, n.d.).

Children from low-income homes have fewer world experiences and the amount of talk at home may be limited, which may account for the continued developmental lag in vocabulary knowledge for such children and is one of the reasons for their poor performance on measures of reading comprehension (Carlisle & Rice, 2002). Students from middle-class homes know twice as many words as students from lower-class homes (Gunning, 1998), indicating the significant impact of experience on vocabulary. Programs for students from economically disadvantaged homes need to emphasize vocabulary growth through enrichment experiences.

Some children with language learning disabilities often have reading comprehension problems because they learned to talk late. Their vocabularies are limited, and they use less abstract words than their same-age peers (Stahl, 2004). They also use shorter, less complex sentences in their oral language (Wiig & Semel, 1984). Their foundation of receptive and expressive oral language skills is weak, thereby providing a tenuous structure for building reading and writing skills.

LANGUAGE-BASED READING COMPREHENSION SKILLS

Two areas of language-based reading comprehension need to be systematically taught: vocabulary and syntax. These areas need to be developed independently as well as in relation to each other.

Vocabulary

There are two ways of analyzing the role of vocabulary in reading comprehension. One way is to analyze the role of vocabulary in terms of a student's mastery of *decoding* the print version of the word, and the second way is to analyze the student's mastery of the *word meaning*. Using this type of analysis results in four categories of word knowledge.

1. Students cannot decode the printed word but they know its meaning. For example, students may know the meaning of the word *disappear* but they cannot read the printed word. Teaching such words requires instruction in decoding only because the students already understand the words when they hear or say them. Reading instruction at the pre-reading and early reading stages should emphasize such words because the students have to learn only one skill—decoding—and not two skills—decoding and word meaning.

2. Students can read the printed word but do not know its meaning. For example, students can read the word *gloat* but they do not know what it means. Instruction in teaching the meanings of such words involves comprehension skills, not decoding skills. As students become more adept at word decoding, words with unknown meanings should be included in the instructional program.

3. Students cannot read a printed word nor do they know its meaning. For example, students can neither read nor understand the meaning of the word *chlorophyll*. Teaching of these words would include both word decoding and word comprehension.

4. Students can decode a word but have limited understanding of its meaning. For example, students know the meaning of the word *scab* as a cover for a sore but do not know its other meaning is a worker who breaks a picket line during a strike. They do not have the depth of word comprehension and do not know:
    *   Synonyms
    *   Antonyms
    *   Homonyms, or words that sound alike and have the same spelling but have different meanings (*ball*, meaning an object thrown and a dance)
    *   Homophones, or words that sound alike but have different spellings and meanings (*mail*, *male*)
    *   Homographs, or words that are spelled alike but have different meanings and are spoken differently (*lead*, meaning a metal versus *lead*, meaning to guide)

A second way of analyzing vocabulary is to examine a word based on its type of semantic content. Some words are classified as *function words*, which include articles (*the*, *a*, *an*), conjunctions (*and*, *but*), prepositions (*in*, *on*, *with*), and auxiliary verbs (*is*, *were*). They serve as the glue that holds sentences together (Leu & Kinzer, 2003). They are harder to understand than *content words*, which include nouns, verbs, adjectives, and adverbs. The meanings of such words can be demonstrated with objects, pictures, or actions. For example, for the content word *apple*, an apple can be shown as the word is spoken. Or, for the content word *jump*, jumping can be demonstrated as the word is spoken. It is not possible to show or demonstrate what goes with the function word *were*. In addition, function words are not emphasized in oral language. In a sentence such as, "The stove is hot," the words *the* and *is* are not stressed. Most function words are classified as sight vocabulary words and decoding of them is taught using visual, not phonic, methods. Some students, especially ELLs and those with language-based reading disabilities, have difficulty mastering such sight words because of two factors: they have difficulty discriminating between visually similar words (e.g., *is, in*) and they do not understand their meaning.

Syntax

Syntax is less emphasized than vocabulary in most language-based reading comprehension instructional programs, possibly because of the complexity and abstractness of the concepts underlying grammar or sentence structures. The role of syntax in reading comprehension can be analyzed by examining the following five variables.

1. Sentence length

2. Sentence type

3. Word order

4. Relationship of vocabulary and syntax

5. Metalinguistic skills

The importance of sentence length for reading comprehension has long been recognized. For example, readability formulas place great emphasis on this variable. Obviously, the longer a sentence, the harder it is to process its meaning. Longer sentences increase conceptual density (i.e., many ideas are packed into a long sentence, which places a burden on working memory; Carlisle & Rice, 2002).

A second way of analyzing syntax is based on the types of sentence structures in the reading material. Simple sentences are relatively easy and constitute the primary types of sentences in early reading materials. Simple sentences include identity sentences ("This is a truck."), descriptive sentences ("The truck is red."), and action sentences ("The boy is running."). More difficult sentences include compound and complex sentences. Compound sentences have two independent clauses, both of which can stand alone as sentences ("The Indians grew corn, and later they started to grow tobacco.") Complex sentences have one independent clause, which can stand alone as a sentence, and one dependent clause, which cannot stand alone as a sentence ("After the war, the settlers moved to the West."). Sentences with embedded phrases are especially difficult because they separate the basic ideas in the sentence and add more ideas to the meaning of the sentence ("The settlers, who had lived in the mountains, did not know how to survive when winter came.").

A third aspect of syntax analysis involves the need for students to attend to the order of words. For example, word order is critical for understanding sentences with active and passive voices. In the active voice, the action is clear and the words are in a conventional order with the subject performing the action ("The boy hit the girl."). In the passive voice, the words are not in a conventional order because the object is in the position that is usually occupied by the subject ("The girl was hit by the boy."). Passive sentences are difficult to understand because students must pay close attention to word order and auxiliary verbs. Students must also pay close attention to word order to identify subtle changes in meaning ("He hit the fast ball" versus "He hit the ball fast").

The fourth aspect of syntax analysis involves integrating the analysis of the meaning of words as related to the meaning of sentences. Function words (conjunctions, prepositions, pronouns, and auxiliary verbs) cannot be understood in isolation; they can only be understood by their meanings in sentences. Therefore, mastery of function words and sentence comprehension cannot be separated.

Students must process the meaning of conjunctions to understand the relationships of the clauses in compound and complex sentences. Conjunctions are difficult to understand because they involve temporal or time factors (*before*, *after*), causal relations (*so*), conditional relations (*if*, *then*), and qualifying relations (*but*). Prepositions can only be learned by analyzing the relationship of the ideas within a sentence. For example, the word *behind* cannot be learned unless embedded in a sentence such as, "The boy is behind the tree." It is important for students to understand the meanings of pronouns because they make up 70% of the cohesive ties between sentences in basal readers (Carlisle & Rice, 2002). Students must learn to track the meaning of pronouns from one sentence to the next. For example, in the following sentences, who found the pen and the ownership of the pen is determined by the pronouns. "The boy and the girl lost their pens. He found hers." Finally, students must understand the meaning of auxiliary verbs such as *is, are, was, were, do, did, does, could, would, should, can, may,* and *might*.

The final variable used to analyze the role of syntax in reading comprehension involves metalinguistic skills such as analyzing the role of punctuation marks, analyzing parts of speech and grammatical structures, and monitoring for consistency. Students must learn to integrate the meaning of written punctuation marks as aids for determining the meaning of sentences. For example, the meaning of the question, "Was that a home run?" differs from the meaning of the statement, "Was that a home run!" based on the punctuation marks. These punctuation marks also represent pragmatic linguistic features. The statement with the exclamation point shows that the speaker is expressing excitement.

Students also need metalinguistic skills to analyze the grammatical structures within sentences so that they can understand the meaning of long, complex sentences. They need to analyze lengthy sentences based on the number of complete ideas included. They must have a sense of what a sentence is, which is a highly abstract metalinguistic skill. Such understanding is important for textbooks that are written in formal book language. They also need to apply such analysis to narrative texts that are often "messy" in that they include sentences that are not well organized and cohesive and there are no clear relationships between the sentences (Carlisle & Rice, 2002). It is difficult for some students to switch from analyzing complete sentences in expository text to incomplete sentences often found in narrative text. Finally, students need to use another metacognitive skill—monitoring for the consistency of the meaning of the sentences that they read.

GUIDELINES FOR DESIGNING WORD COMPREHENSION INSTRUCTION

The average child learns approximately 3,000 new words per year from kindergarten through twelfth grade (Carlisle & Rice, 2002). They learn these words incidentally, not through explicit instruction. However, students with reading comprehension difficulties may only learn 1,000 words per year. They do not learn as many words because they do less independent reading, lack strategies to learn words through context, and have superficial word knowledge (Jitendra, Edwards, Sacks, & Jacobson, 2004). Therefore, it is necessary to teach as many words as possible so that these students can "catch up." It is reasonable to aim to teach 10–12 words per week or 300–400 new word meanings per year (Stahl, 2004). Teaching so many words is a daunting task, but it can be done with the right type of instruction (Carlisle & Rice, 2002; Gunning, 1998). The right type of instruction uses S.E.T. to teach students strategies so they can independently master the meanings of unknown words they read by using context (Jitendra et al., 2004).

The following guidelines based on principles of vocabulary instruction proposed by Vacca et al. (2003) can contribute to making students better at learning the meanings of unknown words and can be used to guide the teaching of all aspects of word comprehension.

- Teach comprehension of words that students can decode but do not understand. Therefore, the students will only have to learn one skill—word meaning. After these words are learned, teach words that students cannot decode or understand. The final group of words to be taught involves broadening knowledge of words that the students know. After students master the definition of a word, teach synonyms, antonyms, homonyms, homographs, and homophones.

- Teach receptive mastery of word meaning (i.e., reading) and then expressive mastery (i.e., speaking, writing). Have the students read a new word in different contexts and then create an oral or written sentence demonstrating their understanding of the word. Link reading of new words with writing these new words in sentences.

- Teach unknown everyday words from the students' environment. After these are mastered, teach unknown words from the students' curriculum (both basals and content area textbooks). There may be many unknown curriculum words, so select those that are most important for understanding the main ideas of the academic content and most likely to be used for testing. Teaching reading of everyday words is especially important for ELLs so that they can understand classroom procedures.

- Teach for mastery of the meaning of a word and not just verbalization of the word's definition. This requires that a word be taught in a variety of meaningful contexts. Just saying a definition for a word when the student meets the word while reading will not help the student master the word's meaning. Use repeated presentations of a word and not just one exposure. Integrate the word into different activities and point it out when it is used so that the students can generalize the applicability of the word meaning in different settings.

- Teach word comprehension by having the students actively involved in demonstrating the meaning of the words whenever possible. For example, when teaching the meaning of the word *migrate*, create different environments (cold represented by ice cubes on one side of the room and warm represented by hot water on the other side of the room), and have the students walk from one environment to another.

- Use nonexamples of a word to demonstrate what the word does not mean to highlight its meaning, or use the word incorrectly in a sentence. For example, have the students read the following sentence and determine if the word *executive* is used correctly: "The executive branch of the government includes judges."

- Use graphic organizers to show the interrelationships of word and concepts (i.e., semantic maps, webs, word sorts, word chains).

- Have students use the look-back strategy as a way of teaching them to independently use context to determine word meaning. Require them to find the unknown word in the text and analyze the meaning of the sentence in which it is embedded.

- Provide constant review. When students are not actively using words, they often forget their meanings. Have students keep word banks, and review them periodically to ensure that important vocabulary is retained.

TECHNIQUES FOR TEACHING WORD COMPREHENSION SKILLS

Teaching New Words

The most important strategy students must master to improve their reading vocabularies is use of context clues. Context clues are difficult to learn because students who have difficulty understanding specific words will also have difficulty understanding the surrounding words. Systematically teach students to analyze the sentence in which an unknown word is embedded. If students cannot determine the meaning of an unknown word by analyzing the meaning of the sentence in which it is embedded, then have them analyze the meaning of the preceding sentence. If this is not helpful, then have them analyze the sentence that comes after the sentence containing the unknown word.

Applying structural analysis skills is another useful strategy for helping students determine the meanings of unknown words. For example, if they do not know the meaning of the word *displaced*, then have them analyze the root word of *placed* and the meaning of the prefix *dis* as clues to the word's meaning.

When teaching the meanings of unknown words, select new words from the reading material and teach these at the pre-reading phase. Select the most important words necessary for understanding the major concepts in the material and those that are likely to be the focus of vocabulary testing. First, preteach the words by writing them on the board and demonstrating and explaining their meanings. When the students find these words in their textbooks, they are to note the location so that they tie the preteaching activities on analyzing the meaning of the word with the word as it appears in the text. Fully discuss the meaning of the word at the post-reading phase. Another strategy for teaching students the meanings of unknown words is to use resources such as a dictionary and thesaurus, either in print or electronic form. Learning definitions from the dictionary may not be easy for students with language-based reading difficulties because of the complexity of the definitions. In some cases, the definitions include additional words that the students do not understand. When students say that they do not know the meaning of a word, do not tell students to look it up in the dictionary. They may interpret this as a "brush off" and may become frustrated because they do not understand the dictionary definition. They may simply give up trying to understand the unknown word.

Teach metacognitive skills so students become responsible for identifying words that they do not understand and finding their meanings. Have the students write down words that they do not understand when they are doing independent silent reading. Have them apply context and structural analysis strategies. If these do not help, then have them use a resource or explain the meaning to them.

Have the students create word banks of new words that they have learned. It is helpful for students to write these words on one side of a note card and their definitions on the other side. Then, students can use these to study the meanings of the words for tests.

Strategies for developing word comprehension include use of visual cues such as highlighting or color coding to direct students' attention to unknown words in sentences. Also, use auditory cues when reading sentences with these words by saying the words in a louder voice.

Mini-lessons for training in word comprehension should involve both receptive and expressive tasks. For receptive tasks, use the cloze technique (or fill-in-the-blank activities) in which students have to select a word from several choices for a missing word in a sentence based on the meaning of the sentence. Then, use expressive tasks in which students have to produce all the words that might fit into a sentence with a missing word.

Be sure to provide word comprehension mini-lessons requiring a high level of student engagement. For example, create crossword puzzles using the Discovery Channel web site (http://school.discovery.com/teachingtools/teachingtools.html) with new curriculum words that the students are learning. Create word sorts in which the students have to sort all new words into columns corresponding to the category in which they fit (e.g., for a social studies lesson, have students list new vocabulary words that go under the columns for the three branches of government: judicial, legislative, and executive). Use games such as Jeopardy!, in which the definitions of words are given and students have to ask questions to identify the corresponding words. Also play Pictionary, in which students draw pictures to demonstrate the meanings of new vocabulary.

Teaching Function Words

Systematically teach the meanings of articles, auxiliary verbs, prepositions, and conjunctions. Articles are especially difficult for ELLs to learn because of the different ways that articles are represented in different languages. For example, in Spanish, articles are changed depending on whether they precede singular and plural nouns (the articles *la* and *las*), whereas some articles in English are not changed for singular and plural nouns (e.g., *the* is used for both singular and plural nouns). Help students to differentiate the meanings of the following articles based on these rules: *a* precedes a word starting with a consonant sound versus *an*, which precedes a word starting with a vowel sound; *a* is used the first time a word is mentioned versus *the*, which is used to refer to the word after it has been mentioned. When presenting sentences with these articles, color code or highlight them to direct the student's attention to them. After students learn the meanings of these articles, teach them to skip them when reading sentences to increase their fluency. It is ironic that we teach students to understand these articles so that they can understand the meaning of sentences, and then we teach them to ignore articles. Once students can understand the meaning cues of articles, they can primarily attend to the meaning of content words. Demonstrate how knowing the meaning of an article eliminates the need to look at the word when reading (e.g., when reading the sentence, "The boy is running," it is not necessary to look at the word *the*).

Teach students to understand the meanings of the following auxiliary verbs: *am, is, are, was, were, do, did, does, can, may, might, could, would,* and *should*. Explain that *am* only follows the word *I*. Demonstrate how *is* and *was* represent the singular, and *are* and *were* represent the plural. Also, demonstrate how *is* and *are* represent the present, and the corresponding verbs *was* and *were* represent the past tense. The meanings of *can, may, might could, would,* and *should* need to be demonstrated in many situations. For example, to explain the meaning of *can* as the ability to do something, present sentences such as, "Juan can play the piano. Maria can speak Italian. Bill can play soccer."

In the early stages of instruction on prepositions, use sentences in which the prepositions can be visually demonstrated (e.g., The letter is *in* the envelope) and move on to more abstract sentences in which the prepositions cannot be demonstrated (e.g., There is more rain *in* the spring). Be sure to color code the prepositions for visual emphasis.

Teach the following four types of conjunctions to represent different types of relationships: time (*before, after, during*), causal (*because, so*) conditional (*if, then*) and qualifying (*but*). To teach conjunctions with compound sentences, first present two separate sentences and then show how they are combined. In addition, show the role that the conjunction plays in changing the meaning of the combined sentences (e.g., "The Titanic was on its maiden voyage. No one expected it to sink." versus "The Titanic was on its maiden voyage so no one expected it to sink."). Then, teach conjunctions in complex sentences. Give examples of sentences with the same conjunction in different positions (e.g., "Before we ate lunch, we had a test." "We had a test before we ate lunch.").

An effective activity for teaching function words is to use nonexamples in which students have to determine if a function word is correctly placed in a sentence. For example, have the students read the following sentence and identify the incorrect word: "The boys was playing baseball." Other activities that can be used include Mad Libs, in which the students read a story with blanks representing missing function words that they are to fill in. First, use receptive tasks in which the students select function words from a word bank, and then use expressive tasks in which they produce function words to fit into sentences. To make the activity more fun, have them fill in the blanks with incorrect words to make the sentences funny. Use games such as charades, in which the students silently read sentences with different prepositions and then act them out. The other students are to guess the preposition based on the charade.

Teaching Pronouns

Teach personal pronouns (e.g., *he*, *she*, *it*, *we*, *they*), possessive pronouns (e.g., *his*, *hers*, *its*, *our*, *their*), and reflexive pronouns (e.g., *himself*, *ourselves*, *themselves*). Contrast pronouns based on gender (e.g., *he* versus *she*) and singular versus plural (*he* versus *we*). Point out how these different types of pronouns have different uses in sentences. Teach the meanings of the pronouns in simple sentences during the initial stages of instruction. After this is mastered, teach students to track the use of pronouns in one sentence (e.g., "The boy and the girl lost their books.") and then successive sentences (e.g., "The boy and the girl lost their books. She found his, but he did not find hers.") Use the students' basals and textbooks, and have them track all the pronouns that go with a particular word. Have them highlight the noun and related pronouns in one color. Also, have the students do word sorts in which they group pronouns by gender and number.

Teaching Synonyms, Antonyms, Homonyms, Homophones, and Homographs

Start teaching the concepts of synonyms using word pairs that the students understand (e.g., *big*, *large*; *little*, *small*) and then move on to pairs where they know one of the words but not the other (e.g., *fast*, *rapid*). Teach students to use the thesaurus and a dictionary to help them identify synonyms. Point out that the words listed have different connotations and the meaning of a sentence is changed with each word (e.g., *big*, *enormous*).

Initially, when teaching antonyms, use pairs in which the students know the meanings of each of the word pairs (e.g., *big*, *little*) and then move on to pairs in which they only know the meaning of one of the words but not the other (e.g., *hidden*, *overt*). Again, teach the students to use the thesaurus as a reference.

When first teaching the concept of homonyms, use a word with two meanings that the students already know (e.g., *ball*). Then, teach new meanings for a word (e.g., *fence*, for the sport). Teach students to recognize the correct meaning of a homophone by using context clues (e.g., "The girls put on their masks, picked up their swords, and started to fence."). Teach students to recognize the meaning of a homograph by using context clues, especially syntactic cues (e.g., "A pencil is made out of lead." "The usher will lead you to your seat.")

Use analogies in which students know the meanings of four given words but they are to place them in correct relationship based on synonyms (e.g., *big*, *large*; *small*, *little)* or antonyms (e.g., *big*, *little*; *fat*, *skinny*).

Use puns and jokes to teach multiple meanings of words. For example, tell the joke, "Why did Batman climb the tree? To see if Robin laid an egg." Explain the two meanings of the word *robin* and why use of the wrong meaning is funny.

GUIDELINES FOR DESIGNING SENTENCE COMPREHENSION INSTRUCTION

Incorporate the following guidelines to design instruction for developing sentence comprehension skills.

1. Use strategies that teach students to analyze the following characteristics of sentences: length, order of words, and relationship of words. Guide students in analyzing progressively longer sentences. Also, provide sentences that differ in only key words, and guide the students to systematically analyze each word to differentiate the meanings of the sentences. Finally, teach students to analyze sentences based on words that connect different ideas within the sentences.

2. Teach students to understand progressively longer sentences by initially using content that students understand. Then, rewrite the content using longer, more complex sentences. Therefore, the students only have to concentrate on the syntax and not the meaning of the sentences.

3. Have students who speak a different dialect or language try to rephrase the sentence in their own dialect or language as an aid to understanding the meaning.

TECHNIQUES FOR SENTENCE COMPREHENSION INSTRUCTION

Teaching Understanding of Lengthy, Complicated Sentences

In order for students to understand lengthy, complicated sentences, they must be taught to chunk the sentences into smaller sentences. One way of chunking is to teach students to parse sentences, or divide them into subjects and predicates. Flood, Lapp, and Fisher (2002) described the Parsing, Questioning, and Rephrasing (PQR) strategy in which the teacher and students parse sentences with the teacher asking questions to guide the students to look critically at the ideas included within and across sentences. This may be difficult for some students because they cannot identify subjects and predicates due to metalinguistic limitations (i.e., they cannot easily analyze the components of language).

Another strategy for teaching students to analyze the meaning of lengthy, complicated sentences is the R U BART strategy shown in Display 2. This strategy helps students to process the meaning of grammatically complex sentences by chunking them based on whether each chunk expresses a complete idea. Although analysis of sentences using the criterion of complete ideas is a metalinguistic skill, it seems to be a lower level skill because many struggling

R U BART   (Display 2)

Purpose: To help me understand the meaning of long sentences

Read the long sentence that is hard for you to understand.

Use punctuation marks to break the long sentence into chunks.

Break the long sentence into chunks that have complete ideas.

Analyze the meaning of each of the chunks.

Re-analyze the meanings of the chunks to find out if they are related to each other.

Think about the meaning of the long sentence after you re-read it.

students have a sense of what makes a complete sentence. The R U BART strategy is especially helpful for "messy" sentences that are often found in narrative text and do not follow conventional grammatical rules. It is also helpful for analyzing the long, conceptually dense sentences of expository text.

R U BART could be used to analyze this sentence: "Mike, the pitcher for the last place Tigers, was positive that the Tigers would win the championship, you can bet on that." Using the R U BART strategy, the sentence would be analyzed as follows.

Teacher: "We have been using the R U BART strategy to help us analyze the meaning of long sentences by chunking them into smaller sentences. Remember, we had a huge candy bar when we first learned this strategy. We divided it into chunks, and we each ate a chunk. Let's use the R U BART strategy to try to understand the sentence. The first step, which is the R step, tells us to read the long sentence aloud. Please read it aloud."

Student: "Mike, the pitcher for the last place Tigers, was positive that the Tigers would win the championship, you can bet on that."

Teacher: "The second step, which is the U step, tells us to use punctuation marks to break the long sentence into chunks. Find all of the punctuation marks in this sentence . . . Yes, there's a comma after the word *Mike* and after the word *Tigers*. And there's also a comma after the word *championship*. Let's use these commas to break the long sentence into chunks. But we have to pay attention to the third step, the B step, which says that we have to break the long sentence into chunks that have complete ideas. Each of the chunks, or smaller sentences, has to have a complete idea.

"Let's go to the fourth step, the A step. We have to analyze the meaning of each of these smaller sentences. The first two punctuation marks have to do with the chunk that tells that Mike is the pitcher for the Tigers and that the Tigers are in last place, and they can be used to make a sentence such as 'Mike was the pitcher of the last place Tigers.' There's a complete idea in that chunk. The word *was* isn't in the sentence, but it would be if we made this into a complete sentence. Let's write the first sentence down.

"The second chunk would be that Mike was positive that the Tigers would win the championship. That chunk is a complete idea. Let's write that sentence down. The last part of the sentence that is separated by a comma is written in a different way. It's a comment by the author emphasizing that Mike was positive that the Tigers would win the championship even though they were in last place. It's not really a statement that says that somebody would place a bet on that. It would be spoken like this. [Speak the sentence with appropriate affect.] It expresses a complete idea, so let's write the last sentence down.

"Now let's do the R step and re-analyze the meaning of each of the three chunks and find out if they're related to each other. The first chunk tells us that Mike was a pitcher and that the Tigers were last place in the league. The second chunk tells us that Mike was positive that they would win the championship even though they were in last place, so these two chunks are related to each other. The third chunk tells that he is very positive that they will win and is related to the second chunk. It's a way of saying that he is very, very positive.

"Now let's do the T step. Think about the meaning of the sentence after you re-read it. If the author had used three short sentences, the writing would be choppy. [Read the three short sentences and then read the complete sentence.] Writing a long sentence like this is what good writers do to get their ideas across to readers. But it's hard to understand long sentences, so we have to break them into smaller sentences so we can get their meanings."

Teach Identification of the Most Important Parts of Sentences

Many sentences contain information that is not necessary for understanding the main ideas in the sentence. Some students have difficulty discriminating this information and are overwhelmed by unnecessary details. Model how to search for the sentence parts that are necessary for understanding the meaning of a sentence and how to identify parts that are not necessary. Have the students use self-talk and ask themselves the following question to guide their analyses, "Do I need this sentence part to understand the overall sentence meaning?" For example, an analysis of the following sentence would lead to identification of three sentence parts.

> The great yellow-fever discoveries at Cuba, those later dramatized in Sidney Howard's play *Yellow Jack* and in a movie made from the play, were the work of Gorgas' superior officer, Dr. Walter Reed, who had taken his lead from Carlos Finlay (McCullough, 1977, p. 413).

Teacher-led analysis would show that the main idea of the sentence is that the yellow-fever discoveries were the work of Dr. Walter Reed. Further analysis would lead to two details: Walter Reed was Gorgas' superior officer, and Walter Reed based his work on the work of Carlos Finlay. The part of the sentence that discussed the dramatization in a play and a movie is not necessary for the main idea.

Use mini-lessons to teach discrimination of unnecessary information in sentences. Create sentences that initially have one part of nonessential information. Then, add two parts of nonessential information to the sentence. Have the students tell why information is not essential for the overall meaning of a sentence.

Teaching Attention to Word Order in Sentences

Students must pay careful attention to word order to understand the meanings of sentences. Have students who do not pay attention to word order use their fingers to point to each word in a sentence. Also, create mini-lessons involving jumbled sentences in which you present words on word cards, and have the students match the cards to models of sentences written with different word orders. For example, present the two following sentences, and point out that they both contain the same words but in different a order: "The boy hit the red ball" versus "The red ball hit the boy." Discuss how the different word orders changed the meaning of the sentences. Also, use sentences with words written in an incorrect order (e.g., "The sun orbits the planets."), and have students place the words in correct order so the sentence makes sense (e.g., "The planets orbit the sun.").

Teaching Understanding of Sentence Meaning Using Conjunctions

Teach understanding of sentences by emphasizing conjunctions. Create mini-lessons with compound and complex sentences with various types of conjunctions. Have the students read the sentences and discuss the impact the conjunctions have on the meanings of the sentences. Use sentence-combining activities in which the students read simple sentences and then combine them to make a compound or complex sentence. Have them discuss whether the meanings of the separate and combined sentences are the same. For example, present the sentences, "We can play basketball." "We can go to the movies." and "We can play basketball, or we can go to the movies." Discuss that the meaning of the combined sentence is the same as the two small sentences.

10

Teaching Reading Comprehension and Cognitive Processing

CONCEPTS EXPLORED

- Importance of cognitive processes for reading comprehension
- Guidelines for designing instruction for reading comprehension and cognitive processing
- Techniques for developing literal comprehension skills
- Techniques for developing inferential comprehension skills
- Techniques for developing evaluative comprehension skills
- Techniques for developing metacognitive skills to monitor reading performance

Reading and thinking (also called *higher order cognitive processing*) are intricately intertwined. Reading is the major avenue that the educational system uses to develop students' ability to reason and evaluate. The emphasis on thinking skills is exemplified by the dual scope and sequence of the sixth-grade science basal series *Science Explorer*, published by Prentice Hall (1997). The text is designed to provide knowledge and skills based on the National Science Education Standards as well as honing critical thinking skills, such as comparing and contrasting; relating cause and effect; making generalizations; making judgments; and solving problems. This text imparts science knowledge while simultaneously teaching students to think by reading the book content.

The significance of the different types of thinking processes for assessment of reading comprehension is apparent in statewide assessments. On the Virginia Standards of Learning in language arts, thinking processes are assessed in the fourth grade when students are asked to make simple inferences and draw conclusions. By eighth grade, students are expected to compare and contrast authors' styles, analyze authors' viewpoints, and evaluate and synthesize information (*Standards of Learning Currently in Effect*, n.d.).

Mastering reading comprehension skills involving higher order cognitive processes is especially difficult for some struggling learners. Students who are described as slow learners or having mild mental retardation may not be able to master the more abstract aspects of reading comprehension. Students from economically disadvantaged homes or different cultures may not have the background knowledge that is used as the basis for thinking.

IMPORTANCE OF COGNITIVE PROCESSES FOR READING COMPREHENSION

Cognitive processes refer to the mental activities that individuals engage in when understanding and interpreting information and concepts. Lower order cognitive processes involve perception and basic understanding of concepts (e.g., you read the word *stop* on a stop sign while you are driving, understand its meaning, and stop your car). Higher order cognitive processes involve mental manipulation of ideas and concepts using various forms of thinking (e.g., you read the word *detour* on a sign while you are driving and infer that the detour may be caused by a recent flood that washed out the road). In addition to lower and higher order cognitive processes, there are also metacognitive processes, which individuals use to manage and control their cognitive activities and evaluate whether they are performing successfully (Gersten, Fuchs, & Williams, 2001). Instruction for reading comprehension must take into account developing all types of cognitive and metacognitive processing.

There are three types of reading comprehension skills that involve different types of cognitive processing: literal, inferential, and evaluative comprehension. Literal reading comprehension primarily requires lower order cognitive processes, such as identifying main ideas and details. Inferential reading comprehension (also called interpretive comprehension) involves higher order cognitive processes that deal with reasoning (e.g., comparing ideas, determining cause and effect) as well as metacognitive processes to manage and coordinate students' use of various cognitive processing. Evaluative reading comprehension (also called critical comprehension) involves higher order cognitive processes that deal with judgments (e.g., differentiating fact from fiction, evaluating the adequacy of an author's arguments) as well as metacognitive processing to evaluate whether the student is effectively using strategies to learn.

In the early stages of learning to read, literal comprehension is primarily involved in the reading process because children have not yet fully developed adequate higher order cognitive processes for inferential and evaluative comprehension. As children master higher order processing, they apply these to reading. There seems to be a reciprocal relationship between reading and higher order cognitive processing, much like the relationship between vocabulary and reading. Children first develop higher order cognitive processes based on life experiences and verbal interactions with others. They use these as the basis for inferential and evaluative comprehension when they learn to read. As their reading comprehension skills develop, they use these reading skills to further develop their higher order cognitive processes. In other words, higher order processing is necessary to learn to read at advanced levels, and reading at advanced levels results in improved higher order cognitive processing.

Literal reading comprehension refers to understanding the message being conveyed by the author. It does not require the reader to go beyond the meaning of the material. You must make sure that struggling students have basic understanding of material that they read before moving to instruction at the higher levels of inferential and evaluative reading comprehension.

Following is a list of specific literal comprehension skills and examples of teacher questions or commands eliciting such skills taken from *Social Studies in Virginia* (Teacher's Guide, 2003).

- Determining the main idea: "What were the Articles of Confederation?"

- Identifying details and facts: "How old was George Washington when he became President of the United States?"

- Identifying sequences involving space, time, and process: "What happened 14 years after John Mercer Langston's election?"

- Summarizing: Tell the students to examine the vertical time lines. Ask them to summarize the lesson by using these items or other facts from the lesson to complete the class KWL chart.

Inferential comprehension involves using reading material as the basis for reasoning. This type of comprehension involves higher order thinking processes associated with learning abstract academic content. Following is a list of inferential comprehension skills and examples of teacher questions eliciting such skills.

- Making associations: "What would you have done if you had been Robert E. Lee?"

- Comparing and contrasting: "How was the Ironclad different from other warships?"

- Defining and categorizing: "What are different types of mass media?"

- Determining causation: "Why did the states decide to keep more power than they gave to the national government?"

- Determining effects: "What do you think the people who left the Dust Bowl area found when they arrived in California?"

- Inferring: "Why do you think the author wrote this book? Who is telling the story?"

- Predicting: "We've read all the chapters except the last one, what do you think will happen at the end of the book?"

- Problem solving: "What problem did the Confederate navy face? What did they do to solve it?"

Evaluative comprehension requires students to make judgments concerning material they have read. Following is a list of evaluative comprehension skills and examples of teacher questions or commands for responses eliciting such skills.

- Differentiating fact from fiction: "Do you think time travel is possible? Why?"

- Differentiating fact from opinion: "What word did the author use that makes you think this sentence is his opinion and not a fact?"

- Differentiating fact from persuasion: "Are the arguments put forth by the author strong enough to convince you that we did the right thing when we took over the Panama Canal?"

- Evaluating using explicit criteria: "Do you think that Jean Valjean should be viewed as a criminal? Why?"

- Evaluating using unspecified criteria: "Did you like the poem? Why?"

The emergence of these three types of comprehension skills varies at each of the six stages of the reading process. At the pre-reading stage, children develop literal comprehension skills through verbal interactions and being read to orally; at the early reading stage, they develop literal reading comprehension, primarily for narrative text; at the fluency stage, they expand their literal comprehension to all types of texts and start to develop inferential and critical comprehension skills; at the reading to learn stage, they begin to develop strategies so that they can independently apply literal, inferential, and evaluative comprehension skills to all types of texts; and at the advanced reading stage, they expand the skills developed at the previous stage to reading in all content areas at the secondary and postsecondary levels.

GUIDELINES FOR DESIGNING INSTRUCTION FOR READING COMPREHENSION AND COGNITIVE PROCESSING

The nature of instruction for developing reading comprehension skills varies at each of the six stages of the reading process. Reading comprehension skills are best developed through teacher questioning using S.E.T. at the pre-reading, early reading, and fluency stages. There should be a gradual transition from teacher-directed questioning to student self-questioning at the reading to learn stage. Through scaffolding and explicit teaching of specific strategies, struggling students can learn to independently use literal, inferential, and evaluative comprehension skills by the advanced reading stage. Starting at the reading to learn stage, strategy instruction should become the primary means for teaching reading comprehension skills.

1. Plan your questions to elicit different types of cognitive processes from your students. The importance of teacher questioning in developing reading comprehension and cognitive processes cannot be overstated. Research and best practices have shown that teacher modeling of questioning is an effective means for guiding students to ask themselves questions (Gersten, Fuchs, & Williams, 2001). You must learn to become a good questioner and the first step is to always ask yourself what you want your students to do mentally in order to answer the question you are planning to ask. Then, you have to ask yourself how you can best frame a question using the reading material to elicit this response.

You must always consider whether you want to ask a question requiring a receptive response (e.g., multiple choice, true/false, yes/no) or an expressive response (e.g., an open-ended question). Whenever possible, ask an open-ended expressive question. When students have difficulty mastering a particular comprehension skill and cannot answer an open-ended question, lead them to discover the correct response using a question requiring a receptive response. You may want to emphasize questions requiring receptive responses for students with language problems (e.g., ELLs, students with language learning disabilities) to make sure that they understand the material without having their limited expressive language interfere with their oral response.

2. Use a strategy approach in which you teach your students to use steps to guide their comprehension of the reading material. There are strategies provided for each of the reading comprehension skills listed in this chapter. There are steps that the students are to follow to develop the cognitive processes for answering various reading comprehension questions. You are to clearly model each of these steps so that the students know what they have to do in order to use a strategy. Through repeated use of the steps, students will eventually recall their use.

3. Maximize engagement with your students, between your students, and between your students and the author. Extensive, planned verbal interactions between the students and you, each other, and the author lead to improved reading comprehension skills (Gambrell, Block, & Pressley, 2002). Use questions and discussions to actively engage your students. In addition, use classroom activities that allow your students to interact with each other (e.g., cooperative learning, peer tutoring). Finally, encourage your students to talk to the author (e.g., use a tape recorder, and have the students ask the author questions as if the author were present).

4. Use S.E.T. to guide the students to use the strategies independently. First, use S.E.T. to model a strategy using think-alouds. Then, scaffold instruction using guided practice in which the students use the strategy with prompts and support from you. Next, provide independent practice with no cuing or support from you. Finally, provide opportunities for generalization of the strategy in different settings and with different subject matter content.

Before teaching students a strategy, print the strategy shown in each of the displays in this book. Do *not* require students to memorize the steps in a strategy (except for test-taking strategies) because many students with language learning disabilities also have memory problems. Have them keep the strategies that they are learning in a notebook and also keep the strategies visible in the classroom using charts. Use S.E.T. to explain each step of the strategy. Through repeated use, the students will eventually recall how to use the steps.

When you model the use of a strategy, explain the purpose of the strategy and what each of the letters in the acronym in the title stands for (e.g., present the purpose for the RAP-Q strategy shown in Display 3: "The RAP-Q strategy is to help you understand what you read.") Then, explain that the **R** step stands for, "Read the paragraph or the section of the book that you are working on," the **A** step stands for, "Ask yourself what the main ideas are," the **P** step stands for, "Put the book words into your own words," and the **Q** step stands for "Questions about the reading." Model each step using the students' content area reading. For example, model RAP-Q using the first four paragraphs in the students' science book. Then, progress to the guided practice step by having the students apply the step to their content area reading. For example, have the students read the next four paragraphs using RAP-Q while you provide extensive supports, prompts, and cues. Gradually eliminate these as you move the students to independent practice. As they demonstrate mastery, provide opportunities for them to transfer use of the strategy. For ex-

RAP-Q (Display 3)

Purpose: To help me understand the main ideas of what I read

Read a paragraph or a section of material that you are working on.
- Do not read long sections because there may be too much material to consider at one time.

Ask yourself what the main ideas are.
- Try to find the sentences that give the most important ideas in the section that you read.

Put the book words in your own words.
- Paraphrasing is when you put material you read into your own words
- When you paraphrase the main ideas, make sure you try to think of other words to say the same thing as in the book.

Questions about the reading.
- Based on your paraphrasing of the main ideas, write a question on the front of a note card and the answer on the back so that you can use this for studying.
- Compare the note cards that you wrote for the main ideas of previous paragraphs or sections so that you can see how the ideas of one section are related to the next.

ample, if you have been working on use of RAP-Q with the students' science book, require them to apply the strategy to their history books. Evaluate whether they were able to do this so that you can determine whether they have reached the generalization stage and have complete mastery of the strategy. See Minskoff and Allsopp (2003) for a more detailed description of how to teach using S.E.T. and strategy instruction.

5. Make your instruction on thinking explicit and visible. There are two essential elements to teaching the higher order cognitive skills involved in inferential and evaluative comprehension: making thinking explicit and making thinking visible (Minskoff & Allsopp, 2003). You can make thinking explicit by using think-alouds to verbalize the mental processing of information. Thinking is a silent mental activity that is hard to teach so you must make it audible and visible. It is important to use graphic organizers, visualization, and multisensory instruction to visually show the thinking process.

6. Use the students' reading assignments as the content of the reading comprehension instruction. Most of the instruction on reading comprehension starting at the fluency stage should utilize the students' texts in their content area classes. Use of other types of material is not suggested because some students with reading comprehension difficulties have problems with transfer and generalization from nonessential reading material to reading material essential to their classes. In addition, use of other types of material channels instructional time away from working with the reading material that is needed for classroom assignments. This does not mean that you cannot use mini-lessons to develop certain types of comprehension skills; however, such mini-lessons should be secondary to the primary focus on use of classroom instructional materials. Use both narrative text from the students' English classes and expository text from their other classes. Use electronic text as required for their various classroom assignments.

TECHNIQUES FOR DEVELOPING LITERAL COMPREHENSION SKILLS

Literal comprehension skills, which should be developed starting at the pre-reading stage, entail understanding main ideas, details, sequences, and summarization. There must be questioning whenever students are read to orally to ensure that they understand the main ideas, details, and sequences. At the early reading stage, the literal comprehension skills students learned at the previous stage need to be applied to written material. Although the major emphasis at the early reading stage is on word decoding, attention also needs to be given to understanding the meaning of words the students have decoded as well as sentences and paragraphs including these newly learned words. Students must integrate word decoding skills with comprehension skills. At the early reading stage, literal comprehension skills should primarily be applied to narrative text. At the fluency stage, there should be increasingly more attention given to literal comprehension skills as well as expansion of comprehension instruction to expository and electronic text.

Summarizing should be introduced at the fluency stage. Summarizing is an essential reading comprehension skill because it involves selecting what is most important from a reading passage and committing that to memory storage. Summarizing can be compared with managing computer files; we save what we need for our work, and we recycle what we do not need. Recalling all information from a reading passage can result in overload and, consequently, limited or no retention of the reading material.

Teaching Main Ideas

When teaching students to extract the main ideas from their reading, always ask them to identify the most important ideas. Guide them in identifying and listing all the ideas in a reading passage. Then, review the list and guide them in identifying the difference between the main ideas and details. Ask them to evaluate the ideas based on whether they are needed for overall understanding or if they can be dropped without losing overall understanding.

You need to consider the amount of reading students are required to do relative to answering literal comprehension questions. If you wait to ask questions after students have read lengthy passages, then they may not be able to recall all the information or integrate it with other information. Ask literal comprehension questions at the actual reading phase of reading comprehension instruction. It may be necessary to intersperse questions after each sentence read by the students in the early stages of instruction. Gradually ask questions after several sentences, then one paragraph, and then several paragraphs. You may have to continue asking questions after every sentence or paragraph for students with memory problems.

At the read to learn stage, teach students to use strategies so that they can independently identify the main ideas of what they read. One of the major strategies that has been successfully used to teach students with learning disabilities to understand the main ideas and details of paragraphs and passages has been the RAP strategy (Schumaker, Denton, & Deshler, 1984) and an expansion of this—RAP-Q by Minskoff and Allsopp (2003). This strategy incorporates self-questioning and summarizing, both of which have been recognized as effective methods for building reading comprehension (Vaughn, Gersten, & Chard, 2000). The first step of this strategy has the students **r**ead **(R)** the passage, then **a**sk **(A)** themselves questions about what they have read, and finally **p**araphrase **(P)** the answer. Paraphrasing, in which the students restate the ideas using their own words, is needed to prevent students from parroting the author's words without understanding them. If they are using the reading material for studying purposes, then they are to write **q**uestions **(Q)** on one side of note cards and answers on the other sides. The RAP-Q strategy is shown on the Learning Toolbox web site (http://coe.jmu.edu/learningtoolbox), which can be used to show graphics and examples that help students apply RAP-Q.

Teaching Details

An approach that is effective for developing literal comprehension skills for details is to ask questions with the 5 W questions (who, what, where, when, why) and the 1 H question (how). You can ask these questions for orally read material at the pre-reading stage and expand use of these questions to student read material at the early reading stage. You are helping the students to focus their attention on all aspects of the reading material when you ask questions with these words.

Ask questions starting with these words at each of the three phases of the reading process. At the pre-reading phase, ask questions with appropriate question words to direct the students' attention to review details that will be relevant to the upcoming reading ("What did the children find in the cave?"). Or, ask questions about visual cues ("Who do you think the person looking in the window is?") or organizational features ("Why do you think the title of this chapter is the secret in the box?"). At the actual reading phase, ask questions with all question words relevant to the content.

At the post-reading phase, model how you can uncover the main ideas by exploring the relationships between the details identified through the question words. After writing the details based on questions with these words, identify the main ideas that connect all the details. This allows you to show the relationship between the details and the overarching main ideas. Also, use graphic organizers to visually depict relationships between details and main ideas. Put the main idea in the center of a large box and have each of the details radiate out into smaller boxes. Useful visual cues can also be provided by using color coding or different fonts for the main idea and details (e.g., all answers to *who* questions written in red; all answers to *when* questions written in blue).

Teachers often ask questions only at the post-reading phase when students read silently. This is not advisable for struggling learners because they may not have understood the details and main ideas. Use sticky notes to mark important points in the passage and use these to ask questions about material read silently at the actual reading phase. Have students read the questions to themselves and then write the answers, or say the answers to themselves, so that they can repeat them to you at a later time or record them on an audiotape. When you examine the students' answers, you can see where they had difficulty in the actual reading phase.

To make the transition from teacher-led questioning to student self-questioning, use sticky notes with questions along with question words and visual representations, or icons, for each the following question words.

- Who: the word *who* written under a silhouette of a person with a question mark

- What: the word *what* written under a silhouette of an action being performed, such as running, with a question mark

- Where: the word *where* written under a silhouette of the map of the United States with a question mark

- When: the word *when* written under a picture of a clock with a question mark

- Why: the word *why* written under a picture of light bulb with a question mark

- How: the word *how* written under a question mark

To gradually transition students to self-questioning, remove your written questions from the sticky notes, but keep the question words and icons as cues for the students. They can use these to create their own questions starting with the question word on the note. Then, eliminate the question words and just use the visual icons as cues for the students to self-question. Use S.E.T. to teach students to read passages and ask themselves questions with each of question words whenever they find a sticky note with the icon for a particular question.

At the reading to learn stage, transition from teacher-led questioning to students self-questioning using the Ask 5 W's & 1 H & Answer strategy (Minskoff & Allsopp, 2003; see Display 4), which is similar to other frequently used strategies involving question words (e.g., WH Questions Plus How by Bos & Vaughn, 2002). With this strategy, students are taught to ask themselves questions starting with the question words (who, what, where, when, why, and how). To ease students into independent self-questioning, phase out use of the question words and visual icons and have students just think of the 5 W and 1 H question words.

The first step tells the student to ask **(Ask)** questions to get details for each of the main ideas that they have identified in a reading passage. They are to ask themselves **who (W)** the characters in the reading were and to describe the relationships between them. Then, they are to ask **what (W)** events took place and the order. The third **W** refers to **w**here and has the student list all the places in the reading. Time factors are examined using the fourth **W** for **w**hen. The last **W** deals with **w**hy and has the students analyze causes of events in the reading. The **H** step involves examining **h**ow in terms of the relationship among the events in the passage. Finally, the students are to answer **(Answer)** the questions they asked. They are to integrate all the details and transfer them into an outline or graphic organizer. The Ask 5 W's & 1 H & Answer strategy is included in the Learning Toolbox web site (http://coe.jmu.edu/learningtoolbox) and includes helpful graphics and examples.

Teaching Sequencing

Sequencing is another important literal comprehension skill that must be systematically taught, first through explicit teacher questioning and then self-questioning by students. Teach your students to attend to three different types of sequences (time, spatial, and process) using graphic organizers. For time sequences, teach the students to create visual time lines or numbered lists to represent the time factors in a reading passage whether for events (1. Billy found the lost dog. 2. Billy wrote an ad about the dog. 3. Billy pinned the ad on trees in his neighborhood. 4. The owner called Billy. 5. The owner got his dog. 6. The owner paid Billy $10.) or specific dates (December 7, 1941, Japan bombs Pearl Harbor; December 8, 1941, the United States declares war on Japan; December 11, 1941, the United States declares war on Germany and Italy). Have the students explain the relationship between the events in each item to enhance their recall of the sequence (the United States declared war on Japan because of the surprise bombing of Pearl Harbor by Japan).

Ask 5 W'S & 1 H & Answer   (Display 4)

Purpose: To help me understand details of what I read

Ask detailed questions to go with the main ideas of what you read.
- For each of the main ideas that you have identified in a reading section, ask yourself questions starting with the 5 W's & 1 H question words.
- Not all of the question words will fit the information you read. Select the question words that fit the information.

Who?
- Identify and list the characters in the reading.
- Draw connecting lines between the characters as you describe to yourself the relationship between the characters.

What?
- Identify and list the event or actions in the reading.
- Draw connecting lines between the events or actions to show the relationship between them.
- Draw connecting lines between the characters and the events as you describe to yourself the relationship between them.

Where?
- Identify and list all the places in the reading.
- Draw connecting lines between the places, events, and characters as you describe to yourself the relationship among them.

When?
- Identify and list all the time factors in the reading.
- Draw connecting lines between the time factors, places, events, and characters as you describe to yourself the relationship among them.

Why?
- Identify and list causes for events or actions.
- Draw connecting lines from the causes to the effects of the characters, events, places, or times as you describe the relationship among them.

How?
- Identify and list the way events took place.
- Draw connecting lines between the way the events took place and other factors as you describe the relationship to yourself.

Answer the questions using an outline or graphic organizers.
- Review all the details you listed.
- Make an outline of the overall or main ideas, select details from your lists that are important, and write these under the main ideas. You do not have to include every detail that you identified. You may want to use different colored pens (or fonts if you are using a word processor), and write the main idea in one color (green), the *who* details in another color (red),

the *what* details in another (blue), and so forth. This helps you see the relationship between all the ideas. When you finish your outline, you should
have a complete picture of the overall ideas and how the details relate to
these.
- It might also be helpful to draw lines integrating all of the details.

When teaching students to understand spatial sequences, which involve
how things look (e.g., the location of the planets from the sun, the four time
zones in the continental U.S., the relationship between weather and distance
from the equator), have them visualize how information looks when they see it
shown in the reading material. Have them look at the material and then shut
their eyes and try to picture what they saw. Teach them to use self-talk to facilitate recall of the sequences (e.g., "The East Coast is on the right side of the
map, and the West Coast is on the left side. I know that New York is in the east-
ern time zone and that is later than the time in the rest of the country."). Using
color coding and other visual cues may also be helpful (e.g., coloring the countries nearest to the equator in red to represent hot climates), as well as having
the students draw what they saw.

Literal comprehension of sequences involving steps in a process (e.g., the
steps in the digestive process) is often difficult because of the complexity of the
steps and/or the large number of steps. To facilitate understanding and recall of
process sequences, have the students visualize diagrams that they saw in reading
material and/or create visual representations showing the relationship between
each step using arrows, numbers, and lines. Use think-alouds to expand on the
relationship between each step (e.g., "Digestion of food starts in the mouth
and then food is passed to the esophagus on the way to the stomach. . . .").

Use of mnemonics is also helpful. Teach students to create words or sentences using the first letter of the items in a sequence to be recalled. For example, to recall the parts of the digestive system (mouth, esophagus, stomach,
gall bladder, small intestine, large intestine, and rectum), have the students
create a sentence such as, "My eager sister got seven large rocks."

The 1st Stop strategy presented on the Learning Toolbox web site is designed to help students understand sequences when they read. Use the steps in
this strategy to guide them to analyze sequences whenever reading.

Teaching Summarizing

Instruction on summarizing is similar to instruction on identifying main ideas.
Students must evaluate what they have read to discover what information is
vital for understanding the overall meaning. With main ideas and summarizing,
the students must identify the big ideas, which has been identified as one of the
most important reading comprehension skills to be developed (Vaughn, Ger-

sten, & Chard, 2000). However, with summarizing, the most important details as well as the main ideas are identified. The following four rules are helpful for teaching students to produce summaries: 1) identify the main ideas, 2) delete trivial information, 3) delete redundant information, and 4) relate the main ideas and supporting information (Pressley et al., 1995).

Have students summarize after reading progressively longer material. First, have them summarize a paragraph, then two paragraphs, then a section, then a chapter, and then a book. Gradually increase the amount of information included in the summary. Initially, have students write a one-sentence summary, then a paragraph with the topic sentence stating the main idea, and then the body of the paragraph giving the important details. For longer material, have the students write the summary in outline form so that they can identify all the major ideas and the subordinate ideas under each. They can also write information on cards and do word sorts in which they match details with corresponding main ideas. Students can create graphic organizers to represent major and subordinate ideas. You can also use the RAP-Q strategy to teach summarizing. For lengthy information, they can also write summaries of summaries to identify only the most essential information.

TECHNIQUES FOR DEVELOPING INFERENTIAL COMPREHENSION SKILLS

Associations

Making associations based on the ideas in reading material is one of the easier types of inferential comprehension skills. This skill requires free association by the reader to various related ideas, and there is often no right answer. Students should first be taught personal associations, which requires them to put themselves in the situation they have read about ("What would you do if you were trapped in Japan during the war?"). These questions require the students to put themselves in the role of others to better understand the characters in the reading passage. Personal association questions should be used at all stages starting with the pre-reading stage when stories are read aloud to students.

Another type of association involves associating ideas in a reading passage to ideas in previously read material. Questions requiring students to make associations to other information from previous reading helps them to integrate information learned at different times and from different sources ("In what other book did we read about time travel?).

Comparing and Contrasting

Comparing and contrasting are among the most frequently required cognitive processes for analyzing information. Always ask for similarities and differences when framing questions for comparing and contrasting. Some students with cognitive limitations are concrete thinkers and have difficulty analyzing ideas in multiple ways (i.e., seeing both similarities and differences). Graphic organizers are helpful for demonstrating similarities and differences between ideas and concepts. Use strategies such as written lists with columns for similarities and differences, Venn drawings, and color coding with one color for similarities and another for differences.

Teach the LID strategy at the middle and high school levels of the advanced reading stage (Minskoff & Allsopp, 2003; see Display 5 or http://coe .jmu.edu/learningtoolbox). Students learn to first list **(L)** the items to be compared, **i**dentify the similarities and differences **(I)**, and **d**raw a graphic representation of the relationship **(D)**.

Defining and Categorizing

Defining words and concepts is one of the most basic reading comprehension skills students need to attain if they are to grow their vocabulary through reading. Using context is the most effective way of learning to define words. One

---

LID   (Display 5)

Purpose: To help me compare and contrast ideas

List the items to be compared.
- Make a list of the items to be compared.
- Write these items at the top of a column. For example, if for your science class you were comparing the three fresh water ecosystems, then you would have three columns—one for rivers and streams, another for ponds and lakes, and another for wetlands.

Identify the similarities and differences.
- Use a systematic approach to identify factors for comparing each of the items. These should be based on your readings and lecture notes.
- When making lists, write one factor on each line of the page. Then, go across the columns and ask yourself if this factor applies to the item in a particular column. If it does, then put a check in the column. If it does not, then leave the column blank.
- After you have constructed the listings, verbally describe the similarities and differences among the items to yourself.

Draw a graphic representation of the relationship of the times.
- If you are comparing two items, then draw a Venn diagram with two partially overlapping circles. Write the similarities of the two items in the overlapping part of the circles, and write the differences in the parts of the circles that do not overlap.
- Color coding when writing similarities and differences may be helpful.
- Write the similarities in one color and the differences in another.

---

of the most important elements of the pre-reading phase of teaching reading comprehension is teaching vocabulary that you know the students will not understand (see Chapter 8). When students meet words that they do not understand, they must be taught to systematically analyze context cues (see Chapter 9).

When teaching students to define words and concepts, teach them to analyze the three aspects of a comprehensive definition of a word (i.e., the category, the characteristics, and examples). The Frayer Model is a graphic organizer that includes these aspects by having the students analyze the essential and nonessential characteristics as well as examples and nonexamples (Buehl, 2001). See Figure 8 for an example of the Frayer Model and the definition of the word *vegetable*.

Categorizing is related to defining because a comprehensive definition of a word includes the category placement of the word. Categorization is one of the most frequently required cognitive processes needed for content area learning, especially science (e.g., types of rocks, types of clouds). Categorizing is an extremely important cognitive ability because it helps organize large amounts of complex facts and shows the relationship among the facts. It helps sift through information and extract the most important elements that are

FRAYER MODEL

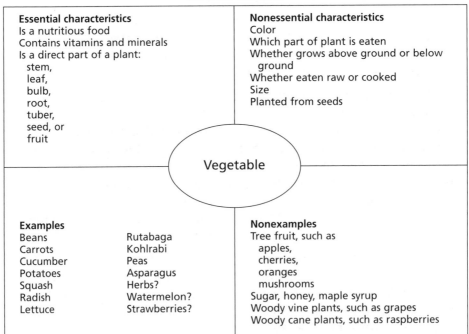

Essential characteristics
Is a nutritious food
Contains vitamins and minerals
Is a direct part of a plant:
    stem,
    leaf,
    bulb,
    root,
    tuber,
    seed, or
    fruit
	Nonessential characteristics
	Color
	Which part of plant is eaten
	Whether grows above ground or below
	    ground
	Whether eaten raw or cooked
	Size
	Planted from seeds

Vegetable	

Examples
Beans   Rutabaga
Carrots   Kohlrabi
Cucumber   Peas
Potatoes   Asparagus
Squash   Herbs?
Radish   Watermelon?
Lettuce   Strawberries?
	Nonexamples
	Tree fruit, such as
	    apples,
	    cherries,
	    oranges
	    mushrooms
	Sugar, honey, maple syrup
	Woody vine plants, such as grapes
	Woody cane plants, such as raspberries

Figure 8.   Example of the Frayer Model for the word *vegetable*. (From Buehl, D. [2001]. *Classroom strategies for interactive learning* [2nd ed., p. 57]. Newark, DE: International Reading Association; reprinted by permission.)

used to form a category. Categorizing is also related to the cognitive abilities of comparing and contrasting because it is necessary to identify similarities as the basis for forming a category and then differentiating the members of a category. Many students with limited cognitive processing skills get lost in the large amount of information in content area reading. You need to use S.E.T. to guide them in the process of giving structure to information by using categorization. Use explicit questions to teach your students to categorize according to the following steps.

1. Title of the category (e.g., biomes)

2. Identify the attribute that is shared by all category members (What is a biome?)

3. Name all category members (What are the six biomes?)

4. Identify what makes each category member different from the others (What is special about a rain forest biome?)

5. Use graphic organizers to represent the category and its members (write *biome* and its definition in a center circle, and then write the six biomes in circles radiating from the center circle along with their distinctive attributes)

Use the CANDY strategy at the middle and high school levels of the advanced stage of reading (Minskoff & Allsopp, 2003; see Display 6 or http://coe.jmu .edu/learningtoolbox) to teach your students to independently categorize content that they have read. This strategy helps students think using a top-down approach in which they start with a general category and then go down to think of specific members of the category. Students first identify the **c**ategory title **(C)**, identify the **a**ttributes shared by all members of the category **(A)**, **n**ame all category members **(N)**, **d**ifferentiate what makes each category member special **(D)**, and then are told that **y**ou can draw the categories **(Y)**.

Determining Cause and Effect

Understanding cause and effect involves seeing two aspects of a relationship. You need to start with an event (a hurricane) or a state (Matilda dislikes her father) and then use *why* questions to demonstrate what made this event or state occur ("Why are hurricanes found in warm climates?" or "What did Mr. Wormwood do to make Matilda dislike him?"). You need to write the event or state and then visually show the causation by using arrows pointing to the left to show causation. Guide the students in discovering that they are reasoning back to find causation.

To demonstrate the meaning of effect, you need to start with an event and show what results from this event using questions such as, "What will happen

CANDY (Display 6)

Purpose: To help me understand how information is organized into categories

Category title.
- Write the title of the category that you are studying. For example, if you are studying different categories of clouds in science class, then you might have to classify clouds on the basis of their altitude. You might write high clouds as the title of your first category, middle clouds for your second category, and low clouds for your third category.

Attribute of all category members.
- Ask yourself why members are grouped together in the category.
- Write down the factor all members have in common. For example, for the category of high clouds, you would write that these are clouds that have bases above 18,000 feet and are composed of ice crystals.

Name all category members.
- Use self-talk and say the different members that belong in the category.
- Write down all the members. For example, you might write cirrus, cirrocumulus, and cirrostratus for members of the high cloud category.

Differentiate the category members.
- Ask yourself how each of the members in the category differs from each other.
- Write a description of each category showing what is common to all members in the category and what is unique about each member. For example, you might describe cirrus as high clouds that have wispy, thin, curled-up ends and cirrocumulus as high clouds that are patchy or wavelike.

You can draw the categories.
- Make a graphic representation of the category title and members that belong in the category. Put the title of the category in the middle of a circle, and write the attribute that is common to all members of the category. Then, draw smaller circles with the names of the category members, and write what is special about them.

---

if we land men on Mars?" You need to write the event or state and then visually show the effects by using arrows pointing to the right to show you are inferring effects. Guide the students in discovering that they are reasoning forward to infer effects.

Students need to be taught to identify both single and multiple causes as well as single and multiple effects. Both require different cognitive processes—single causation leads to one generally accepted cause or effect, and multiple causation leads to numerous alternatives, many of which may be correct.

It is very important to use graphic organizers to show the direction of the reasoning to determine cause and effect. Use arrows to show the direction of the thinking and boxes to show one versus multiple causes or effects.

Cause-and-effect relationships may be stated explicitly in the reading material or they may be inferred based on the reading material. When cause and effect are stated, there are usually certain right answers, but when they are inferred, there may be several right answers.

Determining cause and effect is especially important for prediction questions in the pre-reading phase of reading comprehension instruction. Students should predict the causes or effects in a reading passage based on previous reading, discussions, or picture cues (e.g., "Why do you think this chapter is called 'The One Who Survived?' What do you think will happen to Max in this chapter?")

Use the IFF-C strategy, which is based on the IFF-2 strategy (Minskoff & Allsopp, 2003), to teach students to independently determine causation for material that they read (see Display 7 or http://coe.jmu.edu/learningtoolbox). Students first identify **(I)** the event, find one possible cause **(F),** then find if there is more than one possible cause **(F),** and apply this to causation **(C).**

Identifying effects or making inferences is similar to identifying causation but involves reasoning forward from the event rather than backward from the event. The IFF-E strategy is based on the IFF-2 strategy (Minskoff & Allsopp, 2003) and is similar to the IFF-C strategy but involves identifying effects **(E)** rather than causation (see Display 8).

Inferring

Inferring involves using educated guessing to come to conclusions based on incomplete information. This cognitive skill is especially important when readers interact with the author. For example, when readers ask, "Why did the author write this book?" or "Who is telling the story?" they are making inferences. They cannot ask the author why he or she wrote the book but can only infer why. The narrator is not known in many stories, and readers must infer who it is.

Developing students' ability to make inferences can be started at the pre-reading stage. Use riddles and guessing games to have the students learn to use incomplete information to arrive at a conclusion. Also, read stories, and have the children make inferences based on part of the story and then confirm whether their inferences (or guesses) were supported. This same approach can be used as students read material at the early reading and fluency stages.

Predicting

As we read, we constantly predict what ideas and concepts will come next. We read with an anticipatory set (i.e., based on what we read, we have expectations

IFF-C   (Display 7)

Purpose: To help me find causes

Identify an event.
- Clearly identify the event for which you want to find the cause or causes.
- Write this down so that you are clear about the starting point of your thinking process. For example, you might want to find the cause or causes of avalanches and landslides.

Find one cause.
- Some events have only one cause. Ask yourself if this event fits this category.
- Use self-talk or visual aids to demonstrate to yourself the cause and effect relationship.
- One way to show causation is to write the event and then draw an arrow to the left of the event and write the cause. This will show that you are reasoning backward to find the cause of the event. For example, when identifying the cause of avalanches and landslides, you might say to yourself that substances such as water, ice, and sand overcome friction by making the underlying surface slippery and providing a cushion that snow or rock can move over. This movement is called an avalanche or landslide. Try to visualize in your mind's eye the actions that take place.

Find other causes.
- Some events have more than one cause. Ask yourself if this event fits this category.
- Use self-talk or visual aids to demonstrate to yourself the cause and effect relationship.
- One way to show multiple causation is to write the event and then make a list of all the possible causes to the left of the event. Draw an arrow from the event back to each of the causes to show that your are reasoning backward. For example, if you are studying the Salem witch trials, then you may have learned that there are four major reasons for the trials. You would write the event of the witch trials and then draw arrows to the left to show each of the four reasons.

for what is to come). When these expectations are not met, we either are surprised or we wonder if we have misinterpreted the material. We may go back and re-read a passage to see if we have read it correctly. If we did, then we may revise our interpretation of what we have read.

Prediction is an important skill at the pre-reading phase of reading comprehension instruction. Prediction questions are asked about what will be read based on what has already been read. Prediction is also important at the actual reading phase. As students read, we need to teach them a strategy in

IFF-E   (Display 8)

Purpose: To help me find effects

Identify an event.
- Clearly identify the event for which you want to find the effect or effects.
- Write this down so that you are clear about the starting point of your thinking process.

Find one effect.
- Some events have only one effect. Ask yourself if this event fits this category.
- Use self-talk or visual aids to clearly demonstrate to yourself the nature of the cause and effect relationship.
- One way to show effect is to write down the event and then draw an arrow to the right of the event and write the effect. This will show that you are reasoning forward to project the effect of the event. For example, if you are studying the effects of drinking and driving, then you find that alcohol affects the nervous system by slowing it down.

Find other effects.
- Some events have multiple effects. Ask yourself if this event fits into this category.
- Use self-talk and visual aids to clearly demonstrate to yourself the nature of the cause and effect relationship. Think about why all the effects are likely and why one or a few might not be sufficient to explain the relationship.
- One way to show multiple effects is to write the event and then make a list of all the possible effects of the event to the right. Draw an arrow from the event forward to each of the effects listed to show that you are reasoning forward to project multiple effects. For example, if you are studying the inner body effects of smoking, then you might have read that there are six effects. Draw this and say this aloud to yourself, "There are six effects of smoking on the inner body. These are shortness of breath, coughing, dizziness, cancer, heart disease, and lung problems."

which they predict by constantly asking themselves the question, "What's next?" Then, they can predict the content that they think will come next. They need to use this strategy at the sentence level, paragraph level, and chapter level.

Problem Solving

Problem solving has long been recognized as one of the most important cognitive processes for mastering academic content and solving everyday life problems. The following steps have been used by Minskoff (1994) and Bos and

Vaughn (2002) to teach students to solve social problems; Deshler, Ellis, and Lenz (1996) for academic purposes; and Beyer (1997) and Minskoff and Allsopp (2003) to teach thinking. The steps involved in problem solving require the integration of different literal, inferential, and evaluative comprehension skills. The following are the steps in problem solving and the type of comprehension skills required.

- Identify the problem—requires literal comprehension skill of understanding the main idea

- Project all possible solutions to the problem—requires inferential comprehension skill of projecting effects or consequences

- Evaluate the consequences of the various solutions—requires evaluative comprehension skill of evaluating using a specific criterion (i.e., how effectively was the problem solved based on the projected solutions)

- Put the solution into action—requires inferential comprehension skill of determining cause and effect (i.e., did the solution work)

- Evaluate whether the solution used solved the problem—requires evaluative comprehension

Using explicit teaching of the problem-solving steps as applied to reading should be initiated at the secondary level and continue through the post-secondary levels of the advanced reading stage because of the various higher order cognitive skills required. Use this process to teach students to understand how problems have been solved by others (e.g., how Truman solved the problem of ending the war with the Japanese by dropping the atom bomb) and by having them solve problems identified in their reading material (e.g., how to achieve adequate oil supplies without destroying the environment). Teach the problem-solving steps, one or a few steps at a time, starting with the last steps. For example, first teach students to evaluate whether a problem was solved (e.g., "Did World War II end because Truman dropped the bomb?"). Go through all the steps and model the thinking used at each step.

Teaching students to independently apply problem-solving skills can be accomplished with the SOLVED strategy (Minskoff & Allsopp, 2003; see Display 9 or http://coe.jmu.edu/learningtoolbox). Each of the six steps in this strategy encompasses complex thinking skills and needs to involve different graphic organizers. Because of the complexity of each of the steps, it is important to provide explicit modeling at each step.

The first step of SOLVED has the students set out the problem that they read about **(S).** This requires literal comprehension of all aspects of the problem, so ask main ideas questions to make sure that the students recognize the exact problem. The second step has the students outline **(O)** all possible solutions

SOLVED   (Display 9)

Purpose: To help me with problem solving

Set out the problem
- Identify the problem to be solved.
- Say it in your own words.
- Write it down so you are sure that you understand it. For example, if the problem is how to solve the gasoline crisis, then write "What are all the ways that the gasoline shortage can be solved?"

Outline all possible solutions.
- Brainstorm all the ways that the problem might be solved.
- Do not reject any solution at this step.
- Construct a graphic organizer with the problem written in a circle and all the possible solutions written in circles that come out of the center circle. For example, for the gasoline shortage, the following solutions might be projected:
  Conservation
  Alternate fuels
  Electric cars
  Unlimited exploration of oil in the United States
  Unlimited exploration of oil throughout the world
  More fuel-efficient cars
  More public transportation

List the consequences of each of the solutions that were outlined.
- Think of what will be the likely effect of each solution. Think of the solution as a cause and the consequence as the effect.
- Create a graphic organizer for each solution in which the solution is written in the center circle and the consequences for it are written in circles that project from the center circle. For example, for the consequences of unlimited exploration of oil in the United States, the following consequences might be projected:
  Might result in ecological problems
  Might not be limitless reserves of oil

View the ranking.
- On the basis of the consequences you projected, rank the solutions in terms of what will work with the fewest negative consequences.
- View the rankings and select the highest-ranked solution (or solutions) as the choice to be put into action. There may be no one best solution but several solutions that have to be considered together. For the previous example, you might rank the possible solutions in the following order based on the ease with which they could be put into effect and with the least resistance from the public:

(continued)

Display 9. *(continued)*

> More fuel-efficient cars
> More public transportation
> Conservation
> Alternate fuels
> Electric cars
> Unlimited exploration of oil in the United States
> Unlimited exploration of oil throughout the world

Execute the solution.
- The highest-ranked solution (or solutions) should be put into action.
- Think of all the things that would have to be done to make the solution work.
- Make a list of these. To execute the previous example, the list of actions that would have to be taken might include getting car manufacturers to increase fuel efficiency, getting governments to allocate more money for public transportation, getting the public to change its opinion toward use of public transportation, and so forth.

Did it work?
- If you put the solution into action, then evaluate it to see if it worked. If you did not, then go back and view the other possible solutions and consider which should be tried.
- If it is not possible to put the solution into action, then list questions that need to be answered to determine if the solutions worked. For example, you might ask:
  > Do people use more public transportation if more options are provided?
  > Would auto manufacturers willingly increase fuel efficiency?
  > Who would pay for production of alternate forms of fuel?
- In some cases, you will need to go back and start the problem-solving process again to search for the best solutions to the problem.

---

followed by the next step in which they list the consequences **(L).** Then, they view **(V)** the rankings of what will work best, execute the solution **(E),** and ask themselves **d**id it work **(D).**

TECHNIQUES FOR DEVELOPING EVALUATIVE COMPREHENSION SKILLS

Evaluative comprehension, also called critical reading, involves use of judgments regarding the quality of the information that has been read (Bos & Vaughn, 2002). This type of comprehension requires students to actively engage in self-talk with the author about the content of the reading material. Students ask themselves questions based on whether the reading material is fact or fiction, whether the material states fact or opinion, whether the purpose of the material is to inform or to persuade, and value judgments concerning the material. Carnine et al. (2004) suggested that critical reading is perhaps the most important of all comprehension skills because it is related to the critical thinking that is needed for success in everyday life. Critical comprehension and the related critical thinking skills that are developed are needed for students to become knowledgeable consumers as they negotiate the bombardment of advertisements in all aspects of life and to become educated citizens as they critically analyze political and historical interpretations presented in the media.

The following five areas of evaluative comprehension should be systematically taught.

1. Differentiating fact from fiction

2. Differentiating fact from opinion

3. Differentiating fact from persuasion

4. Evaluating information based on explicit criteria

5. Evaluating information based on unspecified criteria.

There is limited attention to evaluative comprehension skill development in the early grades. But, this area is given greater emphasis as students progress through the stages of learning to read. Evaluative comprehension, especially differentiating fact from opinion and persuasion, is of major importance at the advanced reading stage.

Differentiating Fact from Fiction

There are two aspects to differentiating fact from fiction. One involves judging whether information is true (e.g., fact from fiction), and the other involves judging whether information could be true (e.g., reality from fantasy). When reading fiction with your students, be sure to have them differentiate facts that are true (e.g., the setting of Chicago is a real city) versus facts that may or may not be true (e.g., the main character of the book, Max Smith, was not an actual person). When reading fantasy with students, teach them to differentiate what is reality (e.g., we can fly in airplanes) versus fantasy (e.g., we cannot fly in spaceships to Venus).

Many, if not most, students enjoy fantasy narrative text starting with fairy tales at the early age levels to science fiction and fantasy materials at the higher levels (e.g., *The Lord of the Rings* [Tolkien, 2001]). Instruction for this area needs to focus on teaching students to ask themselves, "Is this real?" And, if they answer no, then they need to ask themselves, "Why isn't this real?" Model asking such questions and gradually move to having the students ask themselves these questions subvocally. For example, when reading *Harry Potter and the Sorcerer's Stone* (Rowling, 1997), ask whether Quidditch is a real sport and why or why not. To broaden the understanding of the material, ask association questions in which the students put themselves into the story content (e.g., "Would you try to walk through a wall like Harry did at the station?"). Developing comprehension skills using fantasy materials should be tied to creative activities involving re-enactments, drawings, and original writing. Also, use of visualization is effective for picturing fantasy materials.

Differentiating Fact from Opinion

Students must be taught to ask themselves, "Is this a fact, or is this the author's opinion?" and then ask, "Why?" You need to model using mini-lessons in which factual information is presented and then the same information is presented with added words or statements that reflect the author's opinion. Focus on teaching students to attend to "loaded" words that subtly express the author's views. For example, lead the student to differentiate between the following two sentences based on the word *unfortunately*: "General Custer was defeated by the Indians at the battle of Little Big Horn" versus "Unfortunately, General Custer was defeated by the Indians at the battle of Little Big Horn." When developing skills in evaluative comprehension, train the students to ask themselves about the purpose of the material (i.e., "Why did the author write this?"). Identifying the author's purpose will help students identify if the author's opinion is being conveyed. They also need to ask themselves if the author is biased in the presentation of the material and if so, why.

Differentiating Fact from Persuasion

Learning to differentiate material that is meant to educate versus material that is meant to persuade is important for dealing with the advertisements that bombard us in everyday life, especially on the Internet. The purpose of advertising is to persuade. Becoming a knowledgeable consumer in our society means learning to discern how facts are presented. Functional content (e.g., advertisements in magazines) and electronic material (e.g., pop-up ads, web sites) should be the focus of instruction for this area. Channel the students' attention to words that are meant to sway the readers' views. For example, in an advertisement about hair spray that reads, "This will lead to a sexier you," point out how the word *sexier* is persuasive. The role of persuasion in political advertisements and reading material should be tied to instruction in social studies. Students need to learn to approach politically based material with an open mind so that they can make informed decisions. They can best do this if they know how to differentiate informational versus persuasive writing, which involves analysis of the trustworthiness of the information. They need to critically look at the sources on which the facts and conclusions are based.

Evaluating Information Based on Explicit Criteria

Students are taught to evaluate reading material based on explicit criteria (e.g., "Was it fair?"), which can involve the criterion of right and wrong (e.g., "Was it right for Jean Valjean to steal?"). Evaluating reading material using this criterion has been integrated with character education in which students are taught moral values of the culture (e.g., stealing is wrong, honesty is right).

Evaluating Information Based on Unspecified Criteria

Students are asked to judge information by imposing their own criterion when they evaluate information based on unspecified criteria. The most common type of question is whether the students liked the reading material and why (e.g. "Did you like the book? Why?"). When asking questions, always use a follow-up question to find out the criterion that the students used to make their decisions. This type of evaluative comprehension question is most frequently used starting at the pre-reading stage.

TECHNIQUES FOR DEVELOPING METACOGNITIVE SKILLS TO MONITOR READING PERFORMANCE

We must develop struggling students' ability to monitor their performance to make them competent readers. They must manage the cognitive processes they are using to read and evaluate whether they are doing so successfully. Obviously, this is an exceedingly difficult skill to develop, but it can be learned with repeated use of a strategy such as SENSE (see Display 10). This strategy is designed to help students to monitor for consistency as they read by analyzing sentences and paragraphs. Although this is a tedious process, it is the only way that certain struggling students can develop these metacognitive skills.

For the **S** step, students read a **s**entence aloud. At the **E** step, they **e**valuate whether the different parts of the sentence make sense. **N**ext, they analyze each of the sentences in a paragraph (**N**). For the **S** step, they see if the sentences in the paragraph make **s**ense in relationship to each other. For the final **E** step, they **e**valuate whether each paragraph they read makes sense in relationship to previously read paragraphs. When they find a sentence or paragraph that does not make sense, they need to use look-backs to try to find out why.

SENSE   (Display 10)

Purpose: To help me tell if the sentences and paragraphs I read make sense

Start with the first sentence and read it aloud.

Evaluate whether the different parts of the sentence make sense by chunking the sentence into smaller sentences and asking yourself if all these make sense.

Next, look at each of the sentences in the paragraph. Read each sentence one at a time.

See if the sentences make sense in relationship to each other.

Evaluate whether each paragraph makes sense in relationship to the earlier paragraphs. If not, go back and re-read to find out why.

11

Teaching Reading Comprehension with Different Text Structures

CONCEPTS EXPLORED

- Reading demands of different text structures

- Techniques for teaching comprehension of narrative text

- Techniques for teaching comprehension of expository text

- Techniques for teaching comprehension of electronic text

READING DEMANDS OF DIFFERENT TEXT STRUCTURES

In Chapters 9 and 10, the language and cognitive processing demands on reading comprehension were considered. This chapter describes the third factor in planning reading comprehension instruction—the structure of the text, or how the text is written. Texts are organized in different ways and require that readers use different language and cognitive processes based on the organizational features of the material. There are three different types of text structures: narrative, expository, and electronic. Narrative text tells a story and is usually organized around understanding of characters and plot. This type of text is used at the pre-reading and early reading stages of learning to read. In the past, most reading comprehension instruction used this type of text, but it has become apparent that students need to learn to understand the type of text that is used in content area classes (Alvermann & Phelps, 2002). Consequently, there has been considerable attention to teaching students to meet the demands of expository text, which includes informational materials, such as content area textbooks, manuals and written directions, and functional or everyday reading materials. Comprehension of expository text becomes most important at the reading to learn stage as well as subsequent stages. Expository text is considered more difficult than narrative text for the following reasons (Westby, 1999):

- The purpose of narrative is to entertain, the purpose of expository is to inform.

- Narrative content is familiar, expository content is not.

- Narrative has a consistent text structure, expository has a variable text structure.

- Narrative text can stand alone, expository text must be integrated with other information.

- Narrative focuses on character, motivation, and so forth, expository focuses on abstract ideas.

Attention has shifted to a third type of text that students are required to read—electronic text (Coiro, 2003), which includes understanding how to negotiate the reading demands of the Internet, such as conducting web searches and reading web sites. Instruction on electronic literacy should begin at the reading to learn stage and continue through the remaining stages.

Students need to be taught to use different strategies to meet the unique demands of each type of text structure. Students need to learn how to analyze the structure of a story (called *the story grammar*) to understand narrative text. This analysis focuses on the characters, setting, action, and problems raised in the story. Students need to learn how to understand the organization of expository text. They need to determine what is important by looking at features such as bold-faced print and the sequence needed to track the presentation of the material. Expository text makes changing demands for many types of higher level cognitive processes, so students must be able to quickly bring forth the cognitive process needed. Electronic text makes unique demands on the reader because it is nonlinear (i.e., information is not presented in a line-by-line manner; Hites & Schrank, 2001a). Rather, the reader must view different spatial presentations of material, such as web sites with nonsequential boxes, and decide which order to read different bits of information. In addition, students must use critical thinking skills to evaluate the information presented.

In a review of studies on reading comprehension, it was found that readers who did not know how to analyze text structures did not have a plan of action when they read, and, consequently, they recalled information randomly. Strategy instruction and modeling were found to be effective in teaching such students how to improve their comprehension of both narrative and expository text (Gersten, Fuchs, & Williams, 2001). There has been little research on training for comprehension of electronic text because it is so new.

TECHNIQUES FOR TEACHING COMPREHENSION OF NARRATIVE TEXT

Narrative text includes stories, poetry, and drama. In this book, attention is only focused on strategies for comprehension of stories because these constitute the overwhelming majority of narrative text structures that students have to read. However, both drama and poetry are important for appreciation of literature and for meeting the language arts demands of the schools and should be included in an overall instructional program for comprehension of narrative text structures.

Narrative text is the easiest of the three types of text structures: It is more familiar to students because they start hearing stories at an early age. From hearing stories read aloud, young children become familiar with the structure of stories: there are main characters who are confronted with problems that are resolved, usually happily. Read stories to your students at the pre-reading stage so that they become familiar with narrative text structure. Use two types of narrative text at the early reading stage: high-interest stories and controlled readers. Continue to read aloud high-interest stories, but also use controlled readers with stories that require students to transfer their mastery of word identification from words in isolation to these words embedded in text. Many of the stories using these words are uninteresting by virtue of the limitations of the words usually learned at the entry levels of reading (e.g., sight words, decodable CVC words). As students gain mastery of word identification, gradually have them read high-interest children's literature.

All children, including those who are struggling, want to read books that are interesting. To many children, reading does not mean reading isolated words; reading means reading books that all children read. Most children feel great pride when they graduate from reading short books to longer, chapter books. Successful reading of these books is the greatest source of motivation for children to continue working on improving their reading. When students successfully read books such as *Harry Potter and the Sorcerer's Stone* (Rowling, 1997), *Matilda* (Dahl, 1990), or *Tales of a Fourth Grade Nothing* (Blume, 2003), they enter the exciting world of children's culture.

Use all types, or genres, of text including fantasy, science fiction, historical fiction, and multicultural when providing instruction using narrative text. Select books from lists of books that have been identified as "good" books for children at different age levels, such as those on the Newbery List (http://www .ala.org/alsc/newbery.html). Also, select reading material in which students have special interests. For example, if a student is interested in baseball, then select reading material about the lives of popular baseball players. Also, use books that are of special interest to groups of struggling students. Use a book such as *Leo the Late Bloomer* (Kraus, 1971) for young students with reading disabilities, *Freak the Mighty* (Philbrick, 1993) for older students with reading disabilities, *The Rainbow Tulip* (Mora, 1999) for students from Hispanic backgrounds, and *Whoever You Are* (Fox, 1997) for students from foreign backgrounds.

Consider both the students' interests and reading levels when selecting reading materials. If you are unsure of a story's reading level, then use a readability formula, such as the Fry formula (see Appendix G). Give students choices when it is time to select a book to read so that they have a sense of ownership in their instructional program.

Most strategies on training students to understand narrative text focus on helping them understand the structure, or story grammar, using graphic organizers. The SPORE strategy (Minskoff & Allsopp, 2003; see Display 11) visually shows the steps in analyzing narrative text. It is similar to the STORE strategy developed by Bos (Bos & Vaughn, 2002). Have the students complete a story map with the title of the book (or chapter title) in the center, and have a circle for the **s**etting **(S)**, another for the **p**roblem **(P)**, another for the **o**rder of actions **(O)**, a fourth for the **r**esolution **(R)**, and the last circle for the **e**nd **(E)**. Examples of how the story map for SPORE should look can be found at the Learning Toolbox web site (http://www.coe.jmu.edu/learningtoolbox).

Graphic organizers can be used to emphasize different aspects of the story structure. For example, draw a center box containing the title of the book and then three boxes radiating out from the center box—one to describe the beginning of the story, another for the middle of the story, and a third for the end of the story. A detailed map can also be made to describe main characters. The character's name can be placed in a center circle and lines can radiate out to smaller circles, which contain information about the character.

There is often a strong demand for students' use of figurative language when working with narrative text because it may contain similes, metaphors,

SPORE   (Display 11)

Purpose: To help me understand stories that I read

Setting
- Make a story web with the center circle containing the name of the story or chapter of the story that was read.
- Make five circles radiating from this center circle. Each of these five circles should contain one of the parts of the SPORE strategy. Just write a word or phrase in each circle. Do not use complete sentences.
- Put the information on the setting in one circle. Write the word *setting* at the top.
- Identify the setting in terms of who (people), what (animals), where (places), and when (times) in the story.
- Write a full description of who, what, where, and when by creating additional circles or boxes and filling in as much detail as possible.

Problem
- Identify the major problems in the story or chapter.
- Analyze the who, what, where, and when in relation to the problem.
- Write words or phrases in the circle to represent the problem.

Order of action
- In this circle, write all of the events that occurred.
- Number the events in the order they occurred.

Resolution
- In this circle, write how the problems were solved.

Ending
- In this circle, identify how the story was wrapped up and what happened to the different characters.
- Review the story web and re-read what you have written in each of the circles so that you can get the overall picture of what was included in the story.

---

puns, and idioms. Whenever possible, pre-teach examples of figurative language contained in material prior to reading it so that the students can understand it when they meet it in context. This is especially important for ELLs.

It is important to have students make different responses to demonstrate their understanding of narrative text. Examples of recommended responses include

- Readers theatre (you and/or the students write a script to enact the story content, and then the students read the script enacting the story content)

- Individual or group drawings of the story content (e.g., murals)

- Book reviews
- Pantomimes of actions of the characters
- Matching photos from a photo book with story content
- Writing activities (e.g., rewriting the end of a book)

TECHNIQUES FOR TEACHING COMPREHENSION OF EXPOSITORY TEXT

Expository text presents information. The major type of expository text that this book focuses on is textbooks. However, it is important to also teach understanding of manuals and directions if they are used in students' courses (e.g., a manual on how to use a piece of equipment in a vocational course on carpentry). For older students who have not attained a high degree of literacy, emphasis should be on reading of functional materials, such as want ads, job application forms, and medicine labels. Students needing instruction on functional skills are frequently in special education classrooms where they are receiving instruction in functional and vocational skills.

There are three types of strategies needed to develop mastery of reading comprehension of textbooks. One type of strategy involves teaching students to preview the material before reading it. The second type is to integrate reading comprehension with study skill strategies. The final type is to make students aware of the thinking process that they have to use to understand the material they read in their textbooks.

Previewing

When many struggling students approach content area textbooks, they do not have a plan. They just start reading and become overwhelmed with the information. These students must be taught how to preview whenever they read a textbook. They need to discover the features of the external text structure of the book (Vacca & Vacca, 2002), which includes overall features of the book (e.g., preface, table of contents, bibliography, glossary) as well as features related to each chapter (e.g., key vocabulary, side headings, graphs, charts, guide questions). Before students start using a textbook, they need to have the external structure of the book explained. They also need knowledge of the overall format of the book as a guide to seeing the "whole picture" of what will be taught in the course. The Chapter Tour strategy guides students through a preview of the major parts of the chapter (Buehl, 2001) as they look at the title, advanced organizers including new vocabulary or concepts, side headings, paragraph headings, bold-faced words, ending questions, and visuals.

Previewing and Study Skills

The PASTE strategy (Minskoff & Allsopp, 2003; see Display 12) is a more in-depth strategy to develop students' ability to preview material and organize

PASTE   (Display 12)

Purpose: To help me read better using aids

Preview the text before reading.
- Always look over the pages you have to read before you start reading.
- Focus on headings and subheadings.
- Also, focus on words that are in bold face or have definitions in parentheses.

Always take notes on main ideas.
- Write down the main ideas and important facts on note cards so that you can study these in the future.

Save time by analyzing unknown words.
- If you do not know the meaning of a word, then try to figure it out using context clues. If this does not work, then look it up in the glossary or a dictionary.
- If you think this is an important word, then write it on the front of a note card and its definition on the back.

Try to highlight important information.
- If you own the book you are using, then highlight the important ideas. If you find highlighting helpful for understanding a book and the book is not your property, then photocopy the pages and highlight them.
- If you do not own the book and have taken notes on what you have read, then highlight the important ideas in your notes.
- *Never highlight everything.* The idea behind highlighting is to identify the most important information. If you highlight everything, then you will not be able to pick out the most important information.

Examine ideas for relationships.
- As you read, try to think about the "big picture." Try to figure out how the information you are reading is related to other information on this topic.
- Try to think about what you have read before on this topic.
- Use graphic organizes to help you show these relationships. For example, if this chapter contains causes for events described in previous chapters, then use cause and effect graphic organizes with arrows going from the causes to the effects.

what they read so that they can study the material and have it readily accessible for testing purposes. Students first **p**review the text **(P)**, **a**lways take notes on main ideas **(A)**, **s**ave time by analyzing unknown words **(S)**, **t**ry to highlight important information **(T)**, and **e**xamine ideas for relationships **(E)**. Examples of the PASTE strategy with accompanying graphics can be found on the Learning Toolbox web site (http://www.coe.jmu.edu/learningtoolbox).

Thinking Processes

In addition to external text structure, students must be taught to analyze the internal text structure of expository material (i.e., various ways used by the author to present information). According to Vacca and Vacca (2002), there are five major internal text structures: 1) description, 2) sequence, 3) comparison and contrast, 4) cause and effect, and 5) problem solving. These five internal text structures are discussed in relationship to literal and inferential questions in Chapter 10. What is so difficult about teaching students to analyze these text structures is that a passage may switch from one type of thinking process to another, often from sentence to sentence. For example, in the following paragraph from the social studies textbook, *The Americas: A History* (Jordan, Greenblanc, & Bowes, 1991), the first sentence presents a description, the second a comparison, and the last a sequence. Students must be cognitively flexible to go from one type of internal structure to another to process the densely packed information.

> The plan provided for a bicameral, or two-house, legislature [*description*]. Instead of the previous unworkable one-state one-vote arrangement, membership in both houses would be allotted among the states according to their free population [*comparison*]. Members of the lower house would be elected by the voters. The lower house in turn would elect members of the upper house. Both houses would then vote for a national executive and national judiciary [*sequence*]. (p. 146)

Students must first have the cognitive processes necessary to understand description, sequences, comparisons, cause and effect, and problem solving. Once they have mastered these processes (developed through inferential comprehension questioning), they need to know when to apply them. They need to ask themselves, "What kind of information is the author presenting—description, sequence, comparison, causation, or problem solving?" They also need to be cognitively flexible so that they can go from one process to another.

TECHNIQUES FOR TEACHING COMPREHENSION OF ELECTRONIC TEXT

Electronic text encompasses a variety of materials and activities read on a computer screen, including electronic textbooks (e-texts), electronic books (e-books), web sites, e-mail, and web searches. Publishers are producing more and more textbooks electronically ("Electronic Textbook Pilot a Success for Florida Public Schools," 2004), and more books are available electronically through web sites such as Project Gutenberg (http://www.gutenberg.net). A popular teaching technique using electronic text is the web quest, which is an inquiry-oriented activity in which information is gathered from the Internet by students doing specific projects (Dodge, n.d.).

Electronic text can be written in linear form, such as conventional reading material, but most frequently, it is written in hypertext, which has been defined as a large set of parallel texts with many possible strategic movements among them (Topping, n.d.). Hypertext includes nodes, or units of information, that are connected by links (Hites & Shrank, 2001a). Coiro (2003) described electronic text as having three essential features: it is nonlinear, interactive, and includes multimedia forms.

Electronic text can be differentiated from narrative and expository text on the following features.

- It is nonlinear, or nonsequential, and, unlike linear text, can be read in any order. Narrative and expository text structures are linear and must be read in order.

- It is interactive. Readers decide what to read and where to go. The authors of narrative and expository text decide what has to be read and readers follow along line by line. With electronic text, readers are given options as to what to read and decide whether to read certain links.

- Hypertext often includes accompanying multimedia (e.g., icons, photos, audiotapes, videotapes, animation). This requires readers to integrate information from these various forms of media with the information gathered from reading the text.

- Hypertext is decontextualized (i.e., it is often read with no background information). There are times when we do web searches and have no idea where the information came from or who wrote it. It is easy to get lost in hyperspace and not get the big picture (Saltzman, n.d.).

- Hypertext has no predetermined organization or structure. Unlike narrative text, which has a story structure, and expository text, which has fairly consistent organizational patterns, electronic text varies greatly. Web sites can have different formats with many different audio-visual media integrated within the text. Search engines have a totally different format in which reading abbreviated summaries based on key words presents a different organizational format.

- Hypertext includes large amounts of information and can result in information glut by the reader. By comparison, narrative and expository text give limited amounts of information.

The process of reading hypertext requires readers to go through the following stages, which are important for developing strategies for struggling students (Hites & Schrank, 2001b).

1. Initially, readers must skim the hypertext to see if the information is useful and if so, why. They must use any organizational features, if present

(e.g., headings, large type, bold text, graphics, bullets). If the organizational features differ, then they must find the unique features of the structure and learn how to use them. Skimming is relatively unimportant for narrative and expository text comprehension, but it is key to electronic text comprehension.

2. Readers must be able to navigate from one link to another. This requires that readers know where they are, where they have been, and where they want to go. This sequential knowledge is not necessary for linear text because the sequence of reading is determined by the nature of the text. Knowing where information has been seen is harder with hypertext than with linear text. When you read linear text, you may not be able to recall specific information, but you remember where in the text you read it (e.g., the bottom of the left-hand page). This ability to recall location is not available with hypertext.

3. Readers must decide if the information is relevant while navigating the links. Readers must use decision-making processes while reading to determine what they want to read. Reading hypertext requires active metacognitive processing and higher order thinking (Topping, n.d.).

So far, few best practices have been identified for developing comprehension of electronic text. However, based on research on reading comprehension with narrative and expository text and analysis of the demands that hypertext makes on readers, the following guidelines are suggested for designing instruction to develop students' mastery of electronic literacy skills.

1. Before teaching students to comprehend electronic text, fully explain the difference in structure between it and linear text. Making students aware of the features of hypertext will help them develop different strategies to meet the unique demands of reading electronic text.

2. Use S.E.T. to model a plan of action for using web site structural cues so that they can systematically read hypertext with different designs. For example, for web sites with boxes, have the students start at the top of the page and go left to right and preview each box. Then they can return to the boxes with the information that they want to pursue and click on the box. Use previewing strategies, such as those described for expository text, to teach the students to scan the material to select what organizational features they can use to help them understand the material.

3. Use literal comprehension and metacognitive strategies to stress sequencing of steps and decision making. Have the students use think-alouds to summarize the information gleaned from each node as they proceed through

a web site. Then, have them verbalize what steps they will follow based on the information they learned (e.g., go backward, go forward).

4. Teach students to actively evaluate each bit of information that they gather as they proceed through a web site. Have them ask themselves if the information is important. Use strategies such as those used to develop main idea and summarization skills. If they think that the information is important, then teach them to save it so it is not lost. Emphasize that information comes and goes on the web and may not be readily accessible in the future. It may be necessary for some students to print important information so that they can review it repeatedly in a different setting, save information in their favorites folder, or record the URL.

5. Use evaluative comprehension questions to have students infer the author of the material and why the author wrote the material, if not evident. Because it is often not possible to determine the author or source of the information on the web, it is important that students use critical comprehension to evaluate the author and reliability of the information. Students need to adopt a questioning attitude about everything they read on the web because of the lack of control over placement of material on the web.

Special instruction on reading hypertext may be important for many struggling learners but especially students from families with economic disadvantages. Children from middle-class homes usually have computers and master basic computer skills even before reading. Children from low-income homes usually do not have computers and may become digitally dispossessed and become members of the information underclass (Topping, n.d.).

Another group of struggling students who will have difficulty with electronic text are those who have problems with metacognitive and higher order cognitive processes, especially students with learning disabilities and mild mental retardation. Students with ADHD will have difficulty sustaining the attention necessary for navigation. They may also be distracted by certain multimedia features (e.g., pop-ups, animation). Although the strategy of multisensory learning has been recommended for many areas of instruction in this book, the bombardment of the senses by the multimedia format may be overwhelming to some struggling students.

The prime role of advertisement in many forms of electronic text changes the nature of the reading material used in schools. Textbooks do not have advertisements, but there are advertisements on many of the web sites used for educational purposes. Students must be taught to critically analyze these in relationship to the purpose of their reading.

For most adults, learning comprehension skills applied to electronic text involves use of reading for lifelong learning. We are at the sixth stage of learning to read, so we have been able to independently develop skills to meet the challenges presented by reading electronic text. We must make sure that we take our students to the sixth stage of learning to read so that they, too, can meet the future changes in reading that we cannot begin to conceptualize today.

12

Assessment for Planning and Monitoring Reading Instruction

CONCEPTS EXPLORED

- Assessment model for planning and monitoring reading instruction
- Collecting information for an educational history
- Role of formal tests in the assessment model
- Role of an IRI in the assessment model
- Role of curriculum-based assessment (CBA) in the assessment model
- Role of informal individualized skill assessment in the assessment model
- Monitoring reading progress

ASSESSMENT MODEL FOR PLANNING AND MONITORING READING INSTRUCTION

There are numerous purposes for assessing reading (e.g., diagnosis of a reading disability, evaluation of reading programs), but this book focuses only on assessment for 1) planning specialized reading instruction to meet the unique needs of struggling learners and 2) monitoring student progress with such instruction. You cannot design specialized reading instruction for a specific student until you have a comprehensive picture of the student's reading performance. The assessment model for planning and monitoring specialized reading instruction for struggling learners (shown in Table 23) provides such a picture.

The first step of the assessment model is to gather an educational history of the student. You need to collect all of the information that affects the student's responsiveness to reading instruction, including school history, instructional history, and background factors. Compiling a school history includes information on schools and grades attended by the student. Information relative to an instructional history includes participation in specialized programs (e.g., Reading First programs, special education), past and present instruction in reading, and the progress made with such instruction. Finally, background information regarding home, cultural, and linguistic factors is collected.

The second step is to gather information that will help you plan individualized reading instruction for a particular student. You are trying to answer the following questions using different types of assessment data.

1. What is the student's level of performance in the major areas of reading instruction (pre-reading skills, word identification, fluency, and comprehension)? Use formal testing to answer this question.

2. What processes does the student use to approach the task of reading (e.g., how does the student try to decode unknown words)? Use an IRI to answer this question.

3. How does the student perform on classroom reading tasks? Use CBA to answer this question.

4. What is a student's level of mastery of specific reading skills? Use individualized informal skill assessment by the teacher to answer this question.

After you gather information relative to these four questions, you integrate the information with the first step on gathering an educational history. Then, you are ready to design an individualized reading program to meet a student's unique instructional needs. As you implement this program, monitor the student's progress to determine if the program is working. At different points in time, the four types of data collected to plan instruction are collected again to monitor the progress the student is making with the individualized reading instruction.

Table 23. Assessment model for planning and monitoring specialized reading instruction for struggling learners

Step 1: Gather an educational history in the following areas:
- School history
- Instructional history
- Background factors (home, cultural, and linguistic factors)

Step 2: Gather information to plan individualized reading instruction.
- Use formal tests to identify performance levels in general areas of reading.
- Use informal reading inventories (IRIs) to obtain detailed information on the processes a student uses to approach reading.
- Use curriculum-based assessment (CBA) to evaluate how a student performs on classroom reading activities.
- Use informal individualized skill assessment to identify the student's level of mastery on specific reading tasks.

Step 3: Design individualized reading instruction for a student by integrating all data from Steps 1 and 2.

Step 4: Monitor student progress with individualized reading instruction on a daily, weekly, and long-term basis using informal teacher assessment, CBA, IRIs, and formal tests.

COLLECTING INFORMATION FOR AN EDUCATIONAL HISTORY

At the initial step of designing an individualized reading program to meet a particular student's needs, it is necessary to gather as much information as possible so you can make decisions based on factors that have impacted the student's mastery of reading in the past or at the present. First, it is necessary to investigate the student's school history. You need to collect information relative to grades completed; grades repeated; and schools attended, as well as attendance records. Some students have moved repeatedly and have attended a number of different schools in a short period of time, which may have resulted in inconsistent reading instruction (e.g., different approaches, different materials, different expectations). Other students may have been absent for long periods of time and missed reading instruction. These students need an instructional program that seeks to fill the holes in their foundation of reading due to lack of consistency.

Collecting information on a student's instructional history is especially important because it gives you clues as to what methods have worked and what have not worked. Knowing what reading methods and materials the student has received in the regular classroom, and their effectiveness, should inform your judgment about what methods and materials to include in your instruction. It is also important to know what specialized services the student has received (e.g., participation in ESL programs, Reading First programs, special education, after-school tutoring) and how effective they have been. It is important to determine the nature of the education provided to immigrant students in their native country. Some students have been taught reading using their native language, and this can be used as a basis for teaching the students to read English. Others may have received no education at all in their native countries.

Background factors should strongly influence the design of your instructional program. Knowing about a student's family and level of literacy is critical. If the student's parents have limited literacy and the home includes no reading material, then you may decide not to try to have the parents provide reading support in the home. Cultural factors, especially economic factors, give you insight as to a student's limited prior knowledge. Linguistic factors, such as the student's and the family's mastery of English skills, are necessary for providing appropriate attention to language factors in the reading program. Finally, all the information gathered for students who have been evaluated for special education services needs to be examined to determine what information is relevant to decisions about reading instruction (e.g., a diagnosis of ADHD for a student may necessitate your designing shorter lessons with more hands-on involvement). You need to integrate the information from these three sources to identify all factors that have a bearing on the nature of the instructional program that you design for your students.

ROLE OF FORMAL TESTS IN THE ASSESSMENT MODEL

You will need four different sources of information to plan an instructional program for a particular student. First, you must identify the student's level of performance in each of the major areas of reading instruction (i.e., pre-reading, word identification, fluency, comprehension) by using formal testing. Two types of formal tests that provide useful information are norm-referenced standardized tests and standards-referenced tests.

Norm-referenced standardized tests include individually administered tests of academic achievement (e.g., the Woodcock-Johnson III [WJ III] Tests of Achievement; Woodcock, McGrew, & Mather, 2001a) and group-administered tests (e.g., the Stanford Achievement Test, Fourth Edition, 1996). Individually administered achievement tests are used for diagnosis of disabilities and to determine eligibility for special education services. Group-administered tests are usually part of schoolwide or statewide assessment for all students. Norm-referenced tests yield scores based on comparing the student being tested with the "average student." A sample of students across the country is tested, and their scores are used to set the norm or "the average" to which all other children tested are compared. Scores such as standard scores (comparing the student's score to an average score of 100), percentiles, grade equivalent scores, and age equivalent scores are obtained from norm-referenced achievement tests.

The two most frequently used individual tests, the WJ III (Woodcock et al., 2001a) and the Wechsler Individual Achievement Test–Second Edition

(WIAT-2; Wechsler, 2001), have reading subtests for the areas of Word Identification and Passage Comprehension. You can make a tentative judgment about whether the student is below average in word identification (which is related to learning words phonetically and/or by sight) and comprehension based on a student's performance on these tests. In addition, you can get information about the student's level of functioning in the area of fluency from the WJ III Fluency subtest. You can get information about a student's phonetic abilities from the WJ III Word Attack subtest and the WIAT-2 Pseudoword Reading subtest. Other formal tests that give additional information for phonological awareness and comprehension are listed in Appendix B.

When you use any of the previous tests, you can compare your student's performance with students nationwide using the standard scores. Generally, a standard score below 90 is considered below average. The grade equivalent score tells you that your student performs like students in that grade on the skill tested. So, if a student who is in the third month of sixth grade received a grade equivalent score of 2.3, this means that the student reads like students in the third month of second grade.

The information that you get from formal tests is not specific enough to plan instruction. The results only give you a starting point to begin your search for more specific information. For example, if a sixth-grade student received a standard score of 80 and a grade equivalent score of mid–third grade on the Passage Comprehension subtest of the WJ III, you would know that he needs specialized instruction in reading comprehension, but you would not have enough information to design such a program. You would not know if problems with language, cognitive processing, and/or text structures were contributing factors to these low scores. You would not know what strategies, if any, the student uses to comprehend reading material.

Some of the problems in using the results of formal tests are inherent in testing. For example, the reading content of tests is artificial (i.e., it may have no relationship to the content that the student is being taught in school). Another shortcoming of formal testing is the limited sampling of behavior. For example, there are 47 items used to test students from first grade through college on the WJ III Passage Comprehension subtest; therefore, it is impossible to obtain much specific information on a student's comprhension skills.

Use the results of standards-referenced testing that is conducted by your state. The items on these tests are usually aligned with the curriculum that students receive in class, so the results are more relevant to inferences about their reading levels. It should be pointed out that standards-referenced testing is criterion-referenced based; an individual student's score is compared with an arbitrary passing score set by the state. There is no comparison to statewide or national norms. Students are compared with other students at their grade level who passed the test. Research collected in most states indicates that most struggling students do poorly on such statewide assessments (RAND Reading Study Group, 2001). Standards-referenced assessment may tell you the areas of failure for a student and, consequently, the need for specialized instruction.

ROLE OF AN IRI IN THE ASSESSMENT MODEL

It is not possible to get detailed information on how a student approaches the task of reading, or the reading process she uses, from formal testing. These tests only give information relative to the reading product (e.g., how many words a student can read, how fast a student can read). The IRI has been designed to obtain detailed information on the reading process. The Qualitative Reading Inventory-3 (Leslie & Caldwell, 2001), one of the most frequently used IRIs, is used to exemplify the rich information gathered from IRIs.

1. A student's word identification grade level is obtained by having the student read isolated words aloud from graded word lists (lists at different grade levels). This grade level can be used to estimate where to start word identification instruction for a student. In addition to determining if students can read each word correctly, it is possible to get an estimate of automaticity by recording whether they read the words quickly or not. The IRI can indicate a need for fluency instruction for children who can read the words but do so slowly.

2. A student's grade level of reading comprehension is obtained from oral and silent reading of passages at different grade levels. The number of errors made and the number of comprehension questions answered correctly are used to determine comprehension levels. This information is important for estimating the instructional level of the material to be used to teach comprehension skills. There are three grade levels obtained for comprehension: independent, instructional, and frustration. The independent level, variously identified as 98%–100% accuracy for word recognition and 90%–100% accuracy for comprehension, is the reading level at which the students can read without assistance. This level can be used to select trade books that students can read for recreational purposes, for SSR, or for DEAR. The instructional level, identified as 95%–98% accuracy for word recognition and 70%–89% accuracy for comprehension, is the reading level you should use for instructional materials for text reading and comprehension skills. The frustration level, usually defined as below 95% accuracy for word recognition and 70% accuracy for comprehension, is the level at which the student cannot identify words or understand content. Compare a student's frustration level with the reading level of the materials that the student is required to read in content area classes and make instructional modifications accordingly. For example, if a sixth-grade student has a third-grade frustration level, then he will not be able to read any of his content area textbooks. You need to provide accommodations so that he can learn the information through channels other than reading (e.g., books on audiotape).

3. A student's mastery of different types of comprehension skills and strategies is obtained from oral reading of passages at different grade levels. IRIs yield a treasure trove of information relative to a student's comprehension skills. First, you can evaluate how well the student answers literal and inferential questions. You can get information on a student's ability to summarize and understand main ideas and details when the student retells a passage just read. You can assess a student's ability to use strategies involving think-alouds and look-backs. Finally, you can get information on how a student responds to both narrative and expository text when read orally and silently.

4. A student's approach to reading, or the processes that the students apply to reading, can be obtained from oral reading of passages at different grade levels. When a student reads a passage aloud, you record the errors that the student makes so that you can do an error analysis, also called miscue analysis, in which you examine the nature of the errors to find out how a student is trying to identify unknown words. You want to find out if the student is making phonological, graphic, or semantic errors or miscues. Phonological miscues are indicated when students mispronounce sounds (e.g., reading *bag* for *bug*); graphic miscues are indicated when a student misreads sight words (e.g., reading *though* for *through*); and semantic miscues are indicated when a student misreads words resulting in a change or loss of meaning (e.g., reading, "The trip was far" for the sentence, "The trip was to a farm").

In order to analyze these types of miscues, the examiner notes the following types of errors as the student reads aloud:

- Omissions of sounds or words (e.g., the word *very* for the word *every*; the sentence, "The rabbit got his horn" for "The rabbit went and got his horn")

- Substitutions of sounds or words (e.g., using the short *a* sound to read the word *chimp*; reading the word *horse* for *house*)

- Insertion of sounds or words (e.g., reading the word *liked* for *like*; the sentence, "Carlos went to the big lion house" for "Carlos went to the lion house").

- Reversals of letters or words (e.g., the word *bug* for *dug*; the sentence, "Another food group is vegetables and fruit" for "Another food group is fruit and vegetables.")

It is a good idea to use miscue analysis when teaching as well as testing. When-ever a student reads aloud, use the previous approach to record the student's errors. In this way, you can constantly evaluate the processes that the student uses as she reads. Use of miscue analysis for continuous assessment of student's oral reading is called *running records* (Gunning, 1998).

IRIs yield a great deal of information for planning a specialized instruc-tion program; however, there are some drawbacks to their use. First, the read-ing passages still lack authenticity (i.e., they may not be related to the reading that students do in their classes). In addition, IRIs take a long time to admin-ister and require a high level of expertise on the part of the people who ad-minister them.

ROLE OF CBA IN THE ASSESSMENT MODEL

The purpose of CBA is to collect data that is a direct measure of student progress within a curriculum, and the tests come from the materials that are being used in their classes (Pierangelo & Giuliani, 2002). The material is au-thentic (i.e., this is the material that the student faces on a daily basis and is not artificially created for the purpose of testing). Information using CBA can come from tests that are part of a basal series being used as well as teacher-made tests based on what the teacher is teaching in the classroom. CBA may yield useful information if the students are being exposed to an extensive read-ing program. In such cases, it may be possible to obtain useful information to plan specialized reading instruction. For example, if a student is being taught with a phonics program, then it may be possible to tell from the tests included in the program what sounds the student has not mastered. However, if a stu-dent is in an unsystematic reading program (e.g., whole language in which there is little instruction on specific reading skills and little assessment), then there may be little information that can be obtained from CBA.

ROLE OF INFORMAL INDIVIDUALIZED
SKILL ASSESSMENT IN THE ASSESSMENT MODEL

If you have information from formal tests, IRIs, and CBA, then you know the student's grade level of performance in the major areas of reading, you know the student's approach to reading and comprehension skills and strategies, and you know how the student is meeting the reading demands of the classroom. You need to integrate this information so that you can narrow the search for the specific skills to teach. For example, if the results indicate that the student has a problem with phonics, you still do not know what sounds the student has not mastered. You can find this out by informal individualized testing. You would start by assessing the student on each of the sounds in order of mastery (e.g., consonants, short vowels, consonant digraphs). Once you have found the skills the student has not mastered, you know where to begin teaching. For example, if your informal assessment showed that the student had mastered all the consonant sounds, all short vowel sounds except the short *e*, and none of the consonant digraphs, then you would target your instruction toward teaching the short *e* sound and all the digraphs. You would not test any higher level sounds until the student mastered the short *e* sound and consonant digraphs.

Use the Reading Skills Record Form in Appendix E to facilitate your use of informal individualized skill assessment. In addition to using the Record Form, use charting to document in more detail a student's mastery of specific skills. It should be apparent that teacher assessment must be continuous and dynamic. You cannot teach effectively unless you know that the student is learning. If the student is learning, then she is ready to move to higher level skills. If she is not learning, then you need to find out why and change your instruction accordingly.

MONITORING READING PROGRESS

You need to monitor a student's mastery of skills being taught on a daily basis. Keep records of all of the student's responses. For example, if a student is reading 20 cards with CVC words with the short *e* sound, then jot down the correct and incorrect responses. When a student demonstrates a certain level of mastery (e.g., 90% or 18/20 words correctly read) over a certain time span (e.g., 5 days of 90%), then the student is ready to move on to a new skill. However, continuously review previously learned skills so that they are not lost due to disuse.

If a student is not demonstrating progress, then you need to ask yourself why and make changes. The assumption underlying the approach in this book is that struggling students can learn, and it is the teacher's responsibility to constantly search for ways to attain this goal. Perhaps, the student needs different strategies or needs to have a prerequisite skill developed. Do not continue to use a method or approach if a student does not demonstrate mastery. Continuing to use instructional methods when they are not working is educationally irresponsible.

Do not blame the student for not learning. Do not say that he cannot learn a skill because of his cognitive limitations, abusive home life, or language limitations. Your students will rise to the expectations you have for them. If you expect little progess, your students will show little progress. Use daily monitoring, and after each lesson ask yourself, "Did the student learn what I wanted to teach and if not, why? What can I do to help the student learn?"

If a student is making progress, assess whether the student is generalizing the skill to other settings by using curriculum-based measurement (CBM), IRIs, and formal testing. However, these three types of assessment need to be given after a long period of instruction. For example, give an IRI every 6 months or yearly. Do not expect to see improvement with curriculum materials or with unauthentic materials in short periods of time.

Conduct CBM to find out if the student is using the newly acquired reading skills with her content area reading. If not, determine if this is because the student has not generalized the newly learned skills to different settings. You need to plan instruction in these settings to facilitate such generalization. Find out if the student's approach to reading has changed by using an IRI. The last measure of whether a student generalizes reading skills is through use of formal tests. It may take 1 year or longer to see improvement for struggling students on formal reading tests. For example, if you taught a student the five short vowel sounds in a period of 2 months, then the student would only be able to read three more words on the WJ III Word Identification subtest because there are only three words (*in*, *can*, and *get*) that have this pattern. If the student originally read 20 words, then she would attain a grade equivalent score of 1.2. Reading 23 words would get her a grade equivalent score of 1.3. In other words, her score would increase by 1 month for learning all five short vowel sounds. Therefore, you cannot rely on formal tests to show student improvement over short periods of time.

Use charts, informal tests, and the Reading Skills Record Form to demonstrate to the student, the parents, and other educators the progress that the student has made. The instructional approach described in this book is effective. Make sure that there is clear evidence that this effectiveness is apparent to all, especially the student.

References

Adams, M.J. (1990). *Beginning to read: Thinking and learning about print.* Cambridge, MA: MIT Press.

Allington, R.L. (2001). *What really matters for struggling readers: Designing research-based programs.* Boston: Allyn & Bacon.

Alvermann, D.E., & Phelps, S.F. (2002). *Content area reading and literacy: Succeeding in today's diverse classrooms* (3rd ed.). Boston: Allyn & Bacon.

Antunez, B., & Zelasko, N. (2001). *What program models exist to serve English language learners?* Ask NCELA No. 22. Retrieved April 18, 2004, from http://www.ncela.gwu.edu/expert/askncela/22models.htm

Archer, A., Gleason, M.M., & Vachon, V. (2000). *REWARDS (Reading excellence: Word attack and rate development strategies).* Longmont, CO: Sopris West.

Bear, D.R., Invernizzi, M., Templeton, S., & Johnston, F. (2004). *Words their way: Word study for phonics, vocabulary, and spelling instruction.* Upper Saddle River, NJ: Merrill/Prentice Hall.

Beyer, B.K. (1997). *Improving student thinking: A comprehensive approach.* Boston: Allyn & Bacon.

Bloomfield, L., & Barnhart, C.L. (1961). *Let's read: A linguistic approach.* Detroit, MI: Wayne State University Press.

Blume, J. (2003). *Tales of a fourth grade nothing.* New York: Puffin Books.

Bos, C.S., & Vaughn, S. (2002). *Strategies for teaching students with learning and behavior problems* (5th ed.). Boston: Allyn & Bacon.

Brown, V., Hammill, D., & Wiederholt, J.L. (1995). *Test of Reading Comprehension–Third Edition (TORC-3).* Austin, TX: PRO-ED.

Bryant, B.R., Wiederholt, J.L., & Bryant, D.P. (1991). *Gray Diagnostic Reading Tests–Second Edition (GDRT-2)* Austin, TX: PRO-ED.

Buehl, D. (2001). *Classroom strategies for interactive learning* (2nd ed.). Newark, DE: International Reading Association.

California Department of Education. (1995). *Every child a reader: The report of the California task force.* Sacramento, CA: Author.

Campbell, K. (1999). *Great leaps reading program.* Gainesville, FL: Diarmuid.

Carlisle, J.F., & Rice, M.S. (2002). *Improving reading comprehension. Research-based principles and practices.* Baltimore: York Press.

Carnine, D.W. (1999). Bridging the research-to-practice gap. *Exceptional Children, 63,* 513–520.

Carnine, D.W., Silbert, J., Kame'enui, E.J., & Tarver, S.J. (2004). *Direct instruction reading* (4th ed.). Upper Saddle River, NJ: Merrill/Prentice Hall.

Carroll, J. (1963). A model of school learning. *Teachers College Record, 64,* 723–733.

Chall, J.S. (1967). *Learning to read: The great debate.* New York: McGraw-Hill.

Chall, J.S. (1983). *Stages of reading development.* Fort Worth, TX: Harcourt-Brace.

Chard, D.J., Vaughn, S., & Tyler, B.J. (2002). A synthesis of research on effective interventions for building reading fluency with elementary students with learning disabilities. *Journal of Learning Disabilities, 35*(5), 386–406.

Coiro, J. (2003). *Reading comprehension on the Internet: Expanding our understanding of reading comprehension to encompass new literacies.* Retrieved April 29, 2004, from http://www.readingonline.org/electronic/rt/2-03_Column/index.html

Cummins, J. (n.d.). *BICS and CALP.* Retrieved September 6, 2004, from http://www.iteachilearn.com/cummins/bicscalp.html

Dahl, R. (1961). *James and the giant peach.* New York: Penguin Books.

Dahl, R. (1990). *Matilda.* New York: Puffin.

Deshler, D.D., Ellis, E.S., & Lenz, B.K. (1996). *Teaching adolescents with learning disabilities: Strategies and methods* (2nd ed.). Denver: Love Publishing.

Dickson, S. (1992). *Sing, spell, read, and write.* Parsippany, NJ: Pearson Learning Group.

Dodge, B. (n.d.). *Some thoughts about webquests.* Retrieved March 28, 2004, from http://edweb.sdsu.edu/courses/edtec596/about_webquests.html

Dolch, E.W. (1936). Basic sight vocabulary. *Elementary School Journal, 36,* 456–460.

Drucker, M.J. (2003). What reading teachers should know about ESL learners. *The Reading Teacher, 57*(1), 22–29.

Duke, N.K., & Pearson, P.D. (n.d.). *Effective practices in reading comprehension.* Retrieved December 11, 2003, from http://ed-web3.educ.msu.edu/reports/ed-researchrep/03/march_03_3.htm

Edelsky, C., Altwerger, B., & Flores, B. (1991). *Whole language: What's the difference?* Portsmouth, NH: Heinemann.

Electronic textbook pilot a success for a Florida public schools. Pearson Education Press Release. (2004). Retrieved April 14, 2004, from http://www.pearsoned.com/pr_2003/031203.htm

Elkonin, D.B. (1973). U.S.S.R. In J. Downing (Ed.), *Comparative reading* (pp. 551–579). New York: Macmillan.

Engelmann, S., & Bruner, C.E. (1988). *Reading mastery.* Columbus, OH: SRA/McGraw Hill.

Engelmann, S., Osborn, S., & Hanner, S. (2001). *Corrective reading program.* Columbus, OH: SRA/McGraw-Hill.

Flesch, R. (1986). *Why Johnny can't read.* New York: HarperPerennial. (Original work published 1955)

Flood, J., Lapp, D., & Fisher, D. (2002). Phrasing, questioning, and rephrasing (PQR). In C.C. Block, L.B. Gambrell, & M. Pressley (Eds.), *Improving comprehension instruction: Rethinking research, theory, and classroom practice* (pp. 181–198). San Francisco: Jossey-Bass.

Fox, M. (1997). *Whoever you are.* San Diego: Harcourt, Inc.

Gambrell, L.B., Block, C.C., & Pressley, M. (2002). Introduction. In C.C. Block, L.B. Gambrell, & M. Pressley (Eds.), *Improving comprehension instruction: Rethinking research, theory, and classroom practice* (pp. 3–16). San Francisco: Jossey-Bass.

Ganske, K. (2000). *Word journeys: Assessment-guided phonics, spelling, and vocabulary instruction.* New York: Guilford Press.

Gardner, M.F. (1994). *Test of Auditory-Perceptual Skills–Revised (TAPS-R).* Hydesville, CA: Psychological and Educational Publications.

Gersten, R., Fuchs, L.S., & Williams, J.P. (2001). Teaching reading comprehension strategies to students with learning disabilities: a review of research. *Review of Educational Research, 71*(2), 279–320.

Goodman, K.S. (1986). *What's whole in whole language.* Portsmouth, NH: Heinemann.

Graves, M.F., Juel, C., & Graves, B.B. (1998). *Teaching reading in the 21st century.* Boston: Allyn & Bacon.

Greene, J.F. (2000). *Language!* Longmont, CO: Sopris West Educational Services.

Gunning, T.G. (1998). *Assessing and correcting reading and writing difficulties.* Boston: Allyn & Bacon.

Harris, R. (2002). *Word roots and prefixes.* Retrieved March 5, 2003, from http://virtualsalt.com/roots.htm

Hasselbring, T.S. (1999). *Read 180.* New York: Scholastic.

Hegge, T.G., Kirk, S.A., & Kirk, W.D. (1936). *Remedial reading drills.* Champaign, IL: Interstate Publishers.

Hites, J., & Schrank, A. (2001a). *A definition of hypertext.* Retrieved April 20, 2004, from http://lrs.stcloudstate.edu/cim/courses/pine/hypertextdesign2.html

Hites, J., & Schrank, A. (2001b). *Reading electronic text.* Retrieved April 20, 2004, from http://lrs.stcloudstate.edu/cim/courses/pine/hypertextdesign2.html

Humphries, S. (n.d.). *Some features of Appalachian dialects.* Retrieved August 4, 2004, from http://www.ferrum.edu/applit/studyg/dialect/features.htm

Ihnot, C. (1990). *Read naturally.* Saint Paul, MN: Read Naturally.

Jitendra, A.K., Edwards, L.L., Sacks, G., & Jacobson, L.A. (2004). What research says about vocabulary instruction for students with learning disabilities. *Exceptional Children, 70*(3), 299–322.

Johnson, D.D. (1971). The Dolch list reexamined. *The Reading Teacher, 24,* 455–456.

Jordan, W.D., Greenblanc, M., & Bowes, J.S. (1991). *The Americas: A history.* Evanston, IL: McDougal, Littell, and Co.

Juel, C., & Minden-Cupp, C. (2002). *Learning to read words: Linguistic units and strategies.* Retrieved December 5, 2002, from http://www.ciera.org/library/reports/inquiry-1/1-008/Report%201-008.html

Kamhi, A.G., & Catts, H.W. (1999). Language and reading: Convergence and divergence. In H.W. Catts & A.G. Kamhi (Eds.), *Language and reading disabilities* (pp. 1–24). Boston: Allyn & Bacon.

Kaminski, R., & Good, R. (1998). *DIBELS (Dynamic indicators of basic early literacy skills).* Longmont, CO: Sopris West Educational Services.

Kirk, S.A., Kirk, W.D., & Minskoff, E.H. (1985). *Phonic remedial reading lessons.* Novato, CA: Academic Therapy Publications.

Kraus, R. (1971). *Leo the late bloomer.* New York: Windmill Books.

Kuhn, M.R., & Stahl, S.A. (2000). *Fluency: A review of developmental and remedial practices.* Retrieved February 16, 2003, from http://www.ciera.org/library/reports/inquiry-2/2-00812-008.html

Labov, W. (2003). When ordinary children fail to read. *Reading Research Quarterly, 38* (1), 128–131.

LD Online. (n.d.) *Statistics: How many children are in special education programs?* Retrieved October 1, 2003, from http://ldonline.org/ld_indepth/general_info/statistics.html

Leach, J., Scarborough, H., & Rescorla, L. (2003). Late-emerging reading disabilities. *Journal of Educational Psychology, 95*(2), 211–224.

Lee, D.M., & Allen, R.V. (1963). *Learning to read through experience* (2nd ed.). New York: Appleton-Century-Crofts.

L'Engle, M. (1998). *A wrinkle in time.* New York: Yearling.

Lenz, B.K., Ellis, K.S., & Scanlon, D. (1996). *Teaching strategies to adolescents and adults with learning disabilities.* Austin, TX: PRO-ED.

Lerner, J. (2003). *Learning disabilities: Theories, diagnosis, and teaching strategies* (9th ed.). Boston: Houghton Mifflin.

Leslie, L., & Caldwell, J. (2001). *Qualitative Reading Inventory-3.* New York: Longman.

Leu, D.J., & Kinzer, C.K. (2003). *Effective literacy instruction: implementing best practices* (5th ed.). Upper Saddle River, NJ: Merrill/Prentice Hall.

Liberman, I.Y., & Shankweiler, D. (1985). Phonology and the problems of learning to read and write. *Remedial and Special Education, 6*(6), 8–17.

Lindamood, P.A., & Lindamood, P. (1998). *LiPS: The Lindamood phoneme sequencing programs for reading, spelling, and speech–third edition.* San Luis Obispo, CA: Gander Publishing/Lindamood-Bell.

Lyon, G.R., Shaywitz, S.E., & Shaywitz, B.A. (2003). A definition of dyslexia. *Annals of Dyslexia, 53,* 1–14.

Mastropieri, M.A., & Scruggs, T.E. (2000). *The inclusive classroom: Strategies for effective instruction.* Upper Saddle River, NJ: Merrill/Prentice Hall.

McCullough, D. (1977). *The path between the seas: The creation of the Panama Canal 1870–1914.* New York: Simon & Schuster.

Mercer, C.D., & Mercer, A.R. (2001). *Teaching students with learning problems* (6th ed.). Upper Saddle River, NJ: Merrill/Prentice Hall.

Merrill linguist reading program. (1975). New York: McGraw-Hill.

Meyer, R.A. (2002). *Phonics exposed: Understanding and resisting systematic, direct intense phonics instruction.* Mahwah, NJ: Lawrence Erlbaum Associates.

Minskoff, E.H. (1973). Creating and evaluating remediation for the learning disabled. *Focus on Exceptional Children, 5*(5), whole issue.

Minskoff, E.H. (1994). *Workplace social skills training manual.* Fishersville, VA: Woodrow Wilson Rehabilitation Center.

Minskoff, E.H., & Allsopp, D. (2003). *Academic success strategies for adolescents with learning disabilities and ADHD.* Baltimore: Paul H. Brookes Publishing Co.

Mora, P. (1999). *The rainbow tulip.* New York: Viking.

National Center for Education Statistics. (2003). *Concentration of poverty by school district urbanicity.* Retrieved October 1, 2003, from http://nces.ed.gov/programs/coe/2003/section1/indicator02.asp

National Center for Health Statistics. (2002, May). *Attention deficit disorder and learning disability: United States, 1997–98. Data from the National Health Interview Survey, Vital & Health Statistics.* Series 10, No. 206. DHHS Pub No (PHS) 2002-1534.

National Institute of Child Health and Human Development (NICHD). (2000). *Report of the National Reading Panel. Teaching children to read: An evidence-based assessment of the scientific research literature on reading and its implicarions for reading instruction* (NIH Publication No. 00-4769). Washington, DC: U.S. Government Printing Office.

Nation's Report Card: Reading highlights. (n.d.). Retrieved November 1, 2003, from http://nces.ed.gov/pubsearch/pubinfo.asp?pubid=2004452

No Child Left Behind (NCLB) Act of 2001, PL 107-110, 20 U.S.C. 6301 *et seq.*

Ogle, D.M. (1986). K-W-L. A teaching model that develops active reading of exposi-tory text. *The Reading Teacher, 39,* 564–570.

Padolsky, D. (2002, December). *How many school-aged English language learners (ELLs) are there in the U.S.?* (AskNCELA No. 1). Retrieved September 4, 2004, from http://www.ncela.gwu.edu/expert/faq/01leps.htm

The Partnership for Reading. (2001). *Put reading first: The research building blocks for teaching children to read. Kindergarten through grade 3.* Washington, DC: Author.

Philbrick, R. (1993). *Freak the mighty.* New York: Scholastic.

Phonetics: The sounds of Spanish and English (n.d.). Retrieved November, 30, 2004, from http://www.uiowa.edu/~acadtech/phonetics

Pierangelo, R., & Giuliani, G.A. (2002). *Assessment in special education: A practical ap-proach.* Boston: Allyn & Bacon.

Polacco, P. (1998). *Thank you, Mr. Falker.* New York: Philomel Books.

Polloway, E.A., Patton, J.R., & Serna, L. (2001). *Strategies for teaching learners with spe-cial needs.* Upper Saddle River, NJ: Prentice Hall.

Prentice Hall science inquiry–grade 6 (teacher's edition). (1997). Upper Saddle River, NJ: Pearson Education.

Pressley, M., & Cariglia-Bull, T. (1995). Decoding and beginnings of reading. In M. Pressley & T. Cariglia-Bull (Eds.), *Cognitive strategy instruction that really im-proved children's academic performance* (2nd ed., pp. 19–56). Cambridge, MA: Brookline Books.

Pressley, M., Symons, S., McGoldrick, J.A., & Snyder, B.L. (1995). Reading compre-hension strategies. In M. Pressley & T. Cariglia-Bull (Eds.), *Cognitive strategy in-struction that really improved children's academic performance* (2nd ed., pp. 57–100). Cambridge, MA: Brookline Books.

RAND Reading Study Group. (2001). *Reading for understanding: Toward an R & D pro-gram for reading comprehension.* Santa Monica, CA: RAND Corporation.

Rankin-Erickson, J.L., & Pressley, M. (2000). A survey of instruction practices of spe-cial education teachers nominated as effective teachers of literacy. *Learning Disabili-ties Research and Practice, 15*(4), 206–225.

Rathmann, P. (1995). *Officer Buckle and Gloria.* New York: G.P. Putnam and Sons.

Reid, D.K., Hresko, W.P., & Hammill, D.D. (2001). *Test of Early Reading–Third Edi-tion (TERA-3).* Austin, TX: PRO-ED.

Reutzel, D.R., & Cooter, R.B. (2001). *Teaching children to read: Putting the pieces together* (4th ed.). Upper Saddle River, NJ: Merrill/Prentice Hall.

Richek, M.A., Caldwell, J.S., Jennings, J.H., & Lerner, J.W. (2002). *Reading problems: Assessment and teaching strategies* (4th ed.). Boston: Allyn & Bacon.

Roberts, R., & Mather, N. (1997). Orthographic dyslexia: The neglected subtype. *Learning Disabilities Research and Practice, 12*(4), 236–250.

Robertson, C., & Salter, W. (1997). *Phonological Awareness Test.* East Moline, IL: Lingui-Systems.

Romeo, L. (2002). At-risk students: Learning to break through comprehension barri-ers. In C.C. Block, L.B. Gambrell, & M. Pressley (Eds.), *Improving comprehension in-struction: Rethinking research, theory, and classroom practice* (pp. 354–369). San Fran-cisco: Jossey-Bass.

Rowling, J.K. (1997). *Harry Potter and the sorcerer's stone.* New York: Scholastic Press.

Salient features of African American Vernacular English. (n.d.). Retrieved January 18, 2004, from http://www.arches.uga.edu/~bryan/AAVE

Saltzman, A.N. (n.d.). *To facilitate text comprehension in hypertext environments, provide contextual cues and well-structured hypertext.* Retrieved April 2, 2004, from http://coe .sdsu.edu/EDTEC640/POPsample/asaltzman/asaltzman.htm

Schumaker, J.B., Denton, P., & Deshler, D.D. (1984). *The learning strategy curriculum: The paraphrasing strategy.* Lawrence: Institute for Research on Learning Disabilities, University of Kansas.

Scientific Learning Corporation. *Fast ForWord Language.* Oakland, CA: Author.

Dr. Seuss. (1960). *Green eggs and ham.* New York: Random House.

Simmons, L. (2001). *Phonics intervention.* Norman, OK: Saxon Publishers.

Snow, C.E., Burns, S.M., & Griffin, P. (1998). *Recommendations for practice and research: Preventing reading difficulties in young children.* Washington, DC: National Academy Press.

SRA/McGraw-Hill. (2002). *Open Court: Collections for young scholars.* Columbus, OH: Author.

Stahl, S.A. (2004). Scaly? Audacious? Debris? Salubrious? Vocabulary learning and the child with learning disabilities. *Perspectives (International Dyslexia Association), 30*(1), 5–12.

Standards of learning currently in effect in Virginia's schools (n.d.). Retrieved November 30, 2004, from http://www.pen.K12.va.us/VDOE/Superintendent/Sols/home.shtml

Stanford Achievement Test–Ninth Edition. (1996). San Antonio, TX: Harcourt Assessment/ Psych Corp.

Stanovich, K. (2000). *Progress in understanding reading: Scientific foundations and new foundations.* New York: Guilford Press.

Stevens, L.P., & Bean, T.W. (2001). Reading in the digital era: Strategies for building critical literacy. In C.C. Block, L.B. Gambrell, & M. Pressley (Eds.), *Improving comprehension instruction: Rethinking research, theory, and classroom practice* (pp. 308–317). San Francisco: Jossey-Bass.

Swanson, H.L. (1999). Reading research for students with LD: A meta-analysis of intervention strategies. *Journal of Learning Disabilities, 32*(6), 504–532.

Sweet, A.P., & Snow, C. (2002). Reconceptualizing reading comprehension. In C.C. Block, L.B. Gambrell, & M. Pressley (Eds.), *Improving reading comprehension: Rethinking research theory, and practice* (pp. 17–53). San Francisco, CA: Jossey-Bass.

Teacher's guide. (2003). *Social studies in Virginia.* Chicago: Scott Foresman.

Tolkien, J.R.R. (2001). *The lord of the rings.* Boston: Houghton Mifflin.

Tompkins, G.E. (2003). *Literacy for the 21st century* (3rd ed.). Upper Saddle River, NJ: Merrill/Prentice Hall.

Topping, K.J. (n.d.) Electronic literacy in school and home: A look into the future. *Reading online: International perspectives.* Retrieved March 23, 2004, from www.readingon line.org/international/future

Torgesen, J.K. (1999). Assessment and instruction for phonemic awareness and word recognition skills. In H.H. Catts & A.G. Kamhi (Eds.), *Language and reading disabilities* (pp. 128–153). Boston: Allyn & Bacon.

Torgesen, J.K., & Bryant, B. (1994). *Test of Phonological Awareness (TOPA).* Austin, TX: PRO-ED.

Torgesen, J.K., Wagner, R., & Rashotte, C. (1999). *Test of Word Reading Efficiency (TOWRE).* Austin, TX: PRO-ED.

Vacca, J.L., Vacca, R.T., & Gove, M.K. (1995). *Reading to learn and learning to read.* Boston: Allyn & Bacon.

Vacca, J.L., Vacca, R.T., Gove, M.K., Burkey, L., Lenhart, L.A., & McKean, C. (2003). *Reading and learning to read* (5th ed.). Boston: Allyn & Bacon.

Vacca, R.T., & Vacca, J.L. (2002). *Content area reading: Literacy and learning across the curriculum.* Boston: Allyn & Bacon.

Vaughn, S., Gersten, R., & Chard, D. (2000). The underlying message in LD intervention research: Findings from research synthesis. *Exceptional Children, 67*(1), 99–114.

Wagner, R., Torgesen, J., & Rashotte, C. (1999). *Comprehensive Test of Phonological Processing (CTOPP).* Austin, TX: PRO-ED.

Wanzek, J., & Haager, D. (2003). Teaching word recognition with blending and analogizing. *Teaching Exceptional Children, 36*(1), 32–38.

Wasowicz, J. (1997). *Earobics.* Evanston, IL: Cognitive Concepts.

Wechsler, D. (2001). *Wechsler Individual Achievement Test–Second Edition (WIAT-2).* San Antonio, TX: Harcourt Assessment/Psych Corp.

Wechsler, D. (2003). *Wechsler Intelligence Scale for Children–Fourth Edition (WISC-IV).* San Antonio, TX: Harcourt Assessment/Psych Corp.

Westby, C.E. (1999). Assessing and facilitating text comprehension problems. In W.H. Catts & A.G. Kahmi (Eds.), *Language and reading disabilities* (pp. 154–223). Boston: Allyn & Bacon.

White, E.B. (1974). *Charlotte's web.* New York: HarperTrophy.

Wiederholt, J.L., & Blalock, G. (2000). *Gray Silent Reading Tests (GSRT).* Austin, TX: PRO-ED.

Wiederholt, J.L., & Bryant, B.R. (2001). *Gray Oral Reading Tests–Fourth Edition (GORT-4).* Austin, TX: PRO-ED.

Wiig, E.H., & Semel, E.M. (1984). *Language assessment and intervention for the learning disabled* (2nd ed.). Columbus, OH: Charles E. Merrill.

Wilson, B.A. (1998). *Wilson reading system.* Millbury, MA: Wilson Language Training Corp.

Wilson, B.A. (2002). *Fundations: Wilson language basics.* Millbury, MA: Wilson Language Training Corp.

Wolf, M., & Bowers, P.G. (1999). The double deficit hypothesis of developmental dyslexia. *Journal of Educational Psychology, 9*(3), 124.

Woodcock, R.W. (1998). *Woodcock Reading Mastery Tests–Revised/Normative Update (WRMT-R/NU).* Circle Pines, MN: American Guidance Service.

Woodcock, R.W., McGrew, K.S., & Mather, N. (2001a). *Woodcock-Johnson III: Tests of Achievement (WJ III).* Itasca, IL: Riverside Publishing.

Woodcock, R.W., McGrew, K.S., & Mather, N. (2001b). *Woodcock-Johnson III: Tests of Cognitive Abilities (WJ III).* Itasca, IL: Riverside Publishing.

Appendix A

Glossary

advanced organizers   Procedures used to set the stage for teaching a skill; includes linking the skill to previously learned skills or prior knowledge, identifying the objective of the instruction, and providing an explanation for why the skill is important.

affix   A prefix or a suffix.

alphabetic principle   Knowledge that speech sounds (phonemes) correspond to print (graphemes).

analytic phonics   A method that begins with words that students can already read and uses these as the basis for analyzing the sounds in them.

Ask 5 W'S & 1 H & Answer   A reading comprehension strategy to assist students to understand details in what they read.

attention-deficit/hyperactivity disorder (ADHD)   A condition characterized by inattention, hyperactivity, and/or impulsivity.

auditory closure   The ability to complete a word that is spoken with missing sounds.

auditory discrimination   The ability to tell if sounds in orally presented words are the same or different.

automatic words   Words that can be read quickly and accurately.

basal series   Oldest approach to teaching reading; instruction is provided from pre–first-grade level to sixth or eighth grade using sequential books with stories and supportive skill development materials.

BCDE strategy   A reading comprehension strategy used to teach students to ask themselves questions before, during, and after reading.

Basic Interpersonal Communication Skills (BICS)   English that is learned from face-to-face interaction; also called *playground English* or *survival English*; takes approximately 2 years to master.

bidialectal   Speaking more than one dialect, such as "school talk" and "home talk" or Standard American English and African American Vernacular English.

bilingual education   Programs in which instruction is provided in both English and the student's native language.

book language   A formal way of talking that is used in books and contains formal sentence structures and abstract or unfamiliar words.

breve   Diacritical mark over a vowel to show that it is short (e.g., c ă t).

Cognitive Academic Language Proficiency (CALP)   English that is needed to understand textbooks and the formal language of school; takes 5–7 years to master.

CANDY   A reading comprehension strategy to help students understand how information is organized into categories.

closed syllable   A syllable that ends in a consonant and takes the short vowel sound (e.g., tĕn nĭs).

cloze   A procedure for assessing or teaching reading comprehension in which the student has to supply a word that has been deleted from a sentence or paragraph; fill-in-the-blank format.

code-breaking approach   An approach to teaching reading that first teaches sounds and words (phonics) and later emphasizes understanding of words, sentences, and text; contrasted with meaning-based approach.

cognitive processing   Mental activities that individuals engage in when understanding and interpreting information and concepts.

compound word   A word that is made up of two smaller words (e.g., fireman).

comprehension   Understanding the meaning of reading material and using it as the basis for thinking.

consonant blend   Two or three letters that retain their separate sounds and are blended together when read (e.g., *sp*ot, *spr*ing).

consonant digraph   Two or three letters that are spoken with one sound (e.g., *ch*at, pa*tch*).

constructivist approach   Instructional approach in which it is assumed that students learn independently and the teacher plays a limited role; also called *the discovery method.*

content words   Words that can be demonstrated with pictures, objects, or actions; nouns, verbs, adjectives, and adverbs.

criterion-referenced testing   Assessment in which students are compared to predetermined pass rates (e.g., teacher-made tests, standards-referenced tests).

curriculum-based assessment (CBA)   Direct measures of a student's progress with the methods and materials used in the classroom.

diacritical mark   Mark over a letter to signify the sound that it makes.

dialect   A variation of the major language used in a culture (e.g., Standard American English) involving differences in phonology, morphology, semantics, syntax, and pragmatics.

diphthong   Vowel combinations that have a unique sound that is not associated with either of the vowel letters (e.g., *oil*).

direct instruction   A research-based method of systematic, explicit instruction; usually associated with the DISTAR or Reading Mastery Program and the Corrective Reading Series.

direct phonics   Instruction in which certain time periods are devoted to teaching specific sound–symbol relationships.

directionality   The ability to attend to the direction of letters, words, and text and movement from left to right and up to down when reading.

Dolch list   List of 220 sight words that are most frequently used in basal readers.

Drop Everything and Read (DEAR)   Fixed period of time for silent reading of self-selected materials.

dual deficit theory of dyslexia   Theory that dyslexia can be caused by problems in phonological awareness and rapid automatized naming (RAN).

dyslexia   1) A specific learning disability characterized by difficulties with accurate and/or fluent word recognition and by poor spelling and decoding abilities, resulting from phonological awareness deficits (International Dyslexia Association's definition); 2) disabilities in any of the major areas of the reading process (pre-reading, word identification, fluency, or comprehension) that result in students having difficulty meeting the literacy demands of school, work, or everyday life (Minskoff's definition).

electronic text   Variety of materials read on computer screen (e.g., electronic textbooks, web sites, e-mail, web searches).

embedded phonics   A type of phonics instruction that is used in response to a student demonstrating difficulty reading or writing words with specific sounds.

English as a second language (ESL)   Refers to programs in which instruction for ELLs is in English.

English language learners (ELLs)   Students with limited or no mastery of English; also called *students with limited English proficiency (LEPs)*.

error analysis   Used by the teacher to record oral errors made as a student reads; errors (or miscues) may involve omissions, substitutions, insertions, or reversals; also called *miscue analysis*.

evaluative comprehension   Reading comprehension involving higher order cognitive process that deal with judgments, such as differentiating fact from fiction; critical comprehension.

explicit instruction   Comprehensive, performance-based, systematic approach to teaching; makes visible to students what they need to learn and how to do so.

expository text   Text structure that gives information (e.g., textbooks).

expressive oral language   The ability to express ideas through spoken words and sentences.

1st Stop　A reading comprehension strategy designed to help students understand sequences that they read.

fluency　Refers to both a stage of learning to read and a distinct set of skills involving rapid, smooth reading with expression.

frustration level　Reading level determined from an informal reading inventory (IRI) at which a student attains less than 95% accuracy for word recognition and less than 70% accuracy for comprehension and represents the level at which a student cannot understand material.

function words　Articles, conjunctions, prepositions, and auxiliary verbs that serve as the glue that holds sentences together.

functional literacy　Reading level needed for meeting the demands of everyday living.

functional sight words　Survival words and phrases that are needed for everyday living.

generalization　When students apply newly-learned skills to different settings and different materials.

grapheme　Written symbol representing a letter or sound.

grapheme–phoneme association　Association of a written symbol of a letter with the sound of the letter; also called *sound–symbol association*.

high-frequency sight words　Words that most frequency appear in early reading materials (e.g., basal readers).

homograph　Words that are spelled alike but have different meanings and are spoken differently (e.g., *lead* as in "lead pencil" and as in "an usher can lead").

homonym　Words that sound alike and have the same spelling but different meanings (e.g., *ball* as in an object thrown and as in a dance).

homophone　Words that sound alike but have different spellings and meanings (e.g., *sail* versus *sale*).

hypertext　The structure of electronic text that includes large sets of parallel texts with links between them.

IFF-C　A reading comprehension strategy designed to help students find causes for what they read.

IFF-E　A reading comprehension strategy designed to help students find effects for what they read.

independent level　Reading level determined from an IRI at which a student can read with 98%–100% accuracy for word recognition and with more than 90% accuracy for comprehension and is the reading level at which a student can read material without assistance.

inferential comprehension　Reading comprehension involving higher order cognitive processes such as reasoning, comparing, and contrasting; interpretive comprehension.

informal reading inventory (IRI) An informal method for assessing reading that provides detailed information on how a student reads as well as word identification and independent, instructional, and frustration levels.

instructional level Reading level determined from an IRI at which a student can read with 95%–98% accuracy for word recognition and with 70%–89% accuracy for comprehension and is the reading level for instructional materials used by the teacher.

kinesthetic method (Fernald method) A multistep VAKT (visual, auditory, kinesthetic, and tactile) method for teaching words using writing and tracing.

KWL strategy A reading comprehension strategy using a three-column format in which students write what they know about a topic, what they want to know, and what they learned.

language experience approach (LEA) Meaning-based approach to teaching reading in which students use their experiences and language as the basis for creating reading material.

LEPs Students with limited English proficiency; also called *English language learners (ELLs)*.

LID A reading comprehension strategy designed to help students compare and contrast ideas from reading materials.

literal comprehension Reading comprehension involving lower order cognitive processes such as main ideas and details.

logographic system A writing system not based on sound–symbol association (e.g., Chinese).

macron Diacritical mark over a vowel to show that it is long (e.g., l ā ke).

meaning-based approach An approach to teaching reading that stresses meaning and understanding first (e.g., whole language); contrasted with code-based approach.

miscue analysis Used by the teacher to record oral errors made as a student reads; miscues (or errors) may involve omissions, substations, insertions, or reversals; also called *error analysis*.

modeling Clear demonstration of how to perform a reading skill; making learning explicit through think-alouds, prompts and cues, and multisensory techniques.

morpheme Smallest unit of meaning in language (e.g., there are two morphemes in the word *jumped*: *jump* and *ed*).

morphological awareness Ability to hear, identify, and manipulate words based on their parts (e.g., compound words, contractions, affixes, syllables).

morphology Area of language dealing with morphemes.

narrative text Text structure that tells a story and has characters and a plot.

norm-referenced testing Assessment in which a student's scores are compared with other students' scores; involves scores such as standard scores, percentiles, grade equivalents, and age equivalents.

onset-rime method   The ability to manipulate the sounds in a word by removing an onset (the first consonant in a word) from a rime (the rest of the word containing two or more sounds and a vowel) (e.g., /c-at/).

open syllable   A syllable that ends in a vowel and takes the long vowel sound (e.g., bā con).

orthographic dyslexia   One type of dyslexia associated with visual problems; problems confusing similar letters, mastering sight words, and reading fluently.

PASTE   A reading comprehension strategy for expository text that includes previewing and use of aids.

phoneme   Sounds of a language (e.g., there are two sounds in the word *shoe:* /sh/ and /u/).

phonemic awareness   Ability to hear, identify, and manipulate individual sounds or phonemes in spoken words.

phonics   A word identification method in which written symbols are associated with corresponding sounds.

phonological awareness   A broad term that includes the ability to hear, identify, and manipulate phonemes, syllables, rhymes, words, and onset-rimes.

phonological dyslexia   One type of dyslexia associated with difficulties with phonological awareness, phonics, and spelling.

phonology   Area of language dealing with sounds or phonemes.

pragmatics   Area of language dealing with how language is used for interpersonal communication; how a speaker varies language when speaking to different people in different settings and for different purposes.

prosody   Factors involved in reading with inflection or meaning: pitch (intonation), stress (emphasis), and tempo (rate).

r-controlled vowels   The unique sounds for vowels that are followed by the letter *r* (e.g., c*ar*, f*or*, t*er*m, f*ir*, f*ur*).

rapid automatized naming (RAN)   Ability to name pictures, letters, numbers, and words quickly; associated with the dual deficit theory of dyslexia.

RAP-Q   A reading comprehension strategy designed to help students understand the main ideas of what they read.

receptive oral language   The ability to understand the meaning of spoken words and sentences.

readability formula   Means for determining the grade level of reading material based on the length of sentences and the length of words.

roots   Parts of a word that contain basic meanings and are based on Latin and Greek derivatives.

R U BART   A strategy for teaching students to understand the meaning of long sentences that they read by chunking the sentence into parts.

running record   Use of error or miscue analysis by a teacher whenever a student reads aloud.

scaffold   A teaching technique in which strong support is provided in the early stages of learning and is gradually withdrawn so that a student can perform a skill independently.

schwa   An unaccented vowel sound associated with different letters (e.g., *a*bout, l*o*ve).

semantics   Area of language dealing with the meaning of words.

SENSE   A reading comprehension strategy to help students develop metacognitive skills to monitor if what they read makes sense.

S.E.T.   Strategic, explicit teaching—an instructional approach for teaching reading to struggling learners.

sight words   Words that have to be learned visually.

SOLVED   A reading comprehension strategy designed to help students solve problems based on what they have read.

sound blending   The ability to synthesize sounds in a word that is spoken with separated sounds.

sound segmentation   The ability to isolate and analyze each sound in a word.

SPORE   A reading comprehension strategy for narrative text that helps students understand the setting, problems, actions, and problem resolution.

standards-referenced testing   Compares student's performance on measures that are aligned with the student's curriculum as determined by state or national standards.

story grammar   The structure of narrative text including setting, problem, actions, and problem resolution.

strategy instruction   A research-based teaching approach that teaches students ways to acquire, store, and express information and skills as well as plan, execute, and evaluate their performance on a task and its outcomes.

structural analysis   A word identification method in which the parts of a word are analyzed (e.g., compound words, contractions, affixes, syllables, roots).

sustained silent reading (SSR)   Fixed period of time for silent reading with self-selected material.

syllable blending   The ability to hear an orally presented word spoken with the syllables separated and identify the complete word.

syllable segmentation   The ability to say each of the syllables in a word.

syntax   Area of language dealing with how words are combined to form sentences; also called *grammar.*

synthetic phonics   A method of teaching sounds in isolation and then in decoding words.

systematic instruction   Teaching that is based on a comprehensive scope and sequence of skills using a step-by-step process.

text structure   Unique organizational features of different types of reading materials: narrative, expository, and electronic.

think-alouds   Self-talk; a strategy in which the reader talks through a task so that he or she becomes aware of the processes needed to perform the task.

triple deficit theory of dyslexia   View that orthographic, or visual, problems are a cause of dyslexia in addition to phonological awareness/phonics and RAN.

VAKT   Multisensory approach to teaching using **v**isual, **a**uditory, **k**inesthetic, and **t**actile methods.

visual closure   The ability to see part of a letter or word and generate the complete letter or word.

visual discrimination   The ability to tell if visual stimuli are the same.

visualization   A strategy for mentally constructing visual images for what has been read.

vowel digraph   Two adjacent vowels that usually have the sound of the first one (e.g., r*ai*n)

web   Graphic representation showing the relationship between ideas.

whole language   An approach to teaching reading based on the premise that students naturally learn to read based on exposure to print and immersion in language and books.

whole word method   Technique in which a teacher tells students a word and they repeat it; uses visual skills.

word identification   Skills needed to read words; encompasses phonics, visual methods, structural analysis, and combined methods.

Appendix B

Tests for Assessing Reading

Comprehensive Test of Phonological Processing (CTOPP)
Wagner, Torgesen, and Rashotte (1999)
Available from PRO-ED (http://www.proedinc.com)
Ages: 5 years to 24 years, 11 months
Areas tested: Phonological awareness, phonological memory, rapid naming

DIBELS (Dynamic Indicators of Basic Early Literacy Skills)
Kaminski and Good (1998)
Available from Sopris West (http://www.sopriswest.com)
Ages: Kindergarten through third grade
Areas tested: Phonological awareness, alphabetic principle, fluency with connected text

Gray Diagnostic Reading Tests–Second Edition (GDRT-2)
Bryant, Wiederholt, and Bryant (1991)
Available from PRO-ED (http://www.proedinc.com)
Ages: 6 years to 18 years
Areas tested: Letter/word identification, phonetic analysis, reading vocabulary, meaningful reading, phonological awareness, listening vocabulary, rapid naming

Gray Oral Reading Tests–Fourth Edition (GORT-4)
Wiederholt and Bryant (2001)
Available from PRO-ED (http://www.proedinc.com)
Ages: 6 years to 18 years, 11 months
Areas tested: Fluency, oral reading comprehension

Gray Silent Reading Tests (GSRT)
Wiederholt and Blalock (2000)
Available from PRO-ED (http://www.proedinc.com)
Ages: 7 years to 25 years
Areas tested: Silent reading comprehension

Phonological Awareness Test
Robertson and Salter (1997)
Available from LinguiSystems (http://www.linguisystems.com)
Ages: 5 years to 9 years
Areas tested: Rhyming, segmentation, isolation, deletion, substitution, blending, graphemes, decoding, invented spelling

Test of Auditory Perceptual Skills–Revised (TAPS-R)
Gardner (1994)
Available from PRO-ED (http://www.proedinc.com)
Ages: 4 years to 13 years
Areas tested: Auditory memory, auditory discrimination, auditory thinking and reasoning

Test of Early Reading–Third Edition (TERA-3)
Reid, Hresko, and Hammill (2001)
Available from PRO-ED (http://www.proedinc.com)
Ages: 3 years, 6 months to 8 years, 6 months
Areas tested: Alphabet, convention, meaning

Test of Phonological Awareness (TOPA)
Torgesen and Bryant, 1994
Available from PRO-ED (http://www.proedinc.com)
Ages: Kindergarten through second grade
Areas tested: Awareness of individual sounds in words.

Test of Reading Comprehension–Third Edition (TORC-3)
Brown, Hammill, and Wiederholt (1995)
Available from PRO-ED (http://www.proedinc.com)
Ages: 7 years to 17 years, 11 months
Areas tested: General vocabulary, syntactic similarities, paragraph reading, sentence sequencing, math vocabulary, social studies vocabulary, science vocabulary, reading directions for school

Test of Word Reading Efficiency (TOWRE)
Torgesen, Wagner, and Rashotte (1999)
Available from PRO-ED (http://www.proedinc.com)

Ages: 6 years to 24 years, 11 months
Areas tested: Sight word efficiency, phonetic decoding efficiency

Wechsler Individual Achievement Test–Second Edition (WIAT-2)
Wechsler (2001)
Available from Harcourt Assessment (http://www.harcourtassessment.com)
Ages: 4 years to adult
Areas tested: Word reading, pseudoword decoding, reading comprehension

Woodcock-Johnson III (WJ III) Tests of Achievement
Woodcock, McGrew, and Mather (2001a)
Available from Riverside Publishing (http://www.riverpub.com)
Ages: 3 years to 80 years
Areas tested: Letter–word identification, passage comprehension, reading fluency, word attack, reading vocabulary, sound awareness, spelling of sounds

Woodcock-Johnson III (WJ III) Tests of Cognitive Abilities
Woodcock, McGrew, and Mather (2001b)
Available from Riverside Publishing (http://www.riverpub.com)
Ages: 5 years to 95 years
Areas tested: Sound blending, auditory attention, incomplete words

Woodcock Reading Mastery Tests–Revised/Normative Update (WRMT-R/NU)
Woodcock (1998)
Available from American Guidance Service (AGS) (http://www.agsnet.com)
Ages: 5 years to 75 years
Areas tested: Visual–motor learning, letter identification, word identification, word attack, word comprehension, passage comprehension

Appendix C

Proficiency Tests for Phonological Awareness, Phonics, and Structural Analysis

There are two tests presented in this section, one oral and one written. Take these tests with classmates, colleagues, or professors. The purpose of these tests is to identify any weaknesses you may have in phonological awareness, phonics, or structural analysis. You cannot teach a skill if you do not have mastery of the skill. If you have difficulty with any skill, then get help in mastering it.

ORAL PROFICIENCY TEST

1. Sound segmentation: initial position
   What is the first speech sound in these words: *man, phone, center, known?*

2. Sound segmentation: final position
   What is the last speech sound in these words: *bet, rope, cough, shy, baby?*

3. Sound segmentation: middle position
   What is the middle speech sound in these words: *cop, map, lake, found?*

4. Sound counting
   How many speech sounds are in the following words: *up, bat, stack, plant, show?*

5. Rhyming
   Give a rhyming word for each of the following: *more, ride, net, sail.*

6. Onsets and rimes
   Take off the *b* sound from the word *bang* and add the *r* sound. What word is that? Take off the *s* sound from the word *sing* and add the *w* sound. What word is that?

7. Identification of types of sounds: consonant digraphs
   What is the consonant digraph in each of these words: *shut, chip, tack?*

8. Identification of types of sounds: consonant blends
   What is the consonant blend in each of these words: *green, plow, cast, lump, sprain?*

9. Identification of types of sounds: vowel digraphs
   What is the vowel digraph in each of these words: *boat, cream, sheet?*

10. Identification of types of sounds: vowel diphthongs
    What is the vowel diphthong in each of these words: *toy, cow?*

11. Identification of types of sounds: schwas
    Where is the schwa sound in each of these words: *about, upon?*

12. Auditory discrimination of sounds
    Read these words and tell which word does not belong in a group and why?
    a. *sport, turn, hurt, firm*
    b. *coat, cat, cup, city*
    c. *raise, pass, miss, fuss*
    d. *gentle, go, gate, gun*

13. Identification of silent letters
    What is the silent letter(s) in each of these words: *lamb, wrong, listen, know?*

14. Sound blending of words with separated sounds (have someone read these words with the sounds separated and then you tell what the complete word is)
    Blend these sounds into words: /c-u-t/, /h-o-pe/, /s-t-i-ck/, /p-l-a-tt-er/.

15. Read each of these words with the sounds separated and then blend them into words.

    sh ee p   sh o p   sh a pe   m a sh   m u sh

    ch ea t   ch a t   b ee ch   sh ee t   w a sh

    c oa ch   c a tch   d ar k   b or n   f ir m

16. Syllable segmentation
    How many syllables are in each of these words: *biology, elephant, habit, flies?*

17. Identification of affixes
    What are the affixes in each of these words: *dishonesty, counterclockwise, unprotected?*

18. Identification of short vowel sounds
    Say the five short vowel sounds for *a, e, i, o,* and *u.* Give a word starting with each of these vowel sounds to be used as an aid for recalling the sound.

WRITTEN PROFICIENCY TEST

Phonics

1. Identify two words for each of the five short vowels that start with two-letter initial blends (e.g., *stop*).

2. Identify two words for each of the following long vowel sounds and two-letter initial blend: *a_e, i_e, o_e* (e.g., *slope*).

3. Identify a word with each of the following initial consonant blends: *cl, cr, dr, dw, fl, fr, gl, gr, pl, pr, sc, sk, sl, sm, sn, sp, st, sw, spr, str, tr, tw* (e.g., *spring*).

4. Identify a word with each of the following ending consonant sounds: *nd, nt, st, mp* (e.g., *sand*).

5. Identify two words for each of the following *r* controlled vowels: *ar, ir, er, ur, or* (e.g., *car*).

6. Identify two words for each of the following vowel digraphs that follow the rule of two vowels going "a walking": *ai, ay, oa, ee/ea* (e.g., *sail*).

7. Identify two words with the /aw/ vowel sound (e.g., *jaw*), /ow/ (e.g., *cow*), and /ou/ (e.g., *round*).

8. Identify a word that has the following silent letters: *p* (e.g., *pneumonia*), *w* (e.g., *write*), *k* (e.g., *know*), *gh* (e.g., *fight*), *g* (e.g., *gnome*).

Structural Analysis

1. Identify three one-syllable words that follow the open syllable rule (a syllable has a long vowel sound if it ends with a vowel; e.g., *me*) and three two-syllable words with the first syllable open (e.g., *repeat*).

2. Identify three two-syllable words with both syllables closed that follow the rule of closed syllables (a syllable has a short vowel sound if it ends with a consonant; e.g., *mitten*).

3. Identify two words that have three syllables for each of the following prefixes:

   a. *con* (e.g., *contentment*)

   b. *com* (e.g., *computer*)

   c. *dis* (e.g., *disturbance*)

   d. *mis* (e.g., *mistaken*)

4. Identify three four-syllable words that end with the *tion* suffix (e.g., *education*).

Answer Key

ORAL PROFICIENCY TEST

1. *man:* /m/   *phone:* /f/   *center:* /s/   *known:* /n/

2. *bet:* /t/   *rope:* /p/   *cough:* /f/   *shy:* long /i/   *baby:* long /e/

3. *cop:* short /o/   *map:* short /a/   *lake:* long /a/   *found:* /ou/

4. *up:* two sounds   *bat:* three sounds   *stack:* four sounds
   plant: five sounds   *show:* two sounds

5. These are listings of possible correct responses. Not all responses have
   to be given for a particular rhyme word.
   * *more:* bore, core, door, four, gore, lore, no, pore, roar, sore, tore, wore
   * *ride:* bide, died, guide, hide, lied, side, tied, wide
   * *net:* bet, get, jet, let, met, pet, set, wet
   * *sail:* bail, dale, fail, gale, jail, kale, mail, nail, rail, tail, whale

6. *bang:* rang   *sing:* wing

7. *shut:* /sh/   *chip:* /ch/   *tack:* /k/

8. *green:* /gr/   *plow:* /pl/   *cast:* /st/   *lump:* /mp/   *sprain:* /spr/

9. *boat:* long /o/   *cream:* long /e/   *sheet:* long /e/

10. *toy:* /oy/   *cow:* /ow/

11. *about: a*   *upon: u*

12. a. *sport* (/or/ vowel sound differs)
    b. *city* (soft *c*)
    c. *raise* (ending /z/ sound)
    d. *gentle* (soft *g*)

13. *lamb: b   wrong: w   listen: t   know: k*
14. Do this exercise with a partner or teacher.
15. Do this exercise with a partner or teacher.
16. *biology:* four   *elephant:* three   *habit:* two   *flies:* one
17. *dishonesty: dis, y   counterclockwise: counter, wise   unprotected: un, ed*
18. *a: apple   e: egg   i: itch, igloo, or Indian   o: octopus   u: umbrella*

WRITTEN PROFICIENCY TEST

There are many correct responses to these items. Have your responses to this test graded by a partner or teacher.

Appendix D

Programs for
Teaching Reading
to Struggling Learners

The following programs have been used successfully with some struggling learners. All programs will be successful with some students, although none will be successful with all students. Programs will be successful if they fit the needs of the students and are used by a teacher who is competent in teaching reading.

Corrective Reading Program
Engelmann, Osborn, and Hanner (2001)
Available from SRA/McGraw-Hill (http://www.sraonline.com)
Purpose: To provide 1) decoding instruction for students who do not read accurately and are not fluent and 2) comprehension instruction for students who need skills in vocabulary and reasoning.
Target population: Students in grades 4–12 who are struggling readers
Materials and activities:

- Decoding books and workbooks

- Comprehension books and workbooks

- Mastery tests

Earobics Literacy Launch
Wasowicz (1997)
Available from Cognitive Concepts (http://www.earobics.com)

Purpose: To provide scientifically based instruction for vocabulary, fluency, phonics, and comprehension
Target population: All ages
Materials and activities:

- Software

- Multimedia tools and books

- School-to-home materials

- Reading books

Fast ForWord Language
Scientific Learning Corporation
Available from Scientific Learning Corporation
(http://www.scientificlearning.com)
Purpose: To develop skills in phonological awareness, sustained attention, listening comprehension, and language structures
Target population: Students at the pre-reading level or students who need training in basic language and listening skills
Materials and activities:

- Software uses acoustically modified sound to improve receptive and expressive oral language skills

- Artificial speech, digitized human speech, and digital tones are used in computerized exercises to stretch and emphasize minute speech sounds so that students are better able to distinguish among them

- Software contains training exercises presented in a game-like environment and uses motivational rewards

- Training schedule should be 100 minutes, 5 days per week for 4–8 weeks by trained educator.

Great Leaps Reading Program
Campbell (1999)
Available from Great Leaps (http://www.greatleaps.com)
Purpose: To provide instruction in phonics, sight phrases, and reading fluency, but primarily for fluency
Target population: Kindergarten to adult
Materials and activities:

- Presented individually for 10 minutes a day at least 3 times per week with tutor

- Teacher's manual

- Notebooks with word lists and stories

Language!

Greene (2000)

Available from Language! (http://www.language-usa.net)

Purpose: Comprehensive literacy intervention curriculum for reading, writing, spelling, grammar, language, and vocabulary from first through twelfth grades.

Target population: Students of all ages who have literacy problems

Materials and activities:

- Teacher's manual, resource guide, sounds and letters book, readers, and student mastery books

- Individualized instruction based on student's level of performance and progress

- Activities for phonological and linguistic awareness; decoding and encoding isolated words; and reading sentences, paragraphs, and passages for meaning

LiPS: The Lindamood Phoneme Sequencing Program for Reading, Spelling, and Speech–Third Edition

Lindamood and Lindamood (1998)

Available from Gander Publishing (http://www.ganderpublishing.com)

Purpose: To stimulate phonemic awareness by making students aware of mouth actions that produce speech sounds

Target population: Students from kindergarten through adulthood who have phonological processing problems

Materials and activities:

- Kit with teacher's manual, mouth pictures, manipulatives, and videotape

- Activities focus on lip, tongue, and mouth actions that produce speech sounds

- Presents step-by-step sensory–cognitive procedures to develop the ability to identify and sequence individual sounds and their order in words

Open Court: Collections for Young Scholars

SRA/McGraw-Hill (2002)

Available from SRA/McGraw-Hill (http://www.sraonline.com)

Purpose: Complete curriculum providing systematic, explicit instruction of phonemic awareness, phonics, comprehension, and language arts skills

Target population: Kindergarten through sixth grade

Materials and activities:

- Wide variety of materials to provide instruction for all areas of reading

- Books for all reading levels, with emphasis on fine literature

- Materials for phonics instruction, workbooks, software, and assessment

Phonic Remedial Reading Lessons

Kirk, Kirk, and Minskoff (1985)

Available from Academic Therapy Publications

(http://www.academictherapy.com)

Purpose: Systematic, direct instruction of phonics

Target population: Students of all ages who have failed to learn to decode using methods of the general education classroom

Materials and activities:

- Manual with lessons to develop all sounds

- Controlled stories with decodable words

Phonics Intervention

Simmons (2001)

Available from Saxon Publishers (http://www.saxonpublishers.com)

Purpose: To provide systematic phonics instruction to struggling readers

Target population: Older readers who are struggling with reading and spelling

Materials and activities:

- Use of explicit instruction with scripted lessons

- Teacher's manual, student workbooks, classroom materials (e.g., word cards), and decodable text

READ 180

Hasselbring (1999)

Available from Scholastic (http://teacher.scholastic.com/read180)

Purpose: Comprehensive program designed to meet the needs of students who are below proficient level in reading

Target population: Students at elementary, middle, and high school levels

Materials and activities:

- Software, audio books, and paperback books

- Based on 90-minute block of time. First 20 minutes has whole-group instruction for direct instruction on strategies. Then, there are three 20-minute rotations for independent reading, small-group instruction, and use of READ 180 software. Remaining 10 minutes are for whole-group wrap-up.

Reading Mastery

Engelmann and Bruner (1988)

Available from SRA/McGraw-Hill (http://www.sraonline.com)

Purpose: To provide direct instruction for phonics and comprehension

Target population: Students from first through sixth grade, especially students from economically disadvantaged backgrounds

Materials and activities:

- Explicit, direct instruction using scripted lessons
- Use of nonstandard orthography in the early stages of reading

Read Naturally

Ihnot (1990)

Available from Read Naturally (http://www.readnaturally.com)

Purpose: To provide fluency instruction

Target population: Struggling readers

Materials and activities:

- Three strategies used: teacher modeling, repeated reading, and progress monitoring
- Stories, CDs, audiotapes, and teacher's manual

REWARDS (Reading Excellence: Word Attach and Rate Development Strategies)

Archer, Gleason, and Vachon (2000)

Available from Sopris West

(http://www.sopriswest.com; http://www.rewardsreading.com)

Purpose: To teach intermediate and secondary students a flexible strategy for decoding long words and increasing fluency

Target population: grades 4–12

Materials and activities:

- Lessons and scripts
- Masters
- Assessment tests
- Practice word lists

Sing, Spell, Read, and Write

Dickson (1992)

Available from Pearson Learning Group

(http://www.pearsonlearning.com; http://www.singspell.com)

Purpose: To teach spoken language, reading, spelling, and writing using songs, games and a multisensory approach

Target population: Pre-kindergarten through second grade

Materials and activities:

- Provides sequenced, systematic, explicit phonics instruction
- Use of music and movement with multimodal teaching strategies
- Classroom materials (e.g., charts), student books, storybook readers, and audio cassettes

Fundations: Wilson Language Basics
Wilson (2002)
Available from Wilson Language Training Corp.
(http://www.wilsonlanguage.com)
Purpose: To provide instruction for phonological awareness, phonics, and spelling for prevention or early intervention of reading problems
Target population: Kindergarten through third grade general education classes
Materials and activities:

- Teacher's manual, classroom materials (e.g., posters, puppets), student books

- Student manipulatives provide multisensory learning and "fun"

Wilson Reading System
Wilson (1998)
Available from Wilson Language Training Corp.
(http://www.wilsonlanguage.com)
Purpose: To provide direct, intensive, multisensory structured language training for phonics and spelling
Target population: Students in fourth through twelfth grades and adults who have not learned to read
Materials and activities:

- Structured lessons using explicit lesson plan format

- Instructor materials (e.g., sound cards, word cards), student materials (workbooks), and assessment materials

Reading Skills Record Form

PURPOSE

The purpose of this form is to provide a means for you to maintain a record of a student's present level of performance in all areas of reading and to chart the student's progress as specialized instruction is provided to improve areas of deficiency. This record form is an outline to guide you in keeping detailed information on a student's progress in mastering specific skills. Such information is important for determining precisely what a student is learning from the specialized instructional program you are providing.

DIRECTIONS

1. On the Assessment Summary page of the record form, summarize all information and make recommendations for specialized reading instruction. First present the findings from previous evaluations. Then briefly describe the data from the case history, formal testing, informal reading inventories (IRIs), and curriculum-based assessment (CBA).

2. Only evaluate areas that you will be teaching. For example, if a student only has deficiencies in sight words and fluency, then assess his or her present level of performance in these areas and chart his or her progress as you provide instruction.

3. Record the date of the first assessment to obtain the student's present level of performance so that you have a baseline for starting instruction. There are two progress reporting periods in which you should assess the student's progress toward mastery of the skills. Then, there is a column to record the final evaluation date. This may be the date at which the student mastered the target skills and is ready to move on to instruction for other skills. If a student does not master the skill by the third evaluation point,

then examine the instructional program to make sure the student is progressing adequately and just needs more time. If the student is not progressing adequately, then revise the instructional program. Make comments on the student's progress in the final column.

4. Record detailed information on the results of the assessment on attachments. For example, attach a list of sight words that the student has learned at each evaluation date. Or, if you are teaching consonant blends, then attach a list of the blends that the student mastered at different evaluation dates.

5. On the Progress Evaluation page, record the areas of specialized instruction, evaluate the effectiveness of the instruction, and present recommendations for future instruction.

Teaching Reading to Struggling Learners, by Esther Minskoff.
© 2005 Paul H. Brookes Publishing Co. All rights reserved.

Reading Skills Record Form

Assessment Summary

Name: _____   Date: _____

School: _____   Grade: _____

Teacher providing reading instruction: _____

Summary of previous evaluations:

Case history (school and instructional histories and background factors):

Formal test results:

Informal reading inventory (IRI) results:

Curriculum-based assessment (CBA) results:

Recommendations for specialized reading instruction:

Teaching Reading to Struggling Learners, by Esther Minskoff.
© 2005 Paul H. Brookes Publishing Co. All rights reserved.

	Present-level performance date	First progress evaluation date	Second progress evaluation date	Final evaluation date	Comments
Pre-reading skills					
Phonological awareness for sounds: Auditory discrimination					
Phonological awareness for sounds: Sound segmentation					
Phonological awareness for sounds: Sound blending					
Phonological awareness for sounds: Rhyming					
Phonological awareness for sounds: Sound counting					
Phonological awareness for sounds: Sound deletions and additions					
Phonological awareness for sounds: Onsets and rimes					
Phonological awareness for syllables: Compound words					
Phonological awareness for syllables: Syllable blending					
Phonological awareness for syllables: Syllable segmentation					
Language: Semantics-vocabulary					
Language: Syntax					
Visual skills: Visual discrimination					
Visual skills: Directionality					
Visual skills: Visual memory					
Visual skills: Visual speed					
Visual skills: Visual closure					
Cognitive skills: Experiences					

Teaching Reading to Struggling Learners, by Esther Minskoff.

	Present-level performance date	First progress evaluation date	Second progress evaluation date	Final evaluation date	Comments
Cognitive skills: Understanding of main ideas, details, and sequences					
Phonics skills					
Consonants					
Vowels: Short					
Vowels: Long					
Vowels: Digraphs					
Vowels: Diphthongs					
Vowels: *R*-controlled					
Vowels: Combinations					
Vowels: Schwa					
Consonant digraphs					
Consonant blends					
Onsets and rimes					
Silent letters					
Structural analysis skills					
Compound words					
Affixes					
Contractions					
Syllables					

	Present-level performance date	First progress evaluation date	Second progress evaluation date	Final evaluation date	Comments
Root words					
Visual skills					
Letter identification					
Attention to visual details					
Directionality					
Sight words: High frequency					
Sight words: Content areas					
Sight words: Functional words					
Sight words: Irregular words					
Fluency skills					
Automatic word recognition					
Oral reading with expression					
Fluent oral reading					
Rapid silent reading					
General comprehension skills					
Use of strategies before, during, and after reading					
Monitoring reading for meaning					
Monitoring attention to reading					

	Present-level performance date	First progress evaluation date	Second progress evaluation date	Final evaluation date	Comments
Language-based comprehension skills					
Vocabulary					
Function words (conjunctions and prepositions) and pronouns					
Word enrichment (synonyms, antonyms, homonyms, homophones, and homographs)					
Context clues					
Analysis of lengthy, complicated sentences					
Most important sentence parts					
Comprehension and cognitive skills					
Literal comprehension					
Inferential comprehension					
Evaluative comprehension					
Comprehension and text structures					
Narrative text					
Expository text					
Electronic text					

Teaching Reading to Struggling Learners, by Esther Minskoff.
© 2005 Paul H. Brookes Publishing Co. All rights reserved.

Reading Skills Record Form

Progress Evaluation

Student: _____   Date: _____

Teacher providing reading instruction: _____

Summary of areas of specialized reading instruction:

Evaluation of effectiveness of specialized reading instruction:

Recommendations for future instruction:

Appendix F

Games for Making
Reading Instruction Fun

Reading can be a daunting activity for struggling learners. Use games to make reading as much fun as possible to help reduce this anxiety. The chart on the following pages lists games that can be used for teaching all reading skills.

Name	Description	Example 1	Example 2
Board games	1. Create a game board following the Candy Land format in which there is a starting and ending point. Students move along spaces to get to the end space first and win. 2. Students take turns rolling dice. When they land on a space that corresponds to a particular card, they must answer the question on the card. 3. Games can also be played with spinners in which the students move the number of spaces shown by the number that the spinner points to. 4. Make all games re-usable by having cards with different examples. 5. Use themes to decorate the boards (e.g., dinosaurs, cars). 6. Use file folders to make games easy to store.	For phonics practice, have students read a word on a card (e.g., *cop*) and give a word that rhymes with it.	For vocabulary practice, have students read a word on a card (e.g., *fast*) and give a word that is the opposite.

Sports boards	1. Create boards with race tracks, baseball fields, or football fields. 2. Have students answer questions. If they are correct, then they advance on the board (e.g., for every question correctly answered, a student moves ahead 10 yards on a football field). The student who reaches the goal first or has the most points is the winner.	For practice with prefixes, students read words with prefixes and separate the word into the prefix and the base word.	For fluency practice, students time their readings of a passage. Each time they read the passage faster, they move ahead the number of yards corresponding to the number of seconds they read faster.
Memory or Concentration	1. Create pairs of cards that match. 2. Place them face down, and have the students take turns and place cards face up to find matches. If they find a match, then they get another turn. The student with the most matched pairs wins.	For practice of sight words, students read cards to review all previously learned sight words.	For practice identifying specific sounds, students read words on cards and tell if the words have the same vowel sounds (e.g., the long *a* sound in *lake* and *main*).
Bingo	1. Create bingo cards with different words. Velcro the word cards to the bingo cards so that you can re-use the bingo cards. 2. Call the words. If students have them, then they put a chip on the word until someone gets bingo.	For practice reading words phonetically, read pattern words and have students find them on their bingo cards (e.g., *car, part, farm* for the /ar/ sound).	For practice reading compound words, read the words and have students find them on their bingo card (e.g., *fireman, policeman*).

Name	Description	Example 1	Example 2
Camping Trip/ Shopping Trip	1. Each student takes a turn saying what they will take on a camping trip or what they will buy on a shopping trip. Each student has to come up with a word and also remember the words spoken by all previous students. The student who wins is the one who recalls the most words. 2. The word for what they will take has to follow a certain pattern or rule.	For phonics practice, have a student make up a word starting with the sound of the ending sound that was given by the previous student (e.g., if the previous student said that he was taking a backpack, the next student has to think of a word starting with the /k/ sound).	For phonics practice, have the students only use words starting with a particular sound (e.g., for a food shopping trip, have students produce /s/ words such as *salad, soup, salt*)
I Spy	1. You or a student gives clues as to things in the room and the students must guess what they are. 2. This can also be done with pictures in a book.	For practice of sound blending, say a word with blended sounds, and have the students find the object for the corresponding word (e.g., "I spy a /m-ar-k-er/").	For practice of identification of words with specific sounds, use a picture book with many pictures on one page (e.g., *Where's Waldo*), and have the students find pictures that start with certain sounds (e.g., "I spy something that starts with the /n/ sound").
Scavenger Hunt	1. Have students search the room for a list of objects that correspond to certain words. 2. Put the students on teams and the team that identifies all the objects first is the winner.	For practice reading sight words involving color, size, or shape, have the students find objects corresponding to words on the card (e.g., find an object that is red).	For vocabulary practice, have students read definitions of words on cards and find the corresponding objects (e.g., "This is used to cut things").

	Procedure		
Hop Scotch	1. Write a word or sound on each square. 2. Have a student throw a stone (or marker). The student hops to the square and then gives the required word. 3. A student is out if the stone does not fall in a box, if he or she puts both feet down, or does not give the correct word.	For phonics practice, write a different sound in each square. A student throws the stone, hops to the square with the stone, and gives a word with the sound.	For practice with compound words, have students give the second word to make a compound word. The first word is written in the square (e.g., for the word *book* written in a square, the student can say bookcase, bookstore).
Simon Says	1. Give directions for performing actions tied to specific reading rules. Both correct and incorrect examples of the rules should be given. 2. The student who crosses the finish line first wins.	For sound segmentation practice, give a sound and then directions (e.g., "Simon says if the word *bat* ends with the /b/ sound, then take two giant steps back").	For syllable counting practice, give a word and the corresponding number of syllables (e.g., "Simon says if the word *rabbit* has two syllables, then take two baby steps forward").
Fishing Pond	1. Cards with words or questions on the front and magnets on the back are arranged in a fishing pond. Make the cards in the shape of fish. 2. Students have fishing poles with magnets on them. They use their poles to pick up a card and then read the word or question on the card. If they are correct, then they keep the card 3. The student with the most cards (or fish) wins.	For comprehension of a story, have questions on the cards. Students must answer a question correctly or throw the card back in pond.	For sight word practice, use students' current sight words as the "fish" to be caught.

Name		Description	Example 1	Example 2
War (card game)	1.	Two students are dealt an entire deck of cards with words on one side.	For fluency practice, students are to read the sentence on a card as fast as possible. The student who reads the sentence first gets to keep the cards.	For vocabulary practice, students are to read a word and give its synonym.
	2.	Each student holds his or her deck face down with the word not showing.		
	3.	When the teacher says go, both turn one card up and perform a reading activity with it. The student who does it fastest, gets both cards. The student with the most cards at the end of the game is the winner.		
Charades	1.	Have a student read a word on a card and then act it out. The other students must guess the word that is being acted out.	For comprehension of a story, have a student read a sentence about a character performing an action. The other students must guess the character and the action.	For vocabulary practice, have a student read a card with two homophones and then act out one. The other students must guess the spelling of the word being acted out.
	2.	The student who correctly guesses the word, acts out the next word.		
	3.	This can also be played in teams.		
Hangman	1.	Present a line for each letter in an unknown word.	For practice of sight words, use student's current sight words.	For practice reading of words with different spellings of the suffix *tion*, have students guess words such as *education* and *occasion*.
	2.	The student guesses letters. If the letter is in the word, then you write it on the corresponding line. When the student is incorrect, a body part of a hangman is added. The student wins if he or she produces the word before all the body parts are drawn on the hangman.		

Game	Procedure	Applications
Wheel of Fortune	1. Present a phrase or sentence with a line corresponding to each letter in each word and spaces between the words. 2. The students take turns guessing letters. If the letter is in any of the words, then write it on the corresponding line. The student who can read the phrase or sentence first wins.	For comprehension practice, create phrases and sentences that go with the meaning of a story. Once the students read the phrase or sentence, have them determine if it fits the meaning of the story. For practice comprehending sentence structures, use sentences that the students are learning to read (e.g., "The kids went to the movies *because* it was raining").
Mad Libs	1. Create sentences with missing words. 2. The students are to read the sentences and fill in the missing words that fit the meaning.	For phonics practice, have students fill in blanks with words starting with specific sounds. For vocabulary practice, have students fill in blanks with new words that they are learning.
Trivial Pursuit	1. Use a Trivial Pursuit game board but create different questions. 2. Create questions in different categories. Each category is represented by a different color. 3. The student who first completes a circle with the six color pieces wins.	For comprehension practice using the 5 W's and 1 H strategy, create categories for who, what, where, when, why, and how. Questions in these categories should come from books students are reading (e.g., "Who was Matilda's father?"). For phonics practice on teaching exceptions to rules, create categories with different sounds, and have students read words that do or do not follow the sound pattern (e.g., for the category of sounds that represent the letters *ea*, have the students read the card with the word *bread* and tell if it follows the rule).

Name	Description	Example 1	Example 2
Jeopardy!	1. Create a game board with four or five columns corresponding to different content areas. In each column, there are pockets with questions on cards. Each pocket has a different dollar value. The more the dollar value, the harder the question. 2. The teacher gives the answer and students must give the corresponding question. They are to push a buzzer if they know the question. 3. The student who gets the most money wins.	For vocabulary practice, use columns with definitions from different content areas (e.g., *mutation, chromosome, gene*), and have the students ask questions containing the words (e.g., "Is the word *mutation?*").	For comprehension practice, have a column corresponding to who, what, when, where, and why in a story. Give answers to questions about the character, and have the students ask the corresponding question (e.g., "Why does Max carry Kevin?").
Hot Potato	1. Students are in a circle and pass a beanbag around the circle as music is played. When the music stops, the student holding the beanbag has to give a particular word. If correct, the student stays in the game. If not, the student is out.	For phonics practice, students must produce a word starting with a particular sound (e.g., the /r/ sound).	For practice rhyming, students must produce a word rhyming with a given word (e.g., *bat*).

Go Fish	1. Each student is dealt six cards, and the remaining cards are placed face down in a center pile.	For sight word practice, use current and previously learned sight words.	For phonic practice, have students form pairs of words with consonant blends (e.g., "Do you have any cards with the *sp* blend?").
	2. The students try to match cards. If they need a match, then they ask the other student for a particular card. If the student has it, then he or she gives it to first student who has a pair. If not, then the student picks a card from the center pile.		
	3. The student with most matching pairs wins.		
Jenga	1. Place wooden rectangular blocks in a tall, building-like pattern.	For phonics practice, have students identify if a vowel in the word on the block is long or short.	For practice with homophones, have students give a sentence for the word on the block showing the correct meaning (e.g., for the word *sale*, they must make up an appropriate sentence differentiating it from the word *sail*).
	2. Two students take turns reading a word on a block. If they are correct, then they pull the block out. The object is to try to pull out the block and not let the building fall. The student who knocks the building down loses.		

Fry Readability Graph for Estimating Readability—Extended

Readability formulas are used to estimate the reading level of print material. The Fry readability formula uses sentence length as a measure of grammatical complexity and number of syllables as a measure of word length, based on the premise that longer words are more difficult. The graph and directions that follow show how to use this formula

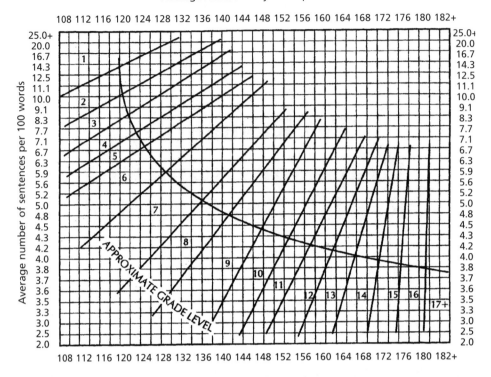

Average number of syllables per 100 words

1. Randomly select three text samples of exactly 100 words, starting with the beginning of a sentence. Count proper nouns, numerals, and initializations as words.

2. Count the number of sentences in each 100-word sample, estimating the length of the last sentence to the nearest one tenth.

3. Count the total number of syllables in each 100-word sample. Count one syllable for each numeral, initial, or symbol; for example, *1990* is one word and four syllables, *LD* is one word and two syllables, and the ampersand symbol (&) is one word and one syllable.

4. Average the number of sentences and number of syllables across the three samples.

5. Enter the average sentence length and average number of syllables on the graph. Put a dot where the two lines intersect. The area in which the dot is plotted will give you an approximate estimated readability.

6. If there is a great deal of variability in the syllable or sentence count across the three samples, more samples can be added.

From Fry, Edward B. (1968, April). A readability formula that saves time. *Journal of Reading* *11*(7), 513–516; adapted by permission; and from Fry, Edward B. (1977, December). Fry's Readability Graph: Clarifications, validity, and extension to level 17. *Journal of Reading, 21*(3), 249; adapted by permission.

Index

Page numbers followed by *f* indicate figures; those followed by *t* indicate tables.